Eyewitness to
Jewish History

Eyewitness to
Jewish History

Rabbi Benjamin Blech

WILEY

John Wiley & Sons, Inc.

Published by John Wiley & Sons, Inc., Hoboken, New Jersey
Published simultaneously in Canada

Permissions appear on page 297.

Design and production by Navta Associates, Inc.

For general information about our other products and services, please contact our Customer Care Department within the United States at (800) 762-2974, outside the United States at (317) 572-3993, or fax (317) 572-4002.

Wiley also publishes its books in a variety of electronic formats. Some content that appears in print may not be available in electronic books. For more information about Wiley products, visit our web site at www.wiley.com.

Library of Congress Cataloging-in-Publication Data:
Blech, Benjamin.
   Eyewitness to Jewish history / Benjamin Blech.
       p. cm.
   ISBN 0-471-46233-0 (cloth)
   1. Jews—History   I. Title.
   DS116 .B54 2004
   909'.04924—dc22   2003025235

Printed in the United States of America

10 9 8 7 6 5 4 3 2 1

I dedicate this book to my grandchildren

Avital Shlomit, Eitan Shimon, and Yair Mordechai Har-Oz

Noam Benzion, Daniel Eli, and Eliana Yonina Lubofsky

Talia Yonit, Ilan Shlomo, and Adin Zion Klein

With the prayer that they be eyewitnesses to a future that makes
all the sacrifices of past generations worthwhile

When all else is lost, the future still remains.

C. N. Bovee

Contents

Introduction

Over three hundred years ago King Louis XIV of France asked Blaise Pascal, the great French philosopher of his day, to give him proof of the existence of miracles. Without a moment's hesitation, Pascal answered, "Why, the Jews, your Majesty—the Jews."

We don't have to speculate what Pascal meant when he gave this answer, because he took the trouble to spell it out. In his masterwork, *Pensées,* he explained that the fact that the Jewish people had survived until the seventeenth century—the time period in which he lived—was nothing short of a supernatural phenomenon.

Pascal is but one of many scholars and students of Jewish history who have been awed by a story that seems inexplicable by the ordinary rules of logic. When Arnold Toynbee completed his classic ten-volume analysis of the rise and fall of human civilizations, *A Study of History,* he was troubled by only one seeming refutation of his universal rules governing the inexorable decline of every people on earth. Only the Jews had survived, in defiance of Toynbee's carefully reasoned analysis. So Toynbee proclaimed the Jews nothing more than "a vestigial remnant," a people destined soon to perish.

But somehow, in spite of the most brutal attempts throughout history to destroy the children of Israel—from crusades, inquisitions, and pogroms to the "Final Solution" of the Holocaust—Jews have defied all predictions of their demise. Like Mark Twain, who read his own obituary in the newspaper, Jews can thankfully respond that the report of their death "is highly exaggerated." With a smile we can remind ourselves of the famous 1964 *Look* magazine cover story that confidently predicted "The Vanishing American Jew" and reflect on the irony that it is *Look* magazine itself that no longer survives.

Jewish history, simply put, defies explanation.

Mark Twain was an agnostic and a self-acknowledged skeptic, yet he could not help but be overwhelmed by this remarkable truth. This is what he wrote in 1899:

> The Egyptian, the Babylonian, and the Persian rose, filled the planet with sound and splendor, then faded to dream-stuff and passed away. The Greek and Roman followed, made a vast noise and they are gone. Other peoples have sprung up, and held their torch high for a time, but it burned out and they sit in twilight now or have vanished. The Jew saw them all, beat them all, and is now what he always was, exhibiting no decadence, no infirmities of age, no weakening of his parts, no slowing of his energies, no dulling of his alert and aggressive mind. All things are mortal but the Jew. All other forces pass, but he remains. What is the secret of his immortality?

The writer Leo Nikolaivitch Tolstoy, best known for *War and Peace,* was not an agnostic. He was a very religious Russian Orthodox Christian. In an 1891 article entitled "What Is a Jew?" he wrote:

> The Jew is the emblem of eternity. He who neither slaughter nor torture of thousands of years could destroy, he who neither fire, nor sword, nor Inquisition was able to wipe off the face of the earth. He who was the first to produce the Oracles of God. He who has been for so long the Guardian of Prophecy and has transmitted it to the rest of the world. Such a nation cannot be destroyed. The Jew is as everlasting as Eternity itself.

Perhaps David Ben Gurion, the first prime minister of the State of Israel, summed it up best when he said, "A Jew who does not believe in miracles is not a realist."

And that's why this book, *Eyewitness to Jewish History,* had to be written. Miracles need to be told. Incredible events have to be publicized. The story of a people that begins with the Bible and continues to be the focus of world attention to this day requires study and understanding.

After all, among the many gifts of the Jews to the world is the very concept of history. Ancients had no appreciation for studying the past. Herodotus, a Greek who lived in the fifth century before the Common

Era, is commonly considered the first historian; he is given the title "the father of history." But as Columbia University historian Joseph Yerushalmi has pointed out, "If Herodotus was the father of history, the father of *meaning* in history was the Jews."

It is the Jewish Bible that introduced the commandment to remember: "Remember the Lord who took you out of Egypt, the house of bondage." "Remember the days of old; understand the years of generation to generation." Remember Amalek and all those who sought to destroy you. Remember what your ancestors taught you. Remembering will make you a better people. Remembering will make you smarter. Remembering will enable you to survive. And remembering will transform you from a people of history to a nation of destiny.

What This Book Is About

Eyewitness to Jewish History is not just another history book. It is unique both in its subject matter and in its approach.

First and foremost, this is a book about in all probability the most unusual, the most influential, and the most creative people on earth. As Ernest Van den Haag has pointed out in *The Jewish Mystique,* if you were asked to make a list of the men who have dominated the thinking of the modern world, most educated people would name Freud, Einstein, Marx, and Darwin. Of these four, only Darwin was not Jewish. In a world where Jews make up one quarter of one percent of the population, Jews consistently make contributions far disproportionate to their numbers. Of the 720 Nobel Prizes awarded since 1901, more than 130 laureates were Jews, an astonishing eighteen percent.

Thomas Cahill was so intrigued by Jewish genius that he wrote *The Gifts of the Jews: How a Tribe of Desert Nomads Changed the Way Everyone Thinks and Feels*—and watched his book rise to the top of the best-seller charts for several years. Clearly, the story of a people who have mastered both the secret of survival and the key to achievements that border on the miraculous has found universal interest and readership.

Eyewitness to Jewish History concentrates on those events that determined the Jewish character—the traits that Albert Einstein had in mind when he wrote, "The pursuit of knowledge for its own sake, an almost fanatical love of justice, and the desire for personal independence—these are the features of Jewish tradition which make me thank my stars that I belong to it."

What makes *Eyewitness to Jewish History* different, however, is its very special way of telling the story. Not by describing the past but by reliving it as if it is all happening in the present. Not by getting hung up on dates or on names but by listening to people passionately recounting major events of their lives. Not by telling you, but by transporting you to the most important moments of history. What you will be reading won't be the words of an author in the twenty-first century but the actual reactions of people who were eyewitnesses to history. From diaries, newspaper accounts, private journals, and public testimonies, you'll get the true flavor of events as the participants experienced them. And that will make *Eyewitness to Jewish History* an incomparable experience for you—a literary journey almost as rewarding as a trip back into the past courtesy of an as-yet-undiscovered time machine.

To underscore the point, let me share with you a speech given by then president of Israel, Ezer Weizman, to both houses of parliament of Germany on January 16, 1996. Weizman spoke these words in Hebrew fifty years after the Holocaust:

> It was fate that delivered me and my contemporaries into this great era when the Jews returned to reestablish their homeland. . . .
>
> I am no longer a wandering Jew who migrates from country to country, from exile to exile. But all Jews in every generation must regard themselves as if they had been there in previous generations, places and events. Therefore, I am still a wandering Jew but not along the far-flung paths of the world. Now I migrate through the expanses of time from generation to generation down the paths of memory. . . .
>
> I was a slave in Egypt. I received the Torah on Mount Sinai. Together with Joshua and Elijah, I crossed the Jordan River. I entered Jerusalem with David and was exiled with Zedekiah. And I did not forget it by the rivers of Babylon. When the Lord returned the captives of Zion, I dreamed along with the builders of its ramparts. I fought the Romans and I was banished from Spain. I was bound to the stake in Mainz. I studied the Torah in Yemen and lost my family in Kishinev.

I was incinerated in Treblinka, I rebelled in Warsaw, and I emigrated to the land of Israel, the country from which I have been exiled and where I have been born and from which I come and to which I return.

I am a wandering Jew who follows in the footsteps of my forebears. And just as I escort them there and now and then, so do my forebears accompany me and stand with me here today.

I am a wandering Jew with the cloak of memory around my shoulders and the staff of hope in my hand. I stand at the great crossroads in time, at the end of the twentieth century. I know whence I come and with hope and apprehension I attempt to find out where I am heading.

We are all people of memory and prayer. We are people of words and hope. We have neither established empires nor built castles and palaces. We have only placed words on top of each other. We have fashioned ideas. We have built memorials. We have dreamed of towers of yearning, of Jerusalem rebuilt, of Jerusalem united, of a peace that will swiftly and speedily establish us in our days.

Reading this speech made me thrill to the president's words as if I were there. And understanding their meaning made me realize how much I need not only to know the past but also to *feel* it as if I had been a participant. Because only if I can believe I was there can the past really have an impact on my present reality.

And that's what I hope *Eyewitness to Jewish History* will be able to transmit to you. So let us together begin the journey.

The Sidebars

Throughout the book you'll notice we've added some sidebars. Indicated by a gray bar along the left side, these are brief comments on the main text that are meant to make you think a little bit more about what you've read. They're observations, insights, or questions I couldn't resist sharing with you. Consider them friendly interruptions offered out of my personal concern that you get the most out of some especially fascinating part of the story.

The Time Frame: What You Need to Know about Dates and Dating Systems

At the beginning of each section of this book, we present a chart of events to put the era into chronological perspective. As we move into recorded history, the dates become more certain. But for the more ancient events, such as those presented in the first Time Frame chart, which appears on page 9, how can we be at all certain about the dates? Remember, we're not dealing with events that are historically verifiable. That's why there are many different opinions as to when they might have happened. But traditional Jewish biblical scholarship derived some important dates by tracking them against other events and clues scattered about the Bible. You can quibble about the exactness of these dates, but at least this method gives us a general idea of the relative timing of the major events.

You'll notice that the first column of the first Time Frame chart is headed "Years after Creation." That's the dating system still used by Jews, a system that puts us today in the sixth millennium from the creation of the universe. To avoid the seeming conflict of this number with the work of scientists who place the age of the world in the billions of years, Jewish scholars have long pointed out that the count rightly begins not with the creation of the world but with the creation of Adam and Eve, the first beings made "in the image of God." What is referred to in the Bible as the "week" of creation is a unit of time that might have lasted billions of years, since the "days" weren't days as we know them, because the sun wasn't created until the fourth "day."

Also, notice the explanation of the Date heading of this first Time Frame chart: "B.C.E.: Before the Common Era." This is how Jews designate that time divide, rather than as B.C., "Before Christ." While Jews—and other non-Christians around the world—necessarily accept the use of the standard Christian-based dating system, they find the designations B.C., "Before Christ," and A.D., the abbreviation for Anno Domini, meaning "in the year of our Lord," referring again to Jesus Christ, inappropriate for obvious reasons. Instead, Jews (and increasingly writers of all backgrounds) refer to these time periods as B.C.E., "Before the Common Era," and C.E., "Common Era."

Jews, Hebrews, or Israelites?

This is a book about the Jewish people, but sometimes you'll meet them under other names. "The Hebrews" and "the children of Israel," or "the Israelites," are all correct ways to identify those we more commonly today call the Jews. Abraham was the first "Hebrew," because—as the rabbis of the Talmud suggest—he dared to be different from the rest of the world when he proclaimed his belief in monotheism. "Hebrew"—or *Ivri* in the language of his time—meant "opposite"; theologically, he was at odds with the rest of mankind. His faith was passed on to his son Isaac, who fathered Jacob. As a result of an encounter with an angel, Jacob's name was changed to *Yisrael,* "Israel"—"the fighter for God." His twelve children became the founders of twelve tribes that together formed a nation. In biblical times they were referred to either as Hebrews, emphasizing their original ancestry, or as Israelites, the children of Israel. When, in the aftermath of a civil war, ten of the twelve tribes were exiled, never to be heard from again ("the Ten Lost Tribes"), only the family of Judah, together with a very small remnant of the family of Benjamin, survived. From the middle of the sixth century B.C.E., the Hebrews and the children of Israel were now almost entirely "Judah"-ites or simply Jews. With the birth of modern-day Israel, Jews who return to their ancient homeland are called "Israelis." We'll try to be historically accurate as we describe the Hebrews/Israelites/Jews/Israelis, but the most important thing to remember is that, just like their God, they are all basically one.

The Sources

The passages from the Bible are from the Revised Standard Version, except for those from Maccabees, which are from the New Revised Standard Version. The passages from the Babylonian Talmud are my own translation from the Aramaic. The passages from the Koran are from *The Holy Qur'an,* translated by M. H. Shakir, published by Tahrike Tarsile Qur'an, Inc., 1983. All other sources are identified at the end of the passage.

Bracketed material that I added to a quoted passage is identified by the note "(Brackets mine.—B. B.)" following the passage. All other bracketed, italicized, or parenthetical material is as it appeared in the source edition.

Book I

The Biblical Period

2000–538 B.C.E.

THE TIME FRAME

Years after Creation	Date (B.C.E.: Before the Common Era)	Event
1948	1812	Birth of Abraham
1996	1764	Tower of Babel
2018	1742	Covenant between God and Abraham
2048	1712	Birth of Isaac
2085	1675	Binding (near-sacrifice) of Isaac
2108	1652	Births of Jacob and Esau
2171	1589	Isaac blesses Jacob
2192	1568	Jacob marries Rachel and Leah
2216	1544	Joseph is sold by his brothers
2229	1531	Joseph becomes Egyptian viceroy
2238	1522	Jacob and his family move to Egypt
2255	1505	Death of Jacob
2309	1451	Death of Joseph
2332	1428	Death of Levi; beginning of servitude in Egypt

Years after Creation	Date (B.C.E.: Before the Common Era)	Event
2368	1392	Birth of Moses
2448	1312	Exodus from Egypt; Revelation at Mt. Sinai
2488	1272	Death of Moses; Joshua leads Jews into Israel
2516	1244	Death of Joshua
2533	1227	Atniel, first of the Judges, leads Israel
2669	1091	Samson judges Israel
2730	1030	Samuel the Prophet judges Israel
2740	1020	Saul becomes king over Israel
2760	1000	King David begins his rule
2800	960	King Solomon begins his rule
2810	950	Construction of First Temple
2832	928	Split of the kingdom; Kings Rehobo'am (Judah) and Jerobo'am (Israel) begin their rule
2889	871	King Ahab begins his rule
3034	726	Exile of the ten tribes to Assyria; northern kingdom (Israel) falls
3174	586	First Temple is destroyed; Babylonian exile

1

In the Beginning

When does Jewish history begin?

The simple answer would seem to be: with the first Jew. But for some scholars that is unacceptable.

Jews look back to Abraham as their founding patriarch. They consider Jacob's twelve children, the children of Israel (Jacob's later-acquired name), the first Jewish family. They believe that the Jewish nation was formed in the chains of Egyptian bondage, followed by divine redemption.

But all of these events present historians with one major difficulty: aside from the Bible's account, they lack confirmation from any other sources. There are no records to validate the biblical report.

We have to remember, though, that the absence of documents corroborating the Bible's version hardly proves its unreliability. Writing at that time was a laborious and specialized task, usually performed by scribes and reserved for events of importance to kings and nobles, and most of the documents that were written on perishable material haven't survived the millennia. And perhaps most important of all, the very concept of history was not yet well understood or appreciated. People lived and died, and what happened to them, they thought, would probably be repeated in cyclical fashion forever. No need, then, to record events if there is never anything new under the sun.

As Thomas Cahill pointed out in his book The Gifts of the Jews: How a Tribe of Desert Nomads Changed the Way Everyone Thinks and Feels, *it is Jews who gave* the world the very notion that life is a process of progression, a linear movement to ever greater heights, a notion that made the idea of history possible. For that reason the Bible told the story while the rest of the world remained silent. The Bible was the groundbreaking work that taught mankind to believe that the future could be different from the past and that remembering was important so that, as George Santayana put it, we won't be condemned to repeat the past.

Some historians, such as J. Alberto Soggin in his book The History of Ancient Israel: A Study in Some Questions of Method, feel that "objective historiography" demands that we begin the story of the Jewish people only when we move from biblical narrative to archeological discovery. But that would leave a huge gap in our knowledge even as it would ignore sacred texts and collective national consciousness.

For Soggin and his similarly minded colleagues, the answer to the old philosophical riddle is that a tree that fell in the forest with no man there to hear it didn't make any noise; an event unrecorded at the time, as far as they're concerned, didn't happen.

I find that view untenable. Historians may debate endlessly with theologians whether the Porgy and Bess lyrics are right and "It ain't necessarily so, De t'ings dat yo' li'ble, To read in de Bible, It ain't necessarily so." What is undeniable is that to the extent that history serves to cultivate collective memories, the Bible has achieved more than countless other recorded sources in that regard. David C. McCullough put it well when he wrote, "History is who we are and why we are the way we are." By that standard, surely the Bible is history.

That's why we won't begin this book, as Soggin would suggest, with the story of the united kingdom under David, when "the history of Israel leaves the realm of prehistory, of cultic and popular tradition, and enters the arena of history proper." We'll start with Abraham and tell the story the way many millions of people believe it really happened, and according to the best and the only account that we have for now.

Abraham Discovers God—and a Land

Here is how the Bible tells the story:

Genesis 12

1: Now the Lord said to Abram, "Go from your country and your kindred and your father's house to the land that I will show you.

2: And I will make of you a great nation, and I will bless you, and make your name great, so that you will be a blessing.

3: I will bless those who bless you, and him who curses you I will curse; and by you all the families of the earth shall bless themselves."

4: So Abram went, as the Lord had told him; and Lot went with him. Abram was seventy-five years old when he departed from Haran.

5: And Abram took Sar'ai his wife, and Lot his brother's son, and all their possessions which they had gathered, and the persons that they had gotten in Haran; and they set forth to go to the land of Canaan. When they had come to the land of Canaan,

6: Abram passed through the land to the place at Shechem, to the oak of Moreh. At that time the Canaanites were in the land.

7: Then the Lord appeared to Abram, and said, "To your descendants I will give this land." So he built there an altar to the Lord, who had appeared to him.

What the Bible doesn't tell us is why God suddenly chose Abraham as his messenger, worthy of divine blessing. Jewish tradition believes that before God chose Abraham, Abraham chose God! The story of man's discovery of monotheism is omitted; what we are told is merely the consequence of that momentous insight.

According to the Midrash, the oral transmission of biblical commentary recorded in Talmudic times, Abraham was led to belief in one God as a result of a sudden awareness, upon seeing a mansion, that just as a carefully constructed building must have had an architect, so too the complex and highly developed universe must be the product of an all-wise Creator. Philosophers and theologians would come to call this the proof from design, or the teleological argument.

Notice that in the initial encounter, Abraham is referred to as Abram. That's because it was only later, when God gave him the mission to spread his newfound belief around the world, that God changed his name to Abraham, a shortened version of the Hebrew phrase meaning "father of many nations."

The Covenant between God and Abraham

Genesis 17

1: When Abram was ninety-nine years old the Lord appeared to Abram, and said to him, "I am God Almighty; walk before me, and be blameless.

2: And I will make my covenant between me and you, and will multiply you exceedingly."

3: Then Abram fell on his face; and God said to him,

4: "Behold, my covenant is with you, and you shall be the father of a multitude of nations.

5: No longer shall your name be Abram, but your name shall be Abraham; for I have made you the father of a multitude of nations.

6: I will make you exceedingly fruitful; and I will make nations of you, and kings shall come forth from you.

7: And I will establish my covenant between me and you and your descendants after you throughout their generations for an everlasting covenant, to be God to you and to your descendants after you.

8: And I will give to you, and to your descendants after you, the land of your sojournings, all the land of Canaan, for an everlasting possession; and I will be their God."

9: And God said to Abraham, "As for you, you shall keep my covenant, you and your descendants after you throughout their generations."

> God made his promise of the land of Canaan (Palestine/Israel) to Abraham's descendants contingent upon their faithfulness to the covenant. Is that the reason Jews were for so long expelled from their divinely promised land?

At the age of one hundred, Abraham fathered Isaac, to whom he transmitted God's blessings and promises. Isaac married Rebecca, and after a period of barrenness Rebecca gave birth to twins, Jacob and Esau. The boys were rivals for the blessings of their birthright—a rivalry that Jacob's descendants would later see as symbolic of their conflict with Rome and with Christianity, which was supposedly descended from Esau. Jacob was chosen to carry on the teachings of Abraham and Isaac. He was blessed with twelve children, who would go on to become the twelve tribes of Israel. Jacob loved Joseph, the firstborn of his beloved wife Rachel, more than the children he sired from his other wife, Leah, and those born to him from his two handmaidens.

Family Hatred

Genesis 37

1: Jacob dwelt in the land of his father's sojournings, in the land of Canaan.

2: This is the history of the family of Jacob. Joseph, being seventeen years old, was shepherding the flock with his brothers; he was a lad with the sons of Bilhah and Zilpah, his father's wives; and Joseph brought an ill report of them to their father.

3: Now Israel loved Joseph more than any other of his children, because he was the son of his old age; and he made him a coat of many colors.

4: But when his brothers saw that their father loved him more than all his brothers, they hated him, and could not speak peaceably to him.

Joseph's favored status in the eyes of his father, as well as his grandiose dreams, inspired envy and hatred. In a shocking act of cruelty toward their own kin, his brothers cast him into a pit and then sold him into slavery. Joseph ended up in Egypt, where his talents and his ability to interpret dreams allowed him to rise to the highest position in the land, next to Pharaoh. Joseph was richly honored for his understanding of economic cycles, as well as for his plan that allowed Egypt to prepare for the projected seven years of famine.

Interpreting the Dreams of Pharaoh

Genesis 41

25: Then Joseph said to Pharaoh, "The dream of Pharaoh is one; God has revealed to Pharaoh what he is about to do.

26: The seven good cows are seven years, and the seven good ears are seven years; the dream is one.

27: The seven lean and gaunt cows that came up after them are seven years, and the seven empty ears blighted by the east wind are also seven years of famine.

28: It is as I told Pharaoh, God has shown to Pharaoh what he is about to do.

29: There will come seven years of great plenty throughout all the land of Egypt,

30: but after them there will arise seven years of famine, and all the plenty will be forgotten in the land of Egypt; the famine will consume the land,

31: and the plenty will be unknown in the land by reason of that famine which will follow, for it will be very grievous.

32: And the doubling of Pharaoh's dream means that the thing is fixed by God, and God will shortly bring it to pass.

33: Now therefore let Pharaoh select a man discreet and wise, and set him over the land of Egypt.

34: Let Pharaoh proceed to appoint overseers over the land, and take the fifth part of the produce of the land of Egypt during the seven plenteous years.

35: And let them gather all the food of these good years that are coming, and lay up grain under the authority of Pharaoh for food in the cities, and let them keep it.

36: That food shall be a reserve for the land against the seven years of famine which are to befall the land of Egypt, so that the land may not perish through the famine."

The Nile's Seven-Year Cycles

From an Egyptian document (purportedly 28th century B.C.E.)

Year 18 of the Horus: Netjer-er-khet; the King of Upper and Lower Egypt: Netjer-er-khet; the Two Godesses: Netjer-er-khet; the Horus of Gold: Djoser, *and under* the Count, Mayor, *Royal Acquaintance,* and Overseer of Nubians in Elephantine, Madir. There was brought to him this royal decree:

To let thee know. I was in distress on the Great Throne and those who are in the palace were in heart's affliction from a very great evil, since the Nile had not come in my time for a space of seven years. Grain was scant, fruits were dried up, and everything which they eat was short. Every man *robbed* his companion. They moved without going *[ahead]*. The infant was wailing; the youth *was waiting;* the heart of the old men was in sorrow, their legs were bent, crouching on the ground, their arms were *folded*. The courtiers were in need. The temples were shut up; the sanctuaries held *[nothing but]*air. Every [thing] was found empty.

James Pritchard, ed., *Ancient Near Eastern Texts Relating to the Old Testament,*
Princeton, N.J., 1969

Joseph's economic plan allowed Egypt to prosper while the countries around it suffered from starvation. Joseph's family was forced to come to Egypt to purchase food. While the brothers no longer recognized the young boy they had so mistreated, Joseph knew they were his family and eventually forgave them. The family of Israel settled in Goshen, a separate area, and were at first welcomed, but with the passage of time all of Joseph's contributions to Egypt were forgotten.

Slavery Begins

Exodus 1

6: Then Joseph died, and all his brothers, and all that generation.

7: But the descendants of Israel were fruitful and increased greatly; they multiplied and grew exceedingly strong; so that the land was filled with them.

8: Now there arose a new king over Egypt, who did not know Joseph.

9: And he said to his people, "Behold, the people of Israel are too many and too mighty for us.

10: Come, let us deal shrewdly with them, lest they multiply, and, if war befall us, they join our enemies and fight against us and escape from the land."

11: Therefore they set taskmasters over them to afflict them with heavy burdens; and they built for Pharaoh store-cities, Pithom and Ra-am'ses.

12: But the more they were oppressed, the more they multiplied and the more they spread abroad. And the Egyptians were in dread of the people of Israel.

13: So they made the people of Israel serve with rigor,

14: and made their lives bitter with hard service, in mortar and brick, and in all kinds of work in the field; in all their work they made them serve with rigor.

> Joseph's brothers sinned by selling him into slavery. Not too many years later, Jews collectively suffered the very same fate, as they were forced into slavery in Egypt. There is a rabbinic belief that divine retribution follows a pattern called "measure for measure." What other incidents from the Bible support or disprove this? What about incidents from your life?

The First Plague of Blood

God appeared to Moses in a burning bush that miraculously was not consumed—a vivid message meant to prophesy the miraculous survival of the Jewish people in the future. Moses was instructed to command Pharaoh to "let my people go." When Pharaoh refused, Egypt was smitten with a series of ten plagues, culminating in the death of Egyptian firstborn children. Compare the account in Exodus with an Egyptian writing that some scholars think may be from the period when the events described in Exodus might have occurred.

Exodus 7

14: Then the Lord said to Moses, "Pharaoh's heart is hardened, he refuses to let the people go.

15: Go to Pharaoh in the morning, as he is going out to the water; wait for him by the river's brink, and take in your hand the rod which was turned into a serpent.

16: And you shall say to him, 'The Lord, the God of the Hebrews, sent me to you, saying, "Let my people go, that they may serve me in the wilderness; and behold, you have not yet obeyed."

17: Thus says the Lord, "By this you shall know that I am the Lord: behold,

I will strike the water that is in the Nile with the rod that is in my hand, and it shall be turned to blood,

18: and the fish in the Nile shall die, and the Nile shall become foul, and the Egyptians will loathe to drink water from the Nile."""

19: And the Lord said to Moses, "Say to Aaron, 'Take your rod and stretch out your hand over the waters of Egypt, over their rivers, their canals, and their ponds, and all their pools of water, that they may become blood; and there shall be blood throughout all the land of Egypt, both in vessels of wood and in vessels of stone.'"

20: Moses and Aaron did as the Lord commanded; in the sight of Pharaoh and in the sight of his servants, he lifted up the rod and struck the water that was in the Nile, and all the water that was in the Nile turned to blood.

21: And the fish in the Nile died; and the Nile became foul, so that the Egyptians could not drink water from the Nile; and there was blood throughout all the land of Egypt.

The Papyrus of Ipuwer

Papyrus 7:4: Behold Egypt is poured out like water. He who poured water on the ground, he has captured the strong man in misery.

Papyrus 2:6: Plague is throughout the land. Blood is everywhere.

Papyrus 2:10: Forsooth, the river is blood.

> "The Admonitions of an Egyptian Sage," in Alan Gardiner,
> *Egypt of the Pharaohs*, Oxford, England, 1961

The Plague of Darkness

Exodus 10

21: Then the Lord said to Moses, "Stretch out your hand toward heaven that there may be darkness over the land of Egypt, a darkness to be felt."

The Papyrus of Ipuwer

Papyrus 9:8–10: Destruction . . . the land is in darkness.

> Gardiner, *Egypt of the Pharaohs*

The festival of Passover commemorates God's "passing over" the houses of the Hebrews as he slew the Egyptian firstborn. Pharaoh feared for his life and urged the Hebrews to leave his land. Many Egyptians, awed by God's miracles, joined the Hebrew people in their exodus.

Exodus 12

38: A mixed multitude also went up with them, and very many cattle, both flocks and herds.

The Papyrus of Ipuwer

Papyrus 3:14: Those who were Egyptians have become foreigners.

Gardiner, *Egypt of the Pharaohs*

Pharaoh changed his mind and pursued the Jews, only to be drowned together with his army in the Sea of Reeds, which had miraculously split for the Jews, allowing their safe passage. The Jews proceeded to Mount Sinai, where they experienced God's revelation and received the Ten Commandments on two tablets of stone. From there they wandered for forty years in the desert, until they reached the site of Canaan, their final destination. Tragically, Moses died before he could fulfill his life's dream of leading the people into the Promised Land. The Five Books of Moses—the Pentateuch—close with this farewell description:

Deuteronomy 34

1: And Moses went up from the plains of Moab to Mount Nebo, to the top of Pisgah, which is opposite Jericho. And the Lord showed him all the land, Gilead as far as Dan,

2: all Naph'tali, the land of E'phraim and Manas'seh, all the land of Judah as far as the Western Sea,

3: the Negeb, and the Plain, that is, the valley of Jericho the city of palm trees, as far as Zo'ar.

4: And the Lord said to him, "This is the land of which I swore to Abraham, to Isaac, and to Jacob, 'I will give it to your descendants.' I have let you see it with your eyes, but you shall not go over there."

5: So Moses the servant of the Lord died there in the land of Moab, according to the word of the Lord,

6: and he buried him in the valley in the land of Moab opposite Beth-pe'or; but no man knows the place of his burial to this day.

7: Moses was a hundred and twenty years old when he died; his eye was not dim, nor his natural force abated.

8: And the people of Israel wept for Moses in the plains of Moab thirty days; then the days of weeping and mourning for Moses were ended.

9: And Joshua the son of Nun was full of the spirit of wisdom, for Moses had laid his hands upon him; so the people of Israel obeyed him, and did as the Lord had commanded Moses.

10: And there has not arisen a prophet since in Israel like Moses, whom the Lord knew face to face,

11: in all the signs and the wonders which the Lord sent him to do in the land of Egypt, to Pharaoh and to all his servants and to all his land,

12: and for all the mighty power and all the great and terrible deeds which Moses wrought in the sight of all Israel.

> Moses' burial site remains unknown to this day. That has prevented the spot from becoming venerated and later generations from being able to worship Moses instead of God. Is that the reason this deservedly holy site remains eternally hidden?

2

Welcome to the Promised Land

The people of Israel mourned the death of Moses, but they knew that their story had just begun. The divine promise was that they would inherit the land that was then occupied by seven nations, chief among whom were the Canaanites. What they needed most of all was a new leader, and Moses had the wisdom to appoint such a man before his death. It is with Joshua that we begin the biblical narrative of the conquest of the Promised Land.

A New Leader

Joshua 1

1: After the death of Moses the servant of the Lord, the Lord said to Joshua the son of Nun, Moses' minister,

2: "Moses my servant is dead; now therefore arise, go over this Jordan, you and all this people, into the land which I am giving to them, to the people of Israel.

3: Every place that the sole of your foot will tread upon I have given to you, as I promised to Moses.

4: From the wilderness and this Lebanon as far as the great river, the river Euphra'tes, all the land of the Hittites to the Great Sea toward the going down of the sun shall be your territory.

5: No man shall be able to stand before you all the days of your life; as I was with Moses, so I will be with you; I will not fail you or forsake you.

6: Be strong and of good courage; for you shall cause this people to inherit the land which I swore to their fathers to give them.

7: Only be strong and very courageous, being careful to do according to all the law which Moses my servant commanded you; turn not from it to the right hand or to the left, that you may have good success wherever you go.

8: This book of the law shall not depart out of your mouth, but you shall meditate on it day and night, that you may be careful to do according to all that is written in it; for then you shall make your way prosperous, and then you shall have good success.

9: Have I not commanded you? Be strong and of good courage; be not frightened, neither be dismayed; for the Lord your God is with you wherever you go."

Joshua at the Battle of Jericho

The first occupied city that stood before the children of Israel was Jericho. Surrounded by a wall and heavily fortified, it seemed almost impregnable. The Bible describes the unusual way Jericho was attacked and conquered:

Joshua 6

1: Now Jericho was shut up from within and from without because of the people of Israel; none went out, and none came in.

2: And the Lord said to Joshua, "See, I have given into your hand Jericho, with its king and mighty men of valor.

3: You shall march around the city, all the men of war going around the city once. Thus shall you do for six days.

4: And seven priests shall bear seven trumpets of rams' horns before the ark; and on the seventh day you shall march around the city seven times, the priests blowing the trumpets.

5: And when they make a long blast with the ram's horn, as soon as you hear the sound of the trumpet, then all the people shall shout with a great shout; and the wall of the city will fall down flat, and the people shall go up every man straight before him."

6: So Joshua the son of Nun called the priests and said to them, "Take up the ark of the covenant, and let seven priests bear seven trumpets of rams' horns before the ark of the Lord."

7: And he said to the people, "Go forward; march around the city, and let the armed men pass on before the ark of the Lord."

8: And as Joshua had commanded the people, the seven priests bearing the seven trumpets of rams' horns before the Lord went forward, blowing the trumpets, with the ark of the covenant of the Lord following them.

9: And the armed men went before the priests who blew the trumpets, and the rear guard came after the ark, while the trumpets blew continually.

10: But Joshua commanded the people, "You shall not shout or let your voice be heard, neither shall any word go out of your mouth, until the day I bid you shout; then you shall shout."

11: So he caused the ark of the Lord to compass the city, going about it once; and they came into the camp, and spent the night in the camp.

12: Then Joshua rose early in the morning, and the priests took up the ark of the Lord.

13: And the seven priests bearing the seven trumpets of rams' horns before the ark of the Lord passed on, blowing the trumpets continually; and the armed men went before them, and the rear guard came after the ark of the Lord, while the trumpets blew continually.

14: And the second day they marched around the city once, and returned into the camp. So they did for six days.

15: On the seventh day they rose early at the dawn of day, and marched around the city in the same manner seven times: it was only on that day that they marched around the city seven times.

16: And at the seventh time, when the priests had blown the trumpets, Joshua said to the people, "Shout; for the Lord has given you the city.

17: And the city and all that is within it shall be devoted to the Lord for destruction; only Rahab the harlot and all who are with her in her house shall live, because she hid the messengers that we sent.

18: But you, keep yourselves from the things devoted to destruction, lest when you have devoted them you take any of the devoted things and make the camp of Israel a thing for destruction, and bring trouble upon it.

19: But all silver and gold, and vessels of bronze and iron, are sacred to the Lord; they shall go into the treasury of the Lord."

20: So the people shouted, and the trumpets were blown. As soon as the people heard the sound of the trumpet, the people raised a great shout, and the wall fell down flat, so that the people went up into the city, every man straight before him, and they took the city.

Were the sounds of the shofar, the ram's horn used as part of religious ritual, meant to frighten the inhabitants of Jericho or to embolden the Israelites through their attachment to God? Was this first, and highly unconventional, method of warfare meant to show that victory or defeat would always be determined by faith rather than military might? And why did the walls "come tumbling down"? The great walls of Jericho have been excavated, and they were found to be twelve feet thick. The assumption of archeologists is that they collapsed as a result of an earthquake. Does that take away from the miracle of the biblical account?

Over a seven-year period, the Israelites became rulers over most of Canaan. They divided the land according to their tribes and developed a loose system of government by independent "judges"—military leaders, moral advisers, inspirational figures, and very often, messengers of God. With varying degrees of success, they maintained a measure of peace and stability. Remarkably enough, especially for an era when the role of women was largely subservient, one of these highly respected judges was a woman, responsible—together with another courageous woman—for a major victory over a powerful enemy.

Deborah the Judge and Ja'el the Warrior

Judges 4

1: And the people of Israel again did what was evil in the sight of the Lord, after Ehud died.

2: And the Lord sold them into the hand of Jabin king of Canaan, who reigned in Hazor; the commander of his army was Sis'era, who dwelt in Haro'sheth-ha-goiim.

3: Then the people of Israel cried to the Lord for help; for he had nine hundred chariots of iron, and oppressed the people of Israel cruelly for twenty years.

4: Now Deb'orah, a prophetess, the wife of Lapp'idoth, was judging Israel at that time.

5: She used to sit under the palm of Deb'orah between Ramah and Bethel in the hill country of E'phraim; and the people of Israel came up to her for judgment.

6: She sent and summoned Barak the son of Abin'o-am from Kedesh in Naph'tali, and said to him, "The Lord, the God of Israel, commands you, 'Go, gather your men at Mount Tabor, taking ten thousand from the tribe of Naph'tali and the tribe of Zeb'ulun.

7: And I will draw out Sis'era, the general of Jabin's army, to meet you by the river Kishon with his chariots and his troops; and I will give him into your hand.'"

8: Barak said to her, "If you will go with me, I will go; but if you will not go with me, I will not go."

9: And she said, "I will surely go with you; nevertheless, the road on which you are going will not lead to your glory, for the Lord will sell Sis'era into the hand of a woman." Then Deb'orah arose, and went with Barak to Kedesh.

10: And Barak summoned Zeb'ulun and Naph'tali to Kedesh; and ten thousand men went up at his heels; and Deb'orah went up with him.

11: Now Heber the Ken'ite had separated from the Ken'ites, the descendants of Hobab the father-in-law of Moses, and had pitched his tent as far away as the oak in Za-anan'nim, which is near Kedesh.

12: When Sis'era was told that Barak the son of Abin'o-am had gone up to Mount Tabor,

13: Sis'era called out all his chariots, nine hundred chariots of iron, and all the men who were with him, from Haro'sheth-ha-goiim to the river Kishon.

14: And Deb'orah said to Barak, "Up! For this is the day in which the Lord has given Sis'era into your hand. Does not the Lord go out before you?" So Barak went down from Mount Tabor with ten thousand men following him.

15: And the Lord routed Sis'era and all his chariots and all his army before Barak at the edge of the sword; and Sis'era alighted from his chariot and fled away on foot.

16: And Barak pursued the chariots and the army to Haro'sheth-ha-goiim, and all the army of Sis'era fell by the edge of the sword; not a man was left.

17: But Sis'era fled away on foot to the tent of Ja'el, the wife of Heber the Ken'ite; for there was peace between Jabin the king of Hazor and the house of Heber the Ken'ite.

18: And Ja'el came out to meet Sis'era, and said to him, "Turn aside, my lord, turn aside to me; have no fear." So he turned aside to her into the tent, and she covered him with a rug.

19: And he said to her, "Pray, give me a little water to drink; for I am thirsty." So she opened a skin of milk and gave him a drink and covered him.

20: And he said to her, "Stand at the door of the tent, and if any man comes and asks you, 'Is any one here?' say, No."

21: But Ja'el the wife of Heber took a tent peg, and took a hammer in her hand, and went softly to him and drove the peg into his temple, till it went down into the ground, as he was lying fast asleep from weariness. So he died.

22: And behold, as Barak pursued Sis'era, Ja'el went out to meet him, and said to him, "Come, and I will show you the man whom you are seeking." So he went in to her tent; and there lay Sis'era dead, with the tent peg in his temple.

23: So on that day God subdued Jabin the king of Canaan before the people of Israel.

24: And the hand of the people of Israel bore harder and harder on Jabin the king of Canaan, until they destroyed Jabin king of Canaan.

Biblical heroes often come with failings. Their imperfections aren't glossed over; they are part of a larger picture acknowledging that human beings are susceptible to sin, to be admired precisely because they must overcome the inclination to give in to their baser instincts. Perhaps the most tragic of these all-too-human heroes is Samson. Renowned for his physical strength, he remains the supreme symbol of masculine weakness in the face of feminine wiles.

Samson and Delilah: Who Is the Weaker Sex?

Judges 16

1: Samson went to Gaza, and there he saw a harlot, and he went in to her.

2: The Gazites were told, "Samson has come here," and they surrounded the place and lay in wait for him all night at the gate of the city. They kept quiet all night, saying, "Let us wait till the light of the morning; then we will kill him."

3: But Samson lay till midnight, and at midnight he arose and took hold of the doors of the gate of the city and the two posts, and pulled them up, bar and all, and put them on his shoulders and carried them to the top of the hill that is before Hebron.

4: After this he loved a woman in the valley of Sorek, whose name was Deli'lah.

5: And the lords of the Philistines came to her and said to her, "Entice him, and see wherein his great strength lies, and by what means we may overpower him, that we may bind him to subdue him; and we will each give you eleven hundred pieces of silver."

6: And Deli'lah said to Samson, "Please tell me wherein your great strength lies, and how you might be bound, that one could subdue you."

7: And Samson said to her, "If they bind me with seven fresh bowstrings which have not been dried, then I shall become weak, and be like any other man."

8: Then the lords of the Philistines brought her seven fresh bowstrings which had not been dried, and she bound him with them.

9: Now she had men lying in wait in an inner chamber. And she said to him, "The Philistines are upon you, Samson!" But he snapped the bowstrings, as a string of tow snaps when it touches the fire. So the secret of his strength was not known.

10: And Deli'lah said to Samson, "Behold, you have mocked me, and told me lies; please tell me how you might be bound."

11: And he said to her, "If they bind me with new ropes that have not been used, then I shall become weak, and be like any other man."

12: So Deli'lah took new ropes and bound him with them, and said to him, "The Philistines are upon you, Samson!" And the men lying in wait were in an inner chamber. But he snapped the ropes off his arms like a thread.

13: And Deli'lah said to Samson, "Until now you have mocked me, and told me lies; tell me how you might be bound." And he said to her, "If you weave the seven locks of my head with the web and make it tight with the pin, then I shall become weak, and be like any other man."

14: So while he slept, Deli'lah took the seven locks of his head and wove them into the web. And she made them tight with the pin, and said to him, "The Philistines are upon you, Samson!" But he awoke from his sleep, and pulled away the pin, the loom, and the web.

15: And she said to him, "How can you say, 'I love you,' when your heart is not with me? You have mocked me these three times, and you have not told me wherein your great strength lies."

16: And when she pressed him hard with her words day after day, and urged him, his soul was vexed to death.

17: And he told her all his mind, and said to her, "A razor has never come upon my head; for I have been a Nazirite to God from my mother's womb. If I be shaved, then my strength will leave me, and I shall become weak, and be like any other man."

18: When Deli'lah saw that he had told her all his mind, she sent and called the lords of the Philistines, saying, "Come up this once, for he has told me all his mind." Then the lords of the Philistines came up to her, and brought the money in their hands.

19: She made him sleep upon her knees; and she called a man, and had him shave off the seven locks of his head. Then she began to torment him, and his strength left him.

20: And she said, "The Philistines are upon you, Samson!" And he awoke from his sleep, and said, "I will go out as at other times, and shake myself free." And he did not know that the Lord had left him.

21: And the Philistines seized him and gouged out his eyes, and brought him down to Gaza, and bound him with bronze fetters; and he ground at the mill in the prison.

22: But the hair of his head began to grow again after it had been shaved.

23: Now the lords of the Philistines gathered to offer a great sacrifice to Dagon their god, and to rejoice; for they said, "Our god has given Samson our enemy into our hand."

24: And when the people saw him, they praised their god; for they said, "Our god has given our enemy into our hand, the ravager of our country, who has slain many of us."

25: And when their hearts were merry, they said, "Call Samson, that he may make sport for us." So they called Samson out of the prison, and he made sport before them. They made him stand between the pillars;

26: and Samson said to the lad who held him by the hand, "Let me feel the pillars on which the house rests, that I may lean against them."

27: Now the house was full of men and women; all the lords of the Philistines were there, and on the roof there were about three thousand men and women, who looked on while Samson made sport.

28: Then Samson called to the Lord and said, "O Lord God, remember me, I pray thee, and strengthen me, I pray thee, only this once, O God, that I may be avenged upon the Philistines for one of my two eyes."

29: And Samson grasped the two middle pillars upon which the house rested, and he leaned his weight upon them, his right hand on the one and his left hand on the other.

30: And Samson said, "Let me die with the Philistines." Then he bowed with all his might; and the house fell upon the lords and upon all the people that were in it. So the dead whom he slew at his death were more than those whom he had slain during his life.

31: Then his brothers and all his family came down and took him and brought him up and buried him between Zorah and Esh'ta-ol in the tomb of Mano'ah his father. He had judged Israel twenty years.

> "Let me die with the Philistines," is a phrase that has come to have contemporary meaning. It's called the Samson Complex: a country faced with the threat of atomic annihilation might unleash its own weaponry against an enemy in an act that would ensure mutual destruction. Is the reality of "mutually assured destruction" a significant deterrent or is it—as its acronym suggests—merely MAD?

3

In the Days of the Kings

I n the ancient world, monarchy was the predominant form of government. The Israelites began their existence as a nation without a king; they believed God was the king of kings, who made a human counterpart unnecessary. Only because they wanted to be more "like all the nations" and because they were tired of corrupt and incompetent local leadership did they begin to desire a king. Yet what makes the birth of Jewish monarchy so remarkable is that it came about at the discretion of their religious leader. Samuel, as both prophet and judge, was respected throughout the land. It was only natural that the people would turn to him for guidance. He didn't agree that monarchy would solve their problems and fulfill their national destiny, but in the end he was told by God to accede to their wishes. He appointed Saul as the first king over the twelve tribes of Israel. Political leadership acquired legitimacy solely by way of its religious backing.

Choosing the First King

1 Samuel 10

17: Now Samuel called the people together to the Lord at Mizpah;

18: and he said to the people of Israel, "Thus says the Lord, the God of Israel, 'I brought up Israel out of Egypt, and I delivered you from the hand of the Egyptians and from the hand of all the kingdoms that were oppressing you.'

19: But you have this day rejected your God, who saves you from all your calamities and your distresses; and you have said, 'No! but set a king over us.' Now therefore present yourselves before the Lord by your tribes and by your thousands."

20: Then Samuel brought all the tribes of Israel near, and the tribe of Benjamin was taken by lot.

21: He brought the tribe of Benjamin near by its families, and the family of the Matrites was taken by lot; finally he brought the family of the Matrites near man by man, and Saul the son of Kish was taken by lot. But when they sought him, he could not be found.

22: So they inquired again of the Lord, "Did the man come hither?" and the Lord said, "Behold, he has hidden himself among the baggage."

23: Then they ran and fetched him from there; and when he stood among the people, he was taller than any of the people from his shoulders upward.

24: And Samuel said to all the people, "Do you see him whom the Lord has chosen? There is none like him among all the people." And all the people shouted, "Long live the king!"

25: Then Samuel told the people the rights and duties of the kingship; and he wrote them in a book and laid it up before the Lord. Then Samuel sent all the people away, each one to his home.

> When the tribes originally entered Canaan, the land was divided among them by means of a lottery. Here, too, the choice of first king was determined by chance. What could have been the motive for this unusual way of handling such important decisions? Is this Judaism's way of teaching that everything—even the throw of the dice or the luck of the draw—is the result of the unseen hand of God?

Saul's reign proved to be unsuccessful in many ways. His story offers vivid testimony to what Shakespeare would many centuries later powerfully portray as the psychological breakdown of King Lear. The Bible describes it simply as "an evil spirit descended upon him." Overwhelmed by melancholy and depression, Saul unwittingly set the stage for his successor by hiring David, a young harpist, to soothe his mood with calming music. The musician from Bethlehem would soon play a far more important role—first on the battlefield and then on the throne.

David and Goliath

1 Samuel 17

1: Now the Philistines gathered their armies for battle; and they were gathered at Socoh, which belongs to Judah, and encamped between Socoh and Aze'kah, in E'phes-dam'mim.

2: And Saul and the men of Israel were gathered, and encamped in the valley of Elah, and drew up in line of battle against the Philistines.

3: And the Philistines stood on the mountain on the one side, and Israel stood on the mountain on the other side, with a valley between them.

4: And there came out from the camp of the Philistines a champion named Goliath, of Gath, whose height was six cubits and a span.

5: He had a helmet of bronze on his head, and he was armed with a coat of mail, and the weight of the coat was five thousand shekels of bronze.

6: And he had greaves of bronze upon his legs, and a javelin of bronze slung between his shoulders.

7: And the shaft of his spear was like a weaver's beam, and his spear's head weighed six hundred shekels of iron; and his shield-bearer went before him.

8: He stood and shouted to the ranks of Israel, "Why have you come out to draw up for battle? Am I not a Philistine, and are you not servants of Saul? Choose a man for yourselves, and let him come down to me.

9: If he is able to fight with me and kill me, then we will be your servants; but if I prevail against him and kill him, then you shall be our servants and serve us."

10: And the Philistine said, "I defy the ranks of Israel this day; give me a man, that we may fight together."

11: When Saul and all Israel heard these words of the Philistine, they were dismayed and greatly afraid.

12: Now David was the son of an Eph'rathite of Bethlehem in Judah, named Jesse, who had eight sons. In the days of Saul the man was already old and advanced in years.

13: The three eldest sons of Jesse had followed Saul to the battle; and the names of his three sons who went to the battle were Eli'ab the first-born, and next to him Abin'adab, and the third Shammah.

14: David was the youngest; the three eldest followed Saul,

15: but David went back and forth from Saul to feed his father's sheep at Bethlehem.

16: For forty days the Philistine came forward and took his stand, morning and evening.

17: And Jesse said to David his son, "Take for your brothers an ephah of this parched grain, and these ten loaves, and carry them quickly to the camp to your brothers;

18: also take these ten cheeses to the commander of their thousand. See how your brothers fare, and bring some token from them."

19: Now Saul, and they, and all the men of Israel, were in the valley of Elah, fighting with the Philistines.

20: And David rose early in the morning, and left the sheep with a keeper, and took the provisions, and went, as Jesse had commanded him; and he came to the encampment as the host was going forth to the battle line, shouting the war cry.

21: And Israel and the Philistines drew up for battle, army against army.

22: And David left the things in charge of the keeper of the baggage, and ran to the ranks, and went and greeted his brothers.

23: As he talked with them, behold, the champion, the Philistine of Gath, Goliath by name, came up out of the ranks of the Philistines, and spoke the same words as before. And David heard him.

24: All the men of Israel, when they saw the man, fled from him, and were much afraid.

25: And the men of Israel said, "Have you seen this man who has come up? Surely he has come up to defy Israel; and the man who kills him, the king will enrich with great riches, and will give him his daughter, and make his father's house free in Israel."

26: And David said to the men who stood by him, "What shall be done for the man who kills this Philistine, and takes away the reproach from Israel? For who is this uncircumcised Philistine, that he should defy the armies of the living God?"

27: And the people answered him in the same way, "So shall it be done to the man who kills him."

28: Now Eli'ab his eldest brother heard when he spoke to the men; and Eli'ab's anger was kindled against David, and he said, "Why have you come down? And with whom have you left those few sheep in the wilderness? I know your presumption, and the evil of your heart; for you have come down to see the battle."

29: And David said, "What have I done now? Was it not but a word?"

30: And he turned away from him toward another, and spoke in the same way; and the people answered him again as before.

31: When the words which David spoke were heard, they repeated them before Saul; and he sent for him.

32: And David said to Saul, "Let no man's heart fail because of him; your servant will go and fight with this Philistine."

33: And Saul said to David, "You are not able to go against this Philistine to fight with him; for you are but a youth, and he has been a man of war from his youth."

34: But David said to Saul, "Your servant used to keep sheep for his father; and when there came a lion, or a bear, and took a lamb from the flock,

35: I went after him and smote him and delivered it out of his mouth; and if he arose against me, I caught him by his beard, and smote him and killed him.

36: Your servant has killed both lions and bears; and this uncircumcised Philistine shall be like one of them, seeing he has defied the armies of the living God."

37: And David said, "The Lord who delivered me from the paw of the lion and from the paw of the bear, will deliver me from the hand of this Philistine." And Saul said to David, "Go, and the Lord be with you!"

38: Then Saul clothed David with his armor; he put a helmet of bronze on his head, and clothed him with a coat of mail.

39: And David girded his sword over his armor, and he tried in vain to go, for he was not used to them. Then David said to Saul, "I cannot go with these; for I am not used to them." And David put them off.

40: Then he took his staff in his hand, and chose five smooth stones from the brook, and put them in his shepherd's bag or wallet; his sling was in his hand, and he drew near to the Philistine.

41: And the Philistine came on and drew near to David, with his shield-bearer in front of him.

42: And when the Philistine looked, and saw David, he disdained him; for he was but a youth, ruddy and comely in appearance.

43: And the Philistine said to David, "Am I a dog, that you come to me with sticks?" And the Philistine cursed David by his gods.

44: The Philistine said to David, "Come to me, and I will give your flesh to the birds of the air and to the beasts of the field."

45: Then David said to the Philistine, "You come to me with a sword and with a spear and with a javelin; but I come to you in the name of the Lord of hosts, the God of the armies of Israel, whom you have defied.

46: This day the Lord will deliver you into my hand, and I will strike you down, and cut off your head; and I will give the dead bodies of the host of the Philistines this day to the birds of the air and to the wild beasts of the earth; that all the earth may know that there is a God in Israel,

47: and that all this assembly may know that the Lord saves not with sword and spear; for the battle is the Lord's and he will give you into our hand."

48: When the Philistine arose and came and drew near to meet David, David ran quickly toward the battle line to meet the Philistine.

49: And David put his hand in his bag and took out a stone, and slung it, and struck the Philistine on his forehead; the stone sank into his forehead, and he fell on his face to the ground.

50: So David prevailed over the Philistine with a sling and with a stone, and struck the Philistine, and killed him; there was no sword in the hand of David.

51: Then David ran and stood over the Philistine, and took his sword and drew it out of its sheath, and killed him, and cut off his head with it. When the Philistines saw that their champion was dead, they fled.

Choosing David as King

While Saul still sat on the throne, Samuel moved to appoint his successor. As prophet, he daringly told the king that God no longer supported Saul as ruler and that he would shortly lose his kingdom. Here is how the Bible describes the way Samuel chose the man destined to be the second king of Israel:

1 Samuel 16

1: The Lord said to Samuel, "How long will you grieve over Saul, seeing I have rejected him from being king over Israel? Fill your horn with oil, and go; I will send you to Jesse the Bethlehemite, for I have provided for myself a king among his sons."

2: And Samuel said, "How can I go? If Saul hears it, he will kill me." And the Lord said, "Take a heifer with you, and say, 'I have come to sacrifice to the Lord.'

3: And invite Jesse to the sacrifice, and I will show you what you shall do; and you shall anoint for me him whom I name to you."

4: Samuel did what the Lord commanded, and came to Bethlehem. The elders of the city came to meet him trembling, and said, "Do you come peaceably?"

5: And he said, "Peaceably; I have come to sacrifice to the Lord; consecrate yourselves, and come with me to the sacrifice." And he consecrated Jesse and his sons, and invited them to the sacrifice.

6: When they came, he looked on Eli'ab and thought, "Surely the Lord's anointed is before him."

7: But the Lord said to Samuel, "Do not look on his appearance or on the height of his stature, because I have rejected him; for the Lord sees not as man sees; man looks on the outward appearance, but the Lord looks on the heart."

8: Then Jesse called Abin'adab, and made him pass before Samuel. And he said, "Neither has the Lord chosen this one."

9: Then Jesse made Shammah pass by. And he said, "Neither has the Lord chosen this one."

10: And Jesse made seven of his sons pass before Samuel. And Samuel said to Jesse, "The Lord has not chosen these."

11: And Samuel said to Jesse, "Are all your sons here?" And he said, "There remains yet the youngest, but behold, he is keeping the sheep." And Samuel said to Jesse, "Send and fetch him; for we will not sit down till he comes here."

12: And he sent, and brought him in. Now he was ruddy, and had beautiful eyes, and was handsome. And the Lord said, "Arise, anoint him; for this is he."

13: Then Samuel took the horn of oil, and anointed him in the midst of his brothers; and the Spirit of the Lord came mightily upon David from that day forward. And Samuel rose up, and went to Ramah.

> In ancient times, primogeniture was a widely accepted principle. The first-born would automatically receive the privileges passed down from his father. A persistent theme in the Bible is the negation of this rule. A younger son who was worthier had a stronger claim than his older brother: Abel over Cain, Isaac over Ishmael, Jacob over Esau, Joseph over Reuben. The biblical ideal repeatedly emphasized the democratic concept that privilege was not the entitlement of people who had done nothing to earn it.

Jerusalem—City of David

Soon thereafter Saul died on the battlefield fighting against the Philistines. David began a reign of forty years that saw an expanded kingdom as well as widespread national unity. David was revered as both a political leader and a spiritual spokesman, the author of the book of Psalms. In one of his most important actions, in 990 B.C.E., David conquered Jerusalem and proclaimed it the national capital. The city, to this day, is still called the City of David, spiritual center of the land of Israel.

2 Samuel 5

1: Then all the tribes of Israel came to David at Hebron, and said, "Behold, we are your bone and flesh.

2: In times past, when Saul was king over us, it was you that led out and brought in Israel; and the Lord said to you, 'You shall be shepherd of my people Israel, and you shall be prince over Israel.'"

3: So all the elders of Israel came to the king at Hebron; and King David made a covenant with them at Hebron before the Lord, and they anointed David king over Israel.

4: David was thirty years old when he began to reign, and he reigned forty years.

5: At Hebron he reigned over Judah seven years and six months; and at Jerusalem he reigned over all Israel and Judah thirty-three years.

6: And the king and his men went to Jerusalem against the Jeb'usites, the inhabitants of the land, who said to David, "You will not come in here, but the blind and the lame will ward you off"—thinking, "David cannot come in here."

7: Nevertheless David took the stronghold of Zion, that is, the city of David.

8: And David said on that day, "Whoever would smite the Jeb'usites, let him get up the water shaft to attack the lame and the blind, who are hated by David's soul." Therefore it is said, "The blind and the lame shall not come into the house."

9: And David dwelt in the stronghold, and called it the city of David. And David built the city round about from the Millo inward.

10: And David became greater and greater, for the Lord, the God of hosts, was with him.

In 1867 the archeologist Charles Warren discovered a water system that gave residents of ancient Jerusalem access to the Gihon Spring from inside the safety of the city walls. The scholars Kathleen Kenyon and John Gray have both suggested that Warren's Shaft is the water shaft mentioned in verse 8 above—the secret to David's conquest of Jerusalem.

But why did David choose Jerusalem? Capital cities were invariably selected because of their proximity to water or to important trade routes. Jerusalem enjoyed neither of these advantages—witness the need to tunnel out to a spring to ensure a supply of water when under siege. What then made it so desirable? The traditional Jewish answer is that Mount Moriah in Jerusalem was the site where God tested Abraham when asking him to sacrifice his son Isaac.

David was a great king, but he was not perfect. The histories written by other ancient peoples often omit any mention of their leaders' failings. Biblical portrayals of heroes often refer to their profound character flaws along with their heroic qualities, thereby making them more human and more real. In the aftermath of an instance where David sins, we witness a historic confrontation between king and prophet. And remarkably enough, it is the prophet who prevails.

Nathan the Prophet versus David the King

2 Samuel 12

1: And the Lord sent Nathan to David. He came to him, and said to him, "There were two men in a certain city, the one rich and the other poor.

2: The rich man had very many flocks and herds;

3: but the poor man had nothing but one little ewe lamb, which he had bought. And he brought it up, and it grew up with him and with his children; it used to eat of his morsel, and drink from his cup, and lie in his bosom, and it was like a daughter to him.

4: Now there came a traveler to the rich man, and he was unwilling to take one of his own flock or herd to prepare for the wayfarer who had come to him, but he took the poor man's lamb, and prepared it for the man who had come to him."

5: Then David's anger was greatly kindled against the man; and he said to Nathan, "As the Lord lives, the man who has done this deserves to die;

6: and he shall restore the lamb fourfold, because he did this thing, and because he had no pity."

7: Nathan said to David, "You are the man. Thus says the Lord, the God of

Israel, 'I anointed you king over Israel, and I delivered you out of the hand of Saul;

8: and I gave you your master's house, and your master's wives into your bosom, and gave you the house of Israel and of Judah; and if this were too little, I would add to you as much more.

9: Why have you despised the word of the Lord, to do what is evil in his sight? You have smitten Uri'ah the Hittite with the sword, and have taken his wife to be your wife, and have slain him with the sword of the Ammonites.

10: Now therefore the sword shall never depart from your house, because you have despised me, and have taken the wife of Uri'ah the Hittite to be your wife.'

11: Thus says the Lord, 'Behold, I will raise up evil against you out of your own house; and I will take your wives before your eyes, and give them to your neighbor, and he shall lie with your wives in the sight of this sun.

12: For you did it secretly; but I will do this thing before all Israel, and before the sun.'"

13: David said to Nathan, "I have sinned against the Lord." And Nathan said to David, "The Lord also has put away your sin; you shall not die."

> David was forgiven because he confessed his sin and acknowledged the truth of Nathan's condemnation. This is one of the most vivid examples of the power of repentance. In the biblical view, it is not sin so much as the subsequent lack of remorse that condemns us.

Building the Temple

In spite of all his accomplishments, David was denied one dream. The successful warrior wanted to build a temple to God as his crowning legacy. But that was not to be. The house of God was supposed to serve as a symbol of peace; David had shed too much blood during his lifetime to be worthy of bringing it into existence. That would be left to his son Solomon, whose name in Hebrew means peace.

1 Chronicles 28

1: David assembled at Jerusalem all the officials of Israel, the officials of the tribes, the officers of the divisions that served the king, the commanders of thousands, the commanders of hundreds, the stewards of all the property and cattle of the king and his sons, together with the palace officials, the mighty men, and all the seasoned warriors.

2: Then King David rose to his feet and said: "Hear me, my brethren and my people. I had it in my heart to build a house of rest for the ark of the covenant of the Lord, and for the footstool of our God; and I made preparations for building.

3: But God said to me, 'You may not build a house for my name, for you are a warrior and have shed blood.'

4: Yet the Lord God of Israel chose me from all my father's house to be king over Israel for ever; for he chose Judah as leader, and in the house of Judah my father's house, and among my father's sons he took pleasure in me to make me king over all Israel.

5: And of all my sons (for the Lord has given me many sons) he has chosen Solomon my son to sit upon the throne of the kingdom of the Lord over Israel.

6: He said to me, 'It is Solomon your son who shall build my house and my courts, for I have chosen him to be my son, and I will be his father.

7: I will establish his kingdom for ever if he continues resolute in keeping my commandments and my ordinances, as he is today.'

8: Now therefore in the sight of all Israel, the assembly of the Lord, and in the hearing of our God, observe and seek out all the commandments of the Lord your God; that you may possess this good land, and leave it for an inheritance to your children after you for ever.

9: And you, Solomon my son, know the God of your father, and serve him with a whole heart and with a willing mind; for the Lord searches all hearts, and understands every plan and thought. If you seek him, he will be found by you; but if you forsake him, he will cast you off for ever."

Is there archeological proof for the Davidic kingdom? For those who seek physical evidence beyond the words of the Bible, a modern-day find offers substantiation. The House of David Inscription, from the First Temple Period, was discovered in excavations of the city of Tel Dan, Israel. It is the first inscription outside of the Bible to mention the Davidic dynasty and King David. The fragment, broken into three pieces, was discovered in 1993 and 1994 and is written in Aramaic with the words separated by dots. It is believed to have been part of a monument built by Hazael, king of Aram, indicating victory over his enemies. The House of David Inscription is the single most important artifact in the State of Israel and is considered a national treasure.

David conquered. Solomon secured. For forty years the land was at peace. Solomon created alliances with his neighbors by way of numerous marriages, forging political links through marital ties. Both Jews and non-Jews considered Solomon wise beyond compare, asking him for advice and assistance. His reign is regarded as the golden age of Israel's history. Highlighting Solomon's success was the magnificence of the temple he built that served to spiritually unite the entire nation.

Solomon's Temple

1 Kings 8

12: Then Solomon said, "The Lord has set the sun in the heavens, but has said that he would dwell in thick darkness.

13: I have built thee an exalted house, a place for thee to dwell in for ever."

14: Then the king faced about, and blessed all the assembly of Israel, while all the assembly of Israel stood.

15: And he said, "Blessed be the Lord, the God of Israel, who with his hand has fulfilled what he promised with his mouth to David my father, saying,

16: 'Since the day that I brought my people Israel out of Egypt, I chose no city in all the tribes of Israel in which to build a house, that my name might be there; but I chose David to be over my people Israel.'

17: Now it was in the heart of David my father to build a house for the name of the Lord, the God of Israel.

18: But the Lord said to David my father, 'Whereas it was in your heart to build a house for my name, you did well that it was in your heart;

19: nevertheless you shall not build the house, but your son who shall be born to you shall build the house for my name.'

20: Now the Lord has fulfilled his promise which he made; for I have risen in the place of David my father, and sit on the throne of Israel, as the Lord promised, and I have built the house for the name of the Lord, the God of Israel.

21: And there I have provided a place for the ark, in which is the covenant of the Lord which he made with our fathers, when he brought them out of the land of Egypt."

22: Then Solomon stood before the altar of the Lord in the presence of all the assembly of Israel, and spread forth his hands toward heaven;

23: and said, "O Lord, God of Israel, there is no God like thee, in heaven above or on earth beneath, keeping covenant and showing steadfast love to thy servants who walk before thee with all their heart;

24: who hast kept with thy servant David my father what thou didst declare to him; yea, thou didst speak with thy mouth, and with thy hand hast fulfilled it this day.

25: Now therefore, O Lord, God of Israel, keep with thy servant David my father what thou hast promised him, saying, 'There shall never fail you a man before me to sit upon the throne of Israel, if only your sons take heed to their way, to walk before me as you have walked before me.'

> Along the eastern wall of the Temple Mount, near the northern end of the wall, is an underlying layer of pre-Herodian stone from which a corner of a very old wall protrudes. The archeologist Leen Ritmeyer has called this unique corner spot the offset. It is clearly a portion of an older wall, believed to be a corner upon which King Herod had his masons build a new wall. Could this offset have been the original northeast corner of the outer courtyard of Solomon's Temple?

In addition to his other accomplishments, Solomon wrote the book of Proverbs. The adage "All good things must come to an end" isn't one of them, yet it could serve as a fitting postscript to his reign. What followed Solomon was a sad story of divisiveness, decline, and ultimate downfall.

4

A Kingdom Divided, a Temple Destroyed

S olomon died leaving a country united politically as the twelve tribes of
Israel and spiritually in the worship of God at the Temple in Jerusalem.
No sooner did Solomon's son Rehobo'am ascend the throne than a civil war broke
out, all because of a very unwise decision.

The Tax Cut That Wasn't

1 Kings 12

1: Rehobo'am went to Shechem, for all Israel had come to Shechem to
make him king.

2: And when Jerobo'am the son of Nebat heard of it (for he was still in
Egypt, whither he had fled from King Solomon), then Jerobo'am returned
from Egypt.

3: And they sent and called him; and Jerobo'am and all the assembly of
Israel came and said to Rehobo'am,

4: "Your father made our yoke heavy. Now therefore lighten the hard service of your father and his heavy yoke upon us, and we will serve you."

5: He said to them, "Depart for three days, then come again to me." So the
people went away.

6: Then King Rehobo'am took counsel with the old men, who had stood before Solomon his father while he was yet alive, saying, "How do you advise me to answer this people?"

7: And they said to him, "If you will be a servant to this people today and serve them, and speak good words to them when you answer them, then they will be your servants for ever."

8: But he forsook the counsel which the old men gave him, and took counsel with the young men who had grown up with him and stood before him.

9: And he said to them, "What do you advise that we answer this people who have said to me, 'Lighten the yoke that your father put upon us'?"

10: And the young men who had grown up with him said to him, "Thus shall you speak to this people who said to you, 'Your father made our yoke heavy, but do you lighten it for us'; thus shall you say to them, 'My little finger is thicker than my father's loins.

11: And now, whereas my father laid upon you a heavy yoke, I will add to your yoke. My father chastised you with whips, but I will chastise you with scorpions.'"

12: So Jerobo'am and all the people came to Rehobo'am the third day, as the king said, "Come to me again the third day."

13: And the king answered the people harshly, and forsaking the counsel which the old men had given him,

14: he spoke to them according to the counsel of the young men, saying, "My father made your yoke heavy, but I will add to your yoke; my father chastised you with whips, but I will chastise you with scorpions."

15: So the king did not hearken to the people; for it was a turn of affairs brought about by the Lord that he might fulfill his word, which the Lord spoke by Ahi'jah the Shi'lonite to Jerobo'am the son of Nebat.

16: And when all Israel saw that the king did not hearken to them, the people answered the king, "What portion have we in David? We have no inheritance in the son of Jesse. To your tents, O Israel! Look now to your own house, David." So Israel departed to their tents.

17: But Rehobo'am reigned over the people of Israel who dwelt in the cities of Judah.

The Northern Kingdom: Israel

Because the new king took the counsel of his young advisers rather than that of his more experienced officials, the entire north, consisting of ten tribes, broke away and formed their own kingdom, which they called Israel. Rehobo'am was left with the

smaller southern portion, comprising Judah and Benjamin, now called simply Judah. The king's stubborn refusal to ease the economic burdens on his populace had severe consequences that eventually affected the very survival of a significant part of the Jewish people.

The northern kingdom of Israel, ruled first by Jerebo'am, would see a succession of nineteen different kings over the next 240 years, each more corrupt and evil than the next. Among the most notorious of them was King Ahab, whose wife Jezebel gave the world the word for a woman who is wicked and scheming. It was during Ahab's reign that the prophet Elijah had his famous confrontation with the idolatrous priests of Ba'al.

Elijah on Mount Carmel

1 Kings 18

17: When Ahab saw Elijah, Ahab said to him, "Is it you, you troubler of Israel?"

18: And he answered, "I have not troubled Israel; but you have, and your father's house, because you have forsaken the commandments of the Lord and followed the Ba'als.

19: Now therefore send and gather all Israel to me at Mount Carmel, and the four hundred and fifty prophets of Ba'al and the four hundred prophets of Ashe'rah, who eat at Jez'ebel's table."

20: So Ahab sent to all the people of Israel, and gathered the prophets together at Mount Carmel.

21: And Elijah came near to all the people, and said, "How long will you waver between two different opinions? If the Lord is God, follow him; but if Ba'al, then follow him." And the people did not answer him a word.

22: Then Elijah said to the people, "I, even I only, am left a prophet of the Lord; but Ba'al's prophets are four hundred and fifty men.

23: Let two bulls be given to us; and let them choose one bull for themselves, and cut it in pieces and lay it on the wood, but put no fire to it; and I will prepare the other bull and lay it on the wood, and put no fire to it.

24: And you call on the name of your god and I will call on the name of the Lord; and the God who answers by fire, he is God." And all the people answered, "It is well spoken."

25: Then Elijah said to the prophets of Ba'al, "Choose for yourselves one bull and prepare it first, for you are many; and call on the name of your god, but put no fire to it."

26: And they took the bull which was given them, and they prepared it, and called on the name of Ba'al from morning until noon, saying, "O Ba'al, answer us!" But there was no voice, and no one answered. And they danced about the altar which they had made.

27: And at noon Elijah mocked them, saying, "Cry aloud, for he is a god; either he is musing, or he has gone aside, or he is on a journey, or perhaps he is asleep and must be awakened."

28: And they cried aloud, and cut themselves after their custom with swords and lances, until the blood gushed out upon them.

29: And as midday passed, they raved on until the time of the offering of the oblation, but there was no voice; no one answered, no one heeded.

30: Then Elijah said to all the people, "Come near to me"; and all the people came near to him. And he repaired the altar of the Lord that had been thrown down;

31: Elijah took twelve stones, according to the number of the tribes of the sons of Jacob, to whom the word of the Lord came, saying, "Israel shall be your name";

32: and with the stones he built an altar in the name of the Lord. And he made a trench about the altar, as great as would contain two measures of seed.

33: And he put the wood in order, and cut the bull in pieces and laid it on the wood. And he said, "Fill four jars with water, and pour it on the burnt offering, and on the wood."

34: And he said, "Do it a second time"; and they did it a second time. And he said, "Do it a third time"; and they did it a third time.

35: And the water ran round about the altar, and filled the trench also with water.

36: And at the time of the offering of the oblation, Elijah the prophet came near and said, "O Lord, God of Abraham, Isaac, and Israel, let it be known this day that thou art God in Israel, and that I am thy servant, and that I have done all these things at thy word.

37: Answer me, O Lord, answer me, that this people may know that thou, O Lord, art God, and that thou hast turned their hearts back."

38: Then the fire of the Lord fell, and consumed the burnt offering, and the wood, and the stones, and the dust, and licked up the water that was in the trench.

39: And when all the people saw it, they fell on their faces; and they said, "The Lord, he is God; the Lord, he is God."

Tourists who go to Mount Carmel today can see a big mountain range. At one end of this range is Haifa, and at the other is a place called Mukhraka, where there is a monastery. In front of the monastery stands a statue of Elijah. This may well be where Elijah challenged the priests of Baal, because the description of the geographic location matches perfectly. Elijah occupies a very special place in Jewish tradition: tradition has it that he is the only prophet who did not die but continues to carry out special missions for God. A chair, "the Chair of Elijah," is reserved for him at every circumcision ceremony. A cup of wine is poured for him, and children are sent to open the door for his arrival, at every Passover seder. According to legend, it is Elijah who will announce the coming of the Messiah. Throughout the centuries, whenever a mysterious stranger has miraculously intervened to help Jews, they would wonder, could that have been Elijah?

Israel in Exile

The northern kingdom of Israel was constantly threatened by its powerful Assyrian neighbor, which occupied most of what today are Syria, Iraq, and Turkey. The Assyrian king Tiglath-pileser III introduced a novel way of dealing with conquered peoples: he exiled them. As a way of pacifying the northern kingdom, Tiglath-pileser took over the lands belonging to the tribes of Zebulun and Naphtali and dispersed them. Soon thereafter, Shalmaneser V, another Assyrian emperor, conquered the lands belonging to the tribes of Reuben, Gad, and Manasseh, and exiled them as well. In 726 B.C.E. Sargon II finished the task, and the whole northern part of the country ceased to exist as a Jewish state.

2 Kings 17

5: Then the king of Assyria invaded all the land and came to Sama'ria, and for three years he besieged it.
6: In the ninth year of Hoshe'a the king of Assyria captured Sama'ria, and he carried the Israelites away to Assyria, and placed them in Halah, and on the Habor, the river of Gozan, and in the cities of the Medes.

The ten northern tribes were dispersed abroad. What happened to them? Where did they end up? Did they maintain any awareness of their origins? Scholars have long been intrigued by the disappearance of the "ten lost tribes." In a fascinating work, *The Thirteenth Gate*, Dr. Tutor Parfait, a professor of history at University College in London, has researched the many people who claim to be descended from these tribes. They range from the Pathans, Muslim fundamentalists who live in northern Afghanistan and Pakistan, to groups from China, Hawaii, Ethiopia, and countless other far-flung communities around the world. According to many scholars, one of the goals of Christopher Columbus's journey was to find the surviving remnants of these long-lost tribes.

The Southern Kingdom: Judah

The southern kingdom of Judah would last another 140 years. When Assyria conquered Israel, Judah was ruled by Hezekiah, the fourteenth king after David, whom the Bible describes in these words: "There was none like him among all the kings of Judah who were after him, nor were there before him" (2 Kings 18:3–5). Hezekiah fortified the city of Jerusalem with a wall that archeologists have excavated, known today as the Broad Wall. The Assyrian king Sennacherib, boasting of his military exploits, wrote this account of his encounter with King Hezekiah:

The Taylor Prism, ii.34–iii.41

But as for Hezekiah, the Jew, who did not bow in submission to my yoke.
. . . He himself I shut up like a caged bird within Jerusalem, his royal city.

James Pritchard, ed., *Ancient Near Eastern Texts Relating to the Old Testament*,
Princeton, N.J., 1969

What Sennacherib did not write about is his conquest of Jerusalem and his victory, neither of which came to pass. That is strong confirmation of the biblical version of the story:

2 Kings 19

35: And that night the angel of the Lord went forth, and slew a hundred and eighty-five thousand in the camp of the Assyrians; and when men arose early in the morning, behold, these were all dead bodies.
36: Then Sennacherib king of Assyria departed, and went home, and dwelt at Nin'eveh.
37: And as he was worshiping in the house of Nisroch his god, Adram'melech and Share'zer, his sons, slew him with the sword, and escaped into the land of Ar'arat. And Esarhad'don his son reigned in his stead.

What happened to Sennacherib's army? Sennacherib's defeat is recorded not only in the Bible; the Greek historian Herodotus gives an account of Sennacherib's humiliation in his *History.* He attributes the miraculous defeat to mice overrunning the camp and wreaking great havoc. "An army of field-mice swarmed over their opponents in the night . . . [and] gnawed through their quivers and their bows, and the handles of their shields, so that on the following day they fled minus their arms and a great number fell" (Book 2:141). Josephus, a first-century Jewish historian, also mentions

Sennacherib's defeat, explaining that it was caused by a plague. He cites an earlier historian who had written: "Now when Sennacherib was returning from his Egyptian war to Jerusalem, he found his army . . . in danger [by a plague], for God had sent a pestilential distemper upon his army; and on the very first night of the siege, a hundred fourscore and five thousand, with their captains and generals, were destroyed" (*Antiquities of the Jews*, Book 10, Chapter 1, Section 5). Some speculate that the mice may have been carriers of the plague. If so, this would not be the only such historical example. Mice were responsible for carrying the black plague in the Middle Ages and could just as easily have transported this deadly malady into the Assyrian camp. The Bible states simply that the destruction came from God and does not mention specifics.

The Assyrian account of Sennacherib's death also confirms the biblical version. The *International Standard Bible Encyclopedia* explains: "According to Esarhaddon's records, his father Sennacherib had named him over his brothers as successor. 'To gain the kingship they slew Sennacherib their father,' forcing Esarhaddon to hasten back from a military campaign to claim the throne" (1988, vol. 4, s.v., "Sennacherib"). A parallel Babylonian account also mentions this assassination.

Destruction

The two saddest words in history, it has often been said, are "if only." If only the kings after Hezekiah had been like him. But Hezekiah's own son, Mannasseh, "did what was evil in the eyes of the Lord. . . . He erected altars to Baal. . . . He passed his son through fire, practiced astrology and read omens, and performed necromancy and conjured spirits. He was profuse in doing what was evil in the eyes of the Lord, to anger Him" (2 Kings 21:2–6). Mannasseh put his own grandfather, the prophet Isaiah, to death. Before long, Babylonia, the major power that replaced Assyria on the world scene, marched against the kingdom of Judah and conquered it. The final defeat was predicted by the prophet Jeremiah (whose name, because of this incident, gave us the word jeremiad*) forty years before it happened.*

2 Kings 25

1: And in the ninth year of his reign, in the tenth month, on the tenth day of the month, Nebuchadnez'zar king of Babylon came with all his army against Jerusalem, and laid siege to it; and they built siege works against it round about.

2: So the city was besieged till the eleventh year of King Zedeki'ah.

3: On the ninth day of the fourth month the famine was so severe in the city that there was no food for the people of the land.

4: Then a breach was made in the city; the king with all the men of war fled by night by the way of the gate between the two walls, by the king's garden, though the Chalde'ans were around the city. And they went in the direction of the Arabah.

5: But the army of the Chalde'ans pursued the king, and overtook him in the plains of Jericho; and all his army was scattered from him.

6: Then they captured the king, and brought him up to the king of Babylon at Riblah, who passed sentence upon him.

7: They slew the sons of Zedeki'ah before his eyes, and put out the eyes of Zedeki'ah, and bound him in fetters, and took him to Babylon.

8: In the fifth month, on the seventh day of the month—which was the nineteenth year of King Nebuchadnez'zar, king of Babylon— Nebu'zarad'an, the captain of the bodyguard, a servant of the king of Babylon, came to Jerusalem.

9: And he burned the house of the Lord, and the king's house and all the houses of Jerusalem; every great house he burned down.

> The Temple burned for several days; on the ninth of the Hebrew month of Av, its destruction was complete. Incredibly enough, the ninth of Av (which falls sometime in July or August, varying from year to year depending on the lunar cycle), would prove to be the very same day the Second Temple was destroyed by the Romans in 70 C.E.; the very same day Jews were expelled from England in 1290 C.E.; the very same day the Jews of Spain were given an ultimatum by the Inquisition—leave, convert, or die in 1492 C.E.; the very same day when World War I, the prelude to the Holocaust, began in 1914; and the very same day when many other calamities were visited upon the Jewish people. Are such coincidences of the calendar proof of God's role in history?

Book II

The Second Temple Period

515 B.C.E.–70 C.E.

THE TIME FRAME

Date (B.C.E.–C.E.)	Event
586 B.C.E.	First Temple destroyed; Babylonian exile
539 B.C.E.	Defeat of Babylonians by Persians
539 B.C.E.	Proclamation of Cyrus: Judean exiles permitted to return
c. 525 B.C.E.	Purim War and victory
515 B.C.E.	Second Temple built
445 B.C.E.	Nehemiah comes to Jerusalem
420 B.C.E.	Ezra introduces religious reforms
332–330 B.C.E.	Alexander the Great conquers Persian Empire
323–322 B.C.E.	After death of Alexander, Judea passes under control of Ptolemy
271 B.C.E.	Translation of Septuagint
200 B.C.E.	Antiochus III of Syria takes control of Judea
175 B.C.E.	Antiochus IV imposes Hellenization

Date (B.C.E.–C.E.)	Event
170–165 B.C.E.	Maccabee rebellion
165 B.C.E.	Hanukkah
104 B.C.E.	Maccabees proclaim themselves kings of Judea
67–63 B.C.E.	Civil war between Maccabee brothers; turn to Rome; Pompey brings Roman troops into Judea
40 B.C.E.	Herod appointed king of Judea by Romans
4 C.E.	Death of Herod
6 C.E.	Judea becomes Roman province; beginning of zealot revolts
30 C.E.	Death of Jesus of Nazareth
66 C.E.	Outbreak of Jewish revolt against the Romans
70 C.E.	Fall of Jerusalem; destruction of Second Temple
73 C.E.	Siege of Masada

5

"These Bones Shall Rise Again"

B y all logic, Jewish history should have come to an end with the destruction of the Temple. The northern kingdom of Israel, comprising ten of the tribes of the children of Israel, had fallen to Assyria in 726 B.C.E. Its inhabitants were exiled, no more to be heard from as a people. Now, in 586 B.C.E., the southern kingdom of Judah met the same fate. Babylonia was the major Mesopotamian power, and after conquering the Jews it forced them out of their land with the expectation that any who remained would soon assimilate into Babylonian society. They did not count on the intensity of Jewish longing for their homeland or, as the Jews would interpret it, the intervention of their God.

A Song of the Exiles

Psalm 137

1: By the waters of Babylon, there we sat down and wept, when we remembered Zion.

2: On the willows there we hung up our lyres.

3: For there our captors required of us songs, and our tormentors, mirth, saying, "Sing us one of the songs of Zion!"

4: How shall we sing the Lord's song in a foreign land?

5: If I forget you, O Jerusalem, let my right hand wither!

6: Let my tongue cleave to the roof of my mouth, if I do not remember you, if I do not set Jerusalem above my highest joy!

> Throughout the centuries, Jews have recited this psalm daily before the grace after meals as a constant reminder that sustenance in exile still leaves us unfulfilled. Perhaps this accounts for the determination of the Jewish people to return to Israel in modern times after a hiatus of close to two thousand years.

The Vision of the Dry Bones

Among the exiles to Babylonia was the prophet Ezekiel. His vision, in the form of a metaphor, gave the people reason to believe in their miraculous redemption.

Ezekiel 37

1: The hand of the Lord was upon me, and he brought me out by the Spirit of the Lord, and set me down in the midst of the valley; it was full of bones.

2: And he led me round among them; and behold, there were very many upon the valley; and lo, they were very dry.

3: And he said to me, "Son of man, can these bones live?" And I answered, "O Lord God, thou knowest."

4: Again he said to me, "Prophesy to these bones, and say to them, O dry bones, hear the word of the Lord.

5: Thus says the Lord God to these bones: Behold, I will cause breath to enter you, and you shall live.

6: And I will lay sinews upon you, and will cause flesh to come upon you, and cover you with skin, and put breath in you, and you shall live; and you shall know that I am the Lord."

7: So I prophesied as I was commanded; and as I prophesied, there was a noise, and behold, a rattling; and the bones came together, bone to its bone.

8: And as I looked, there were sinews on them, and flesh had come upon them, and skin had covered them; but there was no breath in them.

9: Then he said to me, "Prophesy to the breath, prophesy, son of man, and say to the breath, Thus says the Lord God: Come from the four winds, O breath, and breathe upon these slain, that they may live."

10: So I prophesied as he commanded me, and the breath came into them, and they lived, and stood upon their feet, an exceedingly great host.

11: Then he said to me, "Son of man, these bones are the whole house of Israel. Behold, they say, 'Our bones are dried up, and our hope is lost; we are clean cut off.'

12: Therefore prophesy, and say to them, Thus says the Lord God: Behold, I will open your graves, and raise you from your graves, O my people; and I will bring you home into the land of Israel.

13: And you shall know that I am the Lord, when I open your graves, and raise you from your graves, O my people.

14: And I will put my Spirit within you, and you shall live, and I will place you in your own land; then you shall know that I, the Lord, have spoken, and I have done it, says the Lord."

How could slaves dream of freedom? How could the exiled believe they would soon return to their home? The Jews dared to dream because their dreams had been realized before. God had fulfilled his promise when he took them out of Egypt; could he not once again "bring the dead back to life" even though the Jews were subjects of the seemingly invincible Babylonians? Belief made fulfillment of the dream not only possible but inevitable; for the Jews, their destiny was as clear as "the handwriting on the wall"—which is exactly what materialized one night at a magnificent banquet hosted by King Belshazzar of Babylonia:

Daniel and the Handwriting on the Wall

Daniel 5

1: King Belshaz'zar made a great feast for a thousand of his lords, and drank wine in front of the thousand.

2: Belshaz'zar, when he tasted the wine, commanded that the vessels of gold and of silver which Nebuchadnez'zar his father had taken out of the temple in Jerusalem be brought, that the king and his lords, his wives, and his concubines might drink from them.

3: Then they brought in the golden and silver vessels which had been taken out of the temple, the house of God in Jerusalem; and the king and his lords, his wives, and his concubines drank from them.

4: They drank wine, and praised the gods of gold and silver, bronze, iron, wood, and stone.

5: Immediately the fingers of a man's hand appeared and wrote on the plaster of the wall of the king's palace, opposite the lampstand; and the king saw the hand as it wrote.

6: Then the king's color changed, and his thoughts alarmed him; his limbs gave way, and his knees knocked together.

7: The king cried aloud to bring in the enchanters, the Chalde'ans, and the astrologers. The king said to the wise men of Babylon, "Whoever reads this writing, and shows me its interpretation, shall be clothed with purple, and have a chain of gold about his neck, and shall be the third ruler in the kingdom."

8: Then all the king's wise men came in, but they could not read the writing or make known to the king the interpretation.

9: Then King Belshaz'zar was greatly alarmed, and his color changed; and his lords were perplexed.

10: The queen, because of the words of the king and his lords, came into the banqueting hall; and the queen said, "O king, live for ever! Let not your thoughts alarm you or your color change.

11: There is in your kingdom a man in whom is the spirit of the holy gods. In the days of your father light and understanding and wisdom, like the wisdom of the gods, were found in him, and King Nebuchadnez'zar, your father, made him chief of the magicians, enchanters, Chalde'ans, and astrologers,

12: because an excellent spirit, knowledge, and understanding to interpret dreams, explain riddles, and solve problems were found in this Daniel, whom the king named Belteshaz'zar. Now let Daniel be called, and he will show the interpretation."

13: Then Daniel was brought in before the king. The king said to Daniel, "You are that Daniel, one of the exiles of Judah, whom the king my father brought from Judah.

14: I have heard of you that the spirit of the holy gods is in you, and that light and understanding and excellent wisdom are found in you.

15: Now the wise men, the enchanters, have been brought in before me to read this writing and make known to me its interpretation; but they could not show the interpretation of the matter.

16: But I have heard that you can give interpretations and solve problems. Now if you can read the writing and make known to me its interpretation, you shall be clothed with purple, and have a chain of gold about your neck, and shall be the third ruler in the kingdom."

17: Then Daniel answered before the king, "Let your gifts be for yourself, and give your rewards to another; nevertheless I will read the writing to the king and make known to him the interpretation.

18: O king, the Most High God gave Nebuchadnez'zar your father kingship and greatness and glory and majesty;

19: and because of the greatness that he gave him, all peoples, nations, and languages trembled and feared before him; whom he would he slew, and whom he would he kept alive; whom he would he promoted, and whom he would he humbled.

20: But when his heart was lifted up and his spirit was hardened so that he dealt proudly, he was deposed from his kingly throne, and his glory was taken from him;

21: he was driven from among men, and his mind was made like that of a beast, and his dwelling was with the wild asses; he was fed grass like an ox, and his body was wet with the dew of heaven, until he knew that the Most High God rules the kingdom of men, and sets over it whom he will.

22: And you his son, Belshaz'zar, have not humbled your heart, though you knew all this,

23: but you have lifted up yourself against the Lord of heaven; and the vessels of his house have been brought in before you, and you and your lords, your wives, and your concubines have drunk wine from them; and you have praised the gods of silver and gold, of bronze, iron, wood, and stone, which do not see or hear or know, but the God in whose hand is your breath, and all your ways, you have not honored.

24: "Then from his presence the hand was sent, and this writing was inscribed.

25: And this is the writing that was inscribed: MENE, MENE, TEKEL, and PARSIN.

26: This is the interpretation of the matter: MENE, God has numbered the days of your kingdom and brought it to an end;

27: TEKEL, you have been weighed in the balances and found wanting;

28: PERES, your kingdom is divided and given to the Medes and Persians."

29: Then Belshaz'zar commanded, and Daniel was clothed with purple, a chain of gold was put about his neck, and proclamation was made concerning him, that he should be the third ruler in the kingdom.

30: That very night Belshaz'zar the Chalde'an king was slain.

31: And Darius the Mede received the kingdom, being about sixty-two years old.

The Declaration of Cyrus

The warning came true. Babylonia gave way to the rule of the Medes and the Persians. Things changed rapidly for the Jews as they became subjects of the Persian Empire. In 539 B.C.E., the great Cyrus of Persia issued a decree—today on display at the British Museum—that allowed all the indigenous peoples that had been exiled by the now-defunct Babylonian Empire to go back to their homelands. Recorded in cuneiform on what is known as the Cyrus Cylinder, this proclamation, widely acknowledged as the first declaration of human rights, accorded the conquered Babylonians and Jews freedom of worship. For the Jews, it proved Ezekiel right. Dead bones can again stir and come back to life!

Ezra 1

1: In the first year of Cyrus king of Persia, that the word of the Lord by the mouth of Jeremiah might be accomplished, the Lord stirred up the spirit of Cyrus king of Persia so that he made a proclamation throughout all his kingdom and also put it in writing:
2: "Thus says Cyrus king of Persia: The Lord, the God of heaven, has given me all the kingdoms of the earth, and he has charged me to build him a house at Jerusalem, which is in Judah.
3: Whoever is among you of all his people, may his God be with him, and let him go up to Jerusalem, which is in Judah, and rebuild the house of the Lord, the God of Israel—he is the God who is in Jerusalem;
4: and let each survivor, in whatever place he sojourns, be assisted by the men of his place with silver and gold, with goods and with beasts, besides freewill offerings for the house of God which is in Jerusalem."

The Cyrus Cylinder

I am Cyrus. King of the world. When I entered Babylon . . . I did not allow anyone to terrorize the land. . . . I kept in view the needs of people and all its sanctuaries to promote their well being. . . . I put an end to their misfortune. The Great God has delivered all the lands into my hand; the lands that I have made to dwell in a peaceful habitation.

James Pritchard, ed., Ancient Near Eastern Texts Relating to the Old Testament,
Princeton, N.J., 1969

The Song of Deliverance

The Jews who returned could hardly believe their good fortune. They now sang a sequel to the psalm of lament they had sung in Babylonia:

Psalms 126

A Song of Ascents.

1: When the Lord restored the fortunes of Zion, we were like those who dream.

2: Then our mouth was filled with laughter, and our tongue with shouts of joy; then they said among the nations, "The Lord has done great things for them."

3: The Lord has done great things for us; we are glad.

4: Restore our fortunes, O Lord, like streams in the Negeb!

5: May those who sow in tears reap with shouts of joy!

6: He that goes forth weeping, bearing the seed for sowing, shall come home with shouts of joy, bringing his sheaves with him.

> Martin Luther King Jr. captured the vision of the civil rights movement with his impassioned speech featuring the refrain "I have a dream." It was almost certainly inspired by this psalm.

Jews were now allowed to return to their homeland, but not everyone wanted to go back. Of the approximately one million Jews in the empire, only forty-two thousand, approximately 5 percent of those who went into exile seventy years before, were willing to forsake the comfort of their new surroundings. This was the beginning of "Diaspora Jewry" (diaspora is a Greek word meaning "dispersion"), Jews who recognize Israel as the spiritual center of their people but choose nonetheless to reside elsewhere. Those Jews who chose to remain in Persia soon faced the threat of the first genocide in history. Their story is told in the book of Esther and is still celebrated as an annual holiday.

The Purim Story

Esther 1

1: In the days of Ahasu-e'rus, the Ahasu-e'rus who reigned from India to Ethiopia over one hundred and twenty-seven provinces,

2: in those days when King Ahasu-e'rus sat on his royal throne in Susa the capital,

3: in the third year of his reign he gave a banquet for all his princes and servants, the army chiefs of Persia and Media and the nobles and governors of the provinces being before him,

4: while he showed the riches of his royal glory and the splendor and pomp of his majesty for many days, a hundred and eighty days.

Esther 3

5: And when Haman saw that Mor'decai did not bow down or pay him honor, Haman was filled with fury.

6: But he disdained to lay hands on Mor'decai alone. So, as they had made known to him the people of Mor'decai, Haman sought to destroy all the Jews, the people of Mor'decai, throughout the whole kingdom of Ahasu-e'rus.

7: In the first month, which is the month of Nisan, in the twelfth year of King Ahasu-e'rus, they cast Pur, that is the lot, before Haman day after day; and they cast it month after month till the twelfth month, which is the month of Adar.

8: Then Haman said to King Ahasu-e'rus, "There is a certain people scattered abroad and dispersed among the peoples in all the provinces of your kingdom; their laws are different from those of every other people, and they do not keep the king's laws, so that it is not for the king's profit to tolerate them.

9: If it please the king, let it be decreed that they be destroyed, and I will pay ten thousand talents of silver into the hands of those who have charge of the king's business, that they may put it into the king's treasuries."

Haman pressed for a "final solution" to the "problem" of the Jews in the kingdom. Thanks to the influence of the queen, who happened to be Jewish, Haman's plot was foiled, Queen Esther had a biblical book named for her, and the Jews had a new holiday added to the calendar called Purim, after the "lots" that Haman cast for a day of destruction that turned into a day of rejoicing.

> The book of Esther is the only book of the Bible in which God's name does not appear even once. Yet its story is commemorated as a miracle of divine intervention. The message? Miracles don't always have to be obvious. There are times when God chooses to work behind the scenes and perform miracles that might well be called mere coincidence. Purim commemorates the occasion of God's indirect involvement in history; as the saying goes, "Coincidence is just God's way of choosing to remain anonymous."

After numerous delays, such that the work was spread over twenty-three years, the Second Temple was finally completed in 515 B.C.E. and rededicated during the reign of Darius I, emperor of Persia. Far smaller and inferior in many ways to the First Temple, it would have to wait until the reign of King Herod (37–4 B.C.E.) to be beautified in a manner that approximated the splendor of the First Temple. In the century following Cyrus's Proclamation, the Jews floundered without leadership until

the days of Nehemiah and Ezra. Nehemiah, a Jew who occupied the high post of cup-
bearer to the Persian king Artaxerxes, took a voluntary leave of absence from his
royal duties to become military governor of Judea. He was responsible for rebuilding
the wall of Jerusalem in 445 B.C.E. Ezra, a contemporary of Nehemiah and a scholar
and teacher, believed that Judaism could survive only through knowledge. He is
responsible for what is almost certainly the first adult public education program in
history:

Teaching the Masses

Nehemiah 8

1: And all the people gathered as one man into the square before the Water
Gate; and they told Ezra the scribe to bring the book of the law of Moses
which the Lord had given to Israel.
2: And Ezra the priest brought the law before the assembly, both men and
women and all who could hear with understanding, on the first day of the
seventh month.
3: And he read from it facing the square before the Water Gate from early
morning until midday, in the presence of the men and the women and
those who could understand; and the ears of all the people were attentive
to the book of the law.

> Ezra instituted the ritual of reading a portion of the Torah at services three
> times a week, a tradition observed to this day in synagogues around the
> world. How important do you think this practice has been for the survival of
> the Jewish people?

6

The Hebrews and
the Hellenists

The next chapter of Jewish history begins with the rise of Alexander the Great and the Greek Empire. This was the golden age of classical Greek culture—the birth of democracy and the time of Aristotle, Socrates, and Plato. Before dying of a fever at age thirty-three, Alexander conquered most of Asia, the Middle East, and parts of North Africa, dismantling the entire Persian Empire and spreading Hellenism—the Greek lifestyle and culture—wherever he went. According to an eyewitness account of the initial encounter between Alexander the Great and Simeon the Just, a leading rabbi of his generation, the Hebrews and the Hellenists appeared to be headed for an amicable relationship.

Alexander the Great and the Rabbi

Babylonian Talmud, Yoma 69a

The Cutheans demanded from Alexander the Great the right to destroy the House of God, and he had given them permission, whereupon some people came and informed Simeon the Just. What did he do? He put on his priestly garments, some of the noblemen of Israel went with him carrying fiery torches in their hands, and they walked all night until the dawn rose. When Alexander saw them from afar, he asked, "Who are these?" The Samaritans answered, "The Jews who rebelled against you." When the Jews approached and Alexander saw Simeon the Just, he descended from his carriage and bowed down before him. The people said to him in much wonderment: "A great king like yourself should bow down before this Jew?" He answered: "It is his image that constantly appeared before me in my dreams that assured me of victory in all my battles."

Legend has it that at that meeting Alexander asked the Jews to install his statue in the Holy Temple, a practice he established in all the other provinces that he conquered. He either did not know or did not care that doing so would contravene religious law, which precludes Jews from having graven images, especially in the Temple. Simeon the Just came up with a brilliant solution: "O mighty emperor," he said, "of what shall we make this statue? If we make it of metal, it shall someday rust. If we make it from wood it shall someday rot. Statues of stone become covered with pigeon waste. As the emperor can see, throughout our land we have no images, due to religious guidelines. Permit us to provide a substitute that will endure for eternity. We shall make a decree that every boy born this year in Israel shall be named Alexander." And that's how Alexander got to be a Jewish name!

The First Translation of the Bible

After Alexander's death in 323 B.C.E., his newly established empire was soon torn apart by his generals, who each sought to succeed him. Judea passed to the control of Ptolemy, who set up an empire based in Egypt. Thanks to his successor, Ptolemy II (285–247 B.C.E.), Western civilization would be shaped in no small measure by the ideas and the ideals of the Bible. King Ptolemy Philadelphus II, in order to complete his collection of all the world's books for his royal library, needed a copy of the "laws of the Jews." To secure translators for the Hebrew scriptures, Ptolemy agreed to the condition of the Jewish high priest Eleazer, releasing all the Jewish captives in Egypt in exchange for seventy-two men competent to make the translation into Greek. Upon their arrival in Alexandria, Ptolemy hosted a seven-day banquet, during which he posed difficult questions to each translator. Their answers, which reflect Stoic moral philosophy, satisfied Ptolemy. The translation was completed in seventy-two days. The Letter of Aristeas, a Hellenistic Jew, summarizes the events surrounding the production of the Septuagint, the first translation of the Bible into another language.

From "The Letter of Aristeas"

To the Great King, from Demetrius. In accordance with your Majesty's order concerning the library, that books needed to complete the collection should be acquired and added, and that those accidentally damaged should receive suitable attention, I submit the following report, having attended to my responsibility in the matter in no casual manner. Books of the Law of the Jews, with some few others, are absent from the library. For it happens that these books are written in the Hebrew script and language, but, according to the evidence of the experts, have been somewhat carelessly committed to writing and are not in their original form; for they have never had the benefit of royal attention. It is important that these books, duly corrected, should find a place in your library, because this legislation, in as much as it is divine, is of philosophical importance and free from all blemish. For this reason writers and poets and the great majority of historians have avoided reference to the above mentioned books and to the people who have lived and are living in accordance with them, because, as Hecataeus of Abdera says, the view of life presented in them has a certain sanctity and holiness. If, then, your Majesty approves, a letter shall be written to the high priest in Jerusalem, asking him to send elders of exemplary lives, expert in their country's Law, six from each tribe, so that, having established the agreement of the majority and obtained an accurate translation, we may give the book a distinguished place in our library, in keeping both with the importance of the affair and of your own purpose. May you ever prosper! . . .

Three days later Demetrius took the men and passing along the seawall, seven stadia long, to the island, crossed the bridge and made for the northern districts of Pharos. There he assembled them in a house, which had been built upon the seashore, of great beauty and in a secluded situation, and invited them to carry out the work of translation, since everything that they needed for the purpose was placed at their disposal. So they set to work comparing their several results and making them agree, and whatever they agreed upon was suitably copied out under the direction of Demetrius. And the session lasted until the ninth hour; after this they were set free to minister to their physical needs. Everything they wanted was furnished for them on a lavish scale. In addition to this Dorotheus made the same preparations for them daily as were made for the king himself—for thus he had been commanded by the king. In the early morning they appeared daily at the Court, and after saluting the king went back to their own place. And as is the custom of all the Jews, they washed their hands in the sea and prayed to God and then devoted themselves to reading and translating the particular passage upon which they were engaged, and I put the question to them, Why it was that they washed their hands before they prayed? And they explained that it was a token that they had done no evil (for every form of activity is wrought by means of the hands) since in their noble and holy way they regard everything as a symbol of righteousness and truth.

And it so chanced that the work of translation was completed in seventy-two days, just as if this had been arranged of set purpose. When the work was completed, Demetrius collected together the Jewish population in the place where the translation had been made, and read it over to all, in the presence of the translators, who met with a great reception also from the people, because of the great benefits which they had conferred upon them. They bestowed warm praise upon Demetrius, too, and urged him to have the whole law transcribed and present a copy to their leaders. After the books had been read, the priests and the elders of the translators and the Jewish community and the leaders of the people stood up and said, that since so excellent and sacred and accurate a translation had been made, it was only right that it should remain as it was and no alteration should be made in it. And when the whole company expressed their approval, they bade them pronounce a curse in accordance with their custom upon any one who should make any alteration either by adding anything or changing in any way whatever any of the words which had been written or making any omission. This was a very wise precaution to ensure that the book might be preserved for all the future time unchanged.

> *The letter of Aristeas:* translated with an appendix of ancient evidence of the origin of the Septuagint by H. St. J. Thackeray, London/New York, 1918

The rabbis of the Talmud had a strange reaction to the first translation of the Bible. They proclaimed a fast day to commemorate this event! Why? Translations, they believed, inevitably fail to do justice to the original. Also, with a translated Bible available, there was concern that Jews might ignore the study of Hebrew. Is there any validity to their fear?

Ptolemy's Egypt-based empire and the Seleucid kings of Syria waged war over the coastal strip that included Judea. After more than a century, the Seleucid king Antiochus prevailed. To help unify his troubled kingdom, Antiochus the Fourth encouraged all of his subjects to adopt a Greek lifestyle, initiating a period of strong Hellenization. Many Jews responded positively, glorifying their bodies, ceasing to circumcise their sons, and preferring—as some historians would put it—the Greek ideal of "the holiness of beauty" over the Jewish concept of "the beauty of holiness." However, when, circa 170 B.C.E.., Hellenization became enforced as official policy and the practice of Judaism was forbidden, the priestly family of the Hasmoneans, under the leadership of Mattathias and his five sons, led a rebellion for religious freedom. Their goal was to rededicate the Temple, which had become defiled, and to rededicate the Jews to their God and their ancient teachings. Their success is remembered to this day as the holiday of Hanukkah, the Festival of Lights.

The Maccabees and the Holiday of Hanukkah

1 Maccabees 1

41 Then the king wrote to his whole kingdom that all should be one people, [42]and that all should give up their particular customs. [43]All the Gentiles accepted the command of the king. Many even from Israel gladly adopted his religion; they sacrificed to idols and profaned the Sabbath. [44]And the king sent letters by messengers to Jerusalem and the towns of Judah; he directed them to follow customs strange to the land, [45]to forbid burnt offerings and sacrifices and drink offerings in the sanctuary, to profane Sabbaths and festivals, [46]to defile the sanctuary and the priests, [47]to build altars and sacred precincts and shrines for idols, to sacrifice swine and other unclean animals, [48]and to leave their sons uncircumcised. They were to make themselves abominable by everything unclean and profane, [49]so that they would forget the law and change all the ordinances. [50]He added "And whoever does not obey the command of the king shall die."

51 In such words he wrote to his whole kingdom. He appointed inspectors over all the people and commanded the towns of Judah to offer sacrifice, town by town. [52]Many of the people, everyone who forsook the law, joined them, and they did evil in the land; [53]they drove Israel into hiding in every place of refuge they had.

54 Now on the fifteenth day of Kislev, in the one hundred forty-fifth year they erected a desolating sacrilege on the altar of burnt offering. They also built altars in the surrounding towns of Judah, [55]and offered incense at the doors of the houses and in the streets. [56]The books of the law that they found they tore to pieces and burned with fire. [57]Anyone found possessing the book of the covenant, or anyone who adhered to the law, was condemned to death by decree of the king. [58]They kept using violence against Israel, against those who were found month after month in the towns. [59]On the twenty-fifth day of the month they offered sacrifice on the altar that was on top of the altar of burnt offering. [60]According to the

decree, they put to death the women who had their children circumcised, [61]and their families and those who circumcised them; and they hung the infants from their mothers' necks.

62 But many in Israel stood firm and were resolved in their hearts not to eat unclean food. [63]They chose to die rather than to be defiled by food or to profane the holy covenant; and they did die. [64]Very great wrath came upon Israel. . . .

1 Maccabees 2

1 In those days Mattathias son of John son of Simeon, a priest of the family of Joarib, moved from Jerusalem and settled in Modein. [2]He had five sons, John surnamed Gaddi, [3]Simon called Thassi, [4]Judas called Maccabeus, [5]Eleazar called Avaran, and Jonathan called Apphus. [6]He saw the blasphemies being committed in Judah and Jerusalem, [7]and said, "Alas! Why was I born to see this, the ruin of my people, the ruin of the holy city, and to live there when it was given over to the enemy, the sanctuary given over to aliens? [8]Her temple has become like a person without honor [9]her glorious vessels have been carried into exile. Her infants have been killed in her streets, her youths by the sword of the foe. . . ."

1 Maccabees 3

1 Then his son Judas, who was called Maccabeus, took command in his place. [2]All his brothers and all who had joined his father helped him; they gladly fought for Israel. [3]He extended the glory of his people. Like a giant he put on his breastplate; he bound on his armor of war and waged battles, protecting the camp by his sword. [4]He was like a lion in his deeds, like a lion's cub roaring for prey. . . .

1 Maccabees 4

36 Then Judas and his brothers said, "See, our enemies are crushed; let us go up to cleanse the sanctuary and dedicate it." [37]So all the army assembled and went up to Mount Zion. [38]There they saw the sanctuary desolate, the altar profaned, and the gates burned. In the courts they saw bushes sprung up as in a thicket, or as on one of the mountains. They saw also the chambers of the priests in ruins. [39]Then they tore their clothes and mourned with great lamentation; they sprinkled themselves with ashes [40]and fell face down on the ground. And when the signal was given with the trumpets, they cried out to Heaven.

41 Then Judas detailed men to fight against those in the citadel until he had cleansed the sanctuary. [42]He chose blameless priests devoted to the law, [43]and they cleansed the sanctuary and removed the defiled stones to an unclean place. [44]They deliberated what to do about the altar of burnt offering, which had been profaned. [45]And they thought it best to tear it down, so that it would not be a lasting shame to them that the Gentiles had defiled it. So they tore down the altar, [46]and stored the stones in a convenient place on the temple hill until a prophet should come to tell what to do with them. [47]Then they took unhewn stones, as the law directs, and built a new altar like the former one. [48]They also rebuilt the sanctuary and the interior of the temple, and consecrated the courts. [49]They made new holy vessels, and brought the lamp stand, the altar of incense, and the table into the temple. [50]Then they offered incense on the altar and lit the lamps on the lamp stand, and these gave light in the temple. [51]They placed the bread on the table and hung up the curtains. Thus they finished all the work they had undertaken.

Hanukkah means "dedication"; it commemorates the rededication of the Temple. Jewish tradition has it that when the Maccabees needed pure oil to light the menorah, they found a flask with only enough oil to burn for one day. Miraculously, it burned for eight days, until a new supply could be made. That is why, we are told, the holiday is celebrated for eight days— because the light of the menorah lasted far longer than was believed possible. Perhaps symbolically that is the real reason for observing Hanukkah: the light of Judaism, too, continues to shine far beyond expectations.

7

Religious Ferment: Different Visions of Service to God

Histoy is more than the story of kings and rulers, wars and conquests. History is shaped as much by spiritual visions as by military victories. The years immediately preceding the Common Era witnessed a tremendous religious ferment that would not only bring about a new world religion but would also immeasurably influence the story of civilization to the present day. What caused this spiritual upheaval is the subject of much scholarly debate. What is certain, however, is that in the century before the birth of Jesus, a powerful wave of religious fervor made its presence felt, stressing the mystical, the End of Days, the afterlife, and the coming of a Messiah who would usher in a far better world.

We know a great deal about the events of those days thanks to eyewitness accounts from three sources. The first is Philo, an Alexandrian Jewish philosopher who lived from about 20 B.C.E. to 40 C.E. in the large Egyptian Jewish community, which numbered over one million. The second is one of history's most intriguing figures, Joseph, son of Mattathias, known simply as Josephus (37 C.E.–circa 100 C.E.). A Jewish military commander who surrendered to the Romans to save his life, he was called a traitor by many of his people. Taking the name of Flavius in gratitude to the Roman emperor, Flavius Josephus gained fame as a chronicler, regarded in the Christian world as the greatest historian of the Jews. For centuries Josephus's works were more widely read in Europe than any book other than the Bible, as invaluable witness to a momentous turning point in Judaism, Christianity, and Western civilization. The third source for our direct knowledge of those times is the recently discovered Dead Sea Scrolls, affording us for the first time an intimate glimpse into

*the society, the culture, and the thought of the people who in all probability went on
to shape the Christian religion.*

*From these sources we learn about the Ascetics, the Pharisees, the Sadducees, and
the Essenes.*

The Pre-Christian Ascetics of Egypt

Philo, *On the Contemplative Life*

[T]hey have been instructed by nature and the sacred laws to serve the living God. . . .

Then, because of their anxious desire for an immortal and blessed existence, thinking that their mortal life has already come to an end, they leave their possessions to their sons or daughters, or perhaps to other relations, giving them up their inheritance with willing cheerfulness: and those who know no relations give their property to their companions or friends. . . .

When, therefore, men abandon their property without being influenced by any predominant attraction, they flee without even turning their heads back again, deserting their brethren, their children, their wives, their parents, their numerous families, their affectionate bands of companions, their native lands in which they have been born and brought up, though long familiarity is a most attractive bond, and one very well able to allure any one. And they depart, not to another city as those do who entreat to be purchased from those who at present possess them, being either unfortunate or else worthless servants, and as such seeking a change of masters rather than endeavoring to procure freedom (for every city, even that which is under the happiest laws, is full of indescribable tumults, and disorders, and calamities, which no one would submit to who had been even for a moment under the influence of wisdom), but they take up their abode outside of walls, or gardens, or solitary lands, seeking for a desert place, not because of any ill-natured misanthropy to which they have learned to devote themselves, but because of the associations with people of wholly dissimilar dispositions to which they would otherwise be compelled, and which they know to be unprofitable and mischievous. . . .

And in every house there is a sacred shrine which is called the holy place, and the house in which they retire by themselves and perform all the mysteries of a holy life, bringing in nothing, neither meat, nor drink, nor anything else which is indispensable towards supplying the necessities of the body, but studying in that place the laws and the sacred oracles of God enunciated by the holy prophets, and hymns, and psalms, and all kinds of other things by reason of which knowledge and piety are increased and brought to perfection.

Therefore they always retain an imperishable recollection of God, so that not even in their dreams is any other subject ever presented to their eyes except the beauty of the divine virtues and of the divine powers. Therefore many persons speak in their sleep, divulging and publishing the celebrated doctrines of the sacred philosophy. And they are accustomed to pray twice a day, at morning and at evening; when the sun is rising entreating God that the happiness of the coming day may be real happiness, so that their minds may be filled with heavenly light, and when the sun is setting they pray that their soul, being entirely lightened and relieved of the burden of the outward senses, and of the appropriate object of these outward senses, may be able to trace out trust existing in its own consistory and council chamber. And the interval between morning and evening is by them devoted wholly to meditation on and to practice virtue, for they take up the sacred scriptures and philosophy concerning them, investigating the allegories as symbols of some secret meaning of nature, intended to be conveyed in those figurative expressions. . . .

Therefore, during six days, each of these individuals, retiring into solitude by himself, philosophizes by himself in one of the places called monasteries, never going outside the threshold of the outer court, and indeed never even looking out.

But on the seventh day they all come together as if to meet in a sacred assembly, and they sit down in order according to their ages with all becoming gravity, keeping their hands inside their garments, having their right hand between their chest and their dress, and the left hand down by their side, close to their flank; and then the eldest of them who has the most profound learning in their doctrines comes forward and speaks with steadfast look and with steadfast voice, with great powers of reasoning, and great prudence, not making an exhibition of his oratorical powers like the rhetoricians of old, or the sophists of the present day, but investigating with great pains, and explaining with minute accuracy the precise meaning of the laws, which sits, not indeed at the tips of their ears, but penetrates through their hearing into the soul, and remains there lastingly; and all the rest listen in silence to the praises which he bestows upon the law, showing their assent only by nods of the head, or the eager look of the eyes.

Philo, F. H. Colson, trans., Cambridge, Mass., 1954

The Three Philosophies

Josephus, *Antiquities of the Jews,* **Book 18, Chapter 1**

The Jews, from the most ancient times, had three philosophies pertaining to their traditions, that of the Essenes, that of the Sadducees, and, thirdly, that of the group called the Pharisees. . . .

The Pharisees simplify their standard of living, making no concession to luxury. They follow the guidance of that which their doctrine has selected and transmitted as good, attaching the chief importance to the observance of those commandments which it has seen fit to dictate to them. They show respect and deference to their elders, nor do they rashly presume to contradict their proposals. Though they postulate that everything is brought about by fate, still they do not deprive the human will of the pursuit of what is in man's power, since it was God's good pleasure that there should be a fusion and that the will of man with his virtue and vice should be admitted to the council-chamber of fate. They believe that souls have power to survive death and that there are rewards and punishments under the earth for those who have led lives of virtue or vice: eternal imprisonment is the lot of evil souls, while the good souls receive an easy passage to a new life. Because of these views they are, as a matter of fact, extremely influential among the townsfolk; and all prayers and sacred rites of divine worship are performed according to their exposition. This is the great tribute that the inhabitants of the cities, by practicing the highest ideals both in their way of living and in their discourse, have paid to the excellence of the Pharisees.

The Sadducees hold that the soul perishes along with the body. They own no observance of any sort apart from the laws; in fact, they reckon it a virtue to dispute with the teachers of the path of wisdom that they pursue. There are but few men to whom this doctrine has been made known, but these are men of the highest standing. They accomplish practically nothing, however. For whenever they assume some office, though they submit unwillingly and perforce, yet submit they do to the formulas of the Pharisees, since otherwise the masses would not tolerate them.

The doctrine of the Essenes is wont to leave everything in the hands of God. They regard the soul as immortal and believe that they ought to strive especially to draw near to righteousness. They send votive offerings to the temple, but perform their sacrifices employing a different ritual of purification. For this reason they are barred from those precincts of the temple that are frequented by all the people and perform their rites by themselves. Otherwise they are of the highest character, devoting themselves solely to agricultural labor. They deserve admiration in contrast to all others who claim their share of virtue because such qualities as theirs were never found before among any Greek or barbarian people, nay, not even briefly, but have been among them in constant practice and never interrupted since they adopted them from of old. Moreover, they hold their possessions in common, and the wealthy man receives no more enjoyment from his property than the man who possesses nothing. The men who practice this way of life number more than four thousand. They neither bring wives into the community nor do they own slaves, since they believe that the latter practice contributes to injustice and that the former opens the way to a source of dissension. Instead they live by themselves and perform menial tasks for one another. They elect by show of hands good men to receive their revenues and the produce of the earth and priests to prepare bread and other food. Their manner of life does not differ at all from that of the so-called Ctistae among the Dacians, but is as close to it as could be.

Josephus: Antiquities of the Jews, H. St. J. Thackeray, trans., Cambridge, Mass., 1928

The "men of the highest standing" were those who were rich. Why were the wealthy primarily Sadducees? What was it about the philosophy of the Pharisees that most appealed to the masses? Why were the Essenes the minority? Which ideas from these three philosophies have survived? What role do these ideas play in the major religions of our time?

The Life of the Essenes

Some historians suggest that the Essenes were the forerunners of early Christianity. For this reason, their lifestyles are of special interest. Josephus provides us with a fascinating and full account.

Josephus, *Wars of the Jews,* Book 2, Chapter 8

2. For there are three philosophical sects among the Jews. The followers of the first of which are the Pharisees; of the second, the Sadducees; and the third sect, which pretends to a severer discipline, are called Essenes. These

last are Jews by birth, and seem to have a greater affection for one another than the other sects have. These Essenes reject pleasures as an evil, but esteem continence, and the conquest over our passions, to be virtue. They neglect wedlock, but choose out other persons' children, while they are pliable, and fit for learning, and esteem them to be of their kindred, and form them according to their own manners. They do not absolutely deny the fitness of marriage, and the succession of mankind thereby continued; but they guard against the lascivious behavior of women, and are persuaded that none of them preserve their fidelity to one man.

3. These men are despisers of riches, and so very communicative as raises our admiration. Nor is there any one to be found among them who hath more than another; for it is a law among them, that those who come to them must let what they have be common to the whole order, insomuch that among them all there is no appearance of poverty, or excess of riches, but every one's possessions are intermingled with every other's possessions; and so there is, as it were, one patrimony among all the brethren. They think that oil is a defilement; and if any one of them be anointed without his own approbation, it is wiped off his body; for they think to be sweaty is a good thing, as they do also to be clothed in white garments. They also have stewards appointed to take care of their common affairs, who every one of them have no separate business for any, but what is for the uses of them all.

4. They have no one certain city, but many of them dwell in every city; and if any of their sect come from other places, what they have lies open for them, just as if it were their own; and they go in to such as they never knew before, as if they had been ever so long acquainted with them. For which reason they carry nothing at all with them when they travel into remote parts, though still they take their weapons with them, for fear of thieves. Accordingly, there is, in every city where they live, one appointed particularly to take care of strangers, and to provide garments and other necessaries for them. But the habit and management of their bodies is such as children use who are in fear of their masters. Nor do they allow of the change of shoes till be first torn to pieces, or worn out by time. Nor do they either buy or sell any thing to one another; but every one of them gives what he hath to him that wanteth it, and receives from him again in lieu of it what may be convenient for himself; and although there be no requital made, they are fully allowed to take what they want of whomsoever they please.

5. And as for their piety towards God, it is very extraordinary; for before sun-rising they speak not a word about profane matters, but put up certain prayers which they have received from their forefathers, as if they made a supplication for its rising. After this every one of them are sent away by their curators, to exercise some of those arts wherein they are skilled, in which they labor with great diligence till the fifth hour. After which they assemble themselves together again into one place; and when they have clothed themselves in white veils, they then bathe their bodies in cold water. And after this purification is over, they every one meet together in an apartment of their own, into which it is not permitted to any of another sect to enter; while they go, after a pure manner, into the dining-room, as into a certain holy temple, and quietly set themselves down; upon which the baker lays them loaves in order; the cook also brings a single plate of one sort of food, and sets it before every one of them; but a priest says grace before meat; and it is unlawful for any one to taste of the food before grace be said. The same priest, when he hath dined, says grace again after meat; and when they begin, and when they end, they praise God, as he that bestows their food upon them; after which they lay aside their [white] garments, and betake themselves to their labors again till the evening; then they return home to supper, after the same manner; and if there be any strangers there, they sit down with them. Nor is there ever any clamor or disturbance to pollute their house, but they give every one leave to speak in their turn; which silence thus kept in their house appears to foreigners like some tremendous mystery; the cause of which is that perpetual sobriety they exercise, and the same settled measure of meat and drink that is allotted them, and that such as is abundantly sufficient for them. . . .

8. But for those that are caught in any heinous sins, they cast them out of their society; and he who is thus separated from them does often die after a miserable manner; for as he is bound by the oath he hath taken, and by the customs he hath been engaged in, he is not at liberty to partake of that food that he meets with elsewhere, but is forced to eat grass, and to famish his body with hunger, till he perish; for which reason they receive many of them again when they are at their last gasp, out of compassion to them, as thinking the miseries they have endured till they came to the very brink of death to be a sufficient punishment for the sins they had been guilty of.

Josephus: Wars of the Jews, H. St. J. Thackeray, trans., Cambridge, Mass., 1928

Which of these ideas are reflected in Christian thought? How might these ideas have influenced socialism and communism? Which aspects became accepted by the "hippie" movement of the late twentieth century? What makes these ideas so appealing?

The Dead Sea Scrolls

The Dead Sea Scrolls are scrolls and scroll fragments recovered in the area of Qumran, near the Dead Sea in Israel. They represent a voluminous body of Jewish documents dating from the third century B.C.E. to 68 C.E. Considered the greatest manuscript find of the twentieth century, these documents demonstrate the rich literary activity of Second Temple Period Jewry and shed light on an era that was pivotal to both Judaism and Christianity. They contain some books or works in a large number of copies. Others are represented only by fragments or small scraps of parchment. There are tens of thousands of scroll fragments. The number of different compositions represented is almost one thousand, and they are written in three different languages: Hebrew, Aramaic, and Greek. The Dead Sea Scrolls have enhanced our knowledge of both Judaism and Christianity. They are the product of a nonrabbinic form of Judaism and provide a wealth of material, including many important parallels to the Jesus movement, for New Testament scholars. They show Christianity to be rooted in Judaism and have been called the evolutionary link between the two. In addition to biblical books, there are nonbiblical writings that include commentaries, paraphrases that expand on the law, rule books of the community, writings on war conduct, thanksgiving psalms, hymnic compositions, benedictions, liturgical texts, and sapiential (wisdom) writings. The scrolls were most likely written by the Essenes. What follows is a selection from a scroll that is a collection of proverbs.

Fragment 1

It is not advisable to have any kind of legal contract with a person who is not stable. Otherwise, just as a metal like lead that looks intact melts immediately when heated, the unstable person too will change his mind and not keep his word.

Do not lay trust on a lazy man to run an important errand for you, because a lazy person will not feel responsible to do the job given to him, do not ask him to fetch something for you, because he will not follow the specific orders given to him.

Do not ask a dissatisfied person to get any money that you need. It is not wise to trust a man with a deceitful speech for he will definitely manipulate your sayings and give a different meaning to your saying and decisions, for he would not care to keep the truth intact in the words that come out of his mouth.

Do not let a stingy man handle money; for he will not remain loyal and may not give back everything that actually belongs to you and at the time when you need him to repay you, he will turn his face away from you and the short tempered man will for certain cause harm to them.

Geza Vermes, The Complete Dead Sea Scrolls in English, New York, 1997

Fragment 3

An irresponsible person will not do his work carefully and according to his position or even according to his age. A person who gives his verdict before thoroughly examining the situation, and, a person who believes before looking at the evidence, do not give him the power to rule over those who seek for Knowledge, because he will not be able to do justice to his authoritarian position and hence, not being able to understand the judgments of the other wise people under him, he would not be able to distinguish a good man from a wicked person. So he will also be contemptible.

Do not send a man with a vision impairment to observe the upright for he will not be able to look deep into the situation.

Do not send a man who has a hearing impairment to give his opinion about a dispute and try to solve it, because he would not be capable of solving the problem, like someone who winnows in the wind a grain that is not completely separated out. It is not helpful when it comes to talking to an ear that is not ready to listen to you or in other words, a biased person, or, a person who lacks the spirit. . . .

It is futile to ask a person who is narrow-minded or close-minded, to give his judgment for he is not willing to accommodate suggestions and opinions from others and hence, his wisdom remains restricted and is not allowed to evolve, and so he is not able to use his wisdom efficiently. The wise man will be understanding, and he will have the ability to identify wisdom.

Vermes, Complete Dead Sea Scrolls

8

"Veni, Vidi, Vici": Rome and Jerusalem

T he Maccabees proved once again that power corrupts and absolute power corrupts absolutely. From powerful heroes who had restored religious freedom and political independence, their family's rule soon degenerated into the classic behavior of despots. Contrary to religious law, they took for themselves the dual positions of kingship and high priesthood. Conquering neighboring territories, they forcibly converted their subjects to Judaism—a sin for which the Jews would soon pay dearly when Herod, a descendant of one of these Jews-by-force, assumed the throne. Most damaging of all, when the last two Hasmonean rulers, Hyrcanus and Aristobulus, couldn't resolve the dispute over the succession between themselves, they turned to Rome in 63 B.C.E. to mediate. Predictably, the Roman emperor Pompey decided on a better alternative. Rome declared itself sovereign over Judea, effectively bringing the independent Jewish state to an end and turning Judea into a Roman province.

Herod's Rule of Judea

Rome chose Herod to rule, knowing that his allegiance to the empire would be stronger than his ties to a Jewish past that was not part of his ancestry. How right they were is best illustrated by the way in which Herod capped his crowning achievement: he rebuilt a magnificent Temple, ostensibly to the glory of God—and then placed at its top a Roman eagle, which was expressly forbidden by Jewish law in the *second of the Ten Commandments: "Thou shalt not make unto thyself any graven image."*

Josephus, *Antiquities of the Jews,* Book 15, Chapter 11

1. And now Herod, in the eighteenth year of his reign, and after the acts already mentioned, undertook a very great work, that is, to build of himself the temple of God, and make it larger in compass, and to raise it to a most magnificent altitude, as esteeming it to be the most glorious of all his actions, as it really was, to bring it to perfection; and that this would be sufficient for an everlasting memorial of him; but as he knew the multitude were not ready nor willing to assist him in so vast a design, he thought to prepare them first by making a speech to them, and then set about the work itself; so he called them together, and spoke thus to them: "I think I need not speak to you, my countrymen, about such other works as I have done since I came to the kingdom, although I may say they have been performed in such a manner as to bring more security to you than glory to myself; for I have neither been negligent in the most difficult times about what tended to ease your necessities, nor have the buildings I have made not been so proper as to preserve me as well as yourselves from injuries; and I imagine that, with God's assistance, I have advanced the nation of the Jews to a degree of happiness which they never had before; and for the particular edifices belonging to your own country, and your own cities, as also to those cities that we have lately acquired, which we have erected and greatly adorned, and thereby augmented the dignity of your nation, it seems to me a needless task to enumerate them to you, since you well know them yourselves; but as to that undertaking which I have a mind to set about at present, and which will be a work of the greatest piety and excellence that can possibly be undertaken by us, I will now declare it to you. Our fathers, indeed, when they were returned from Babylon, built this temple to God Almighty, yet does it want sixty cubits of its largeness in altitude; for so much did that first temple which Solomon built exceed this temple; nor let any one condemn our fathers for their negligence or want of piety herein, for it was not their fault that the temple was no higher; for they were Cyrus, and Darius the son of Hystaspes, who determined the measures for its rebuilding; and it hath been by reason of the subjection of those fathers of ours to them and to their posterity, and after them to the Macedonians, that they had not the opportunity to follow the original model of this pious edifice, nor could

raise it to its ancient altitude; but since I am now, by God's will, your governor, and I have had peace a long time, and have gained great riches and large revenues, and, what is the principal feeling of all, I am at amity with and well regarded by the Romans, who, if I may so say, are the rulers of the whole world, I will do my endeavor to correct that imperfection, which hath arisen from the necessity of our affairs, and the slavery we have been under formerly, and to make a thankful return, after the most pious manner, to God, for what blessings I have received from him, by giving me this kingdom, and that by rendering his temple as complete as I am able."

Josephus: Antiquities of the Jews, H. St. J. Thackeray, trans., Cambridge, Mass., 1928

The Golden Eagle on the Temple

Josephus, *Wars of the Jews,* Book 1, Chapter 33

2. . . . Now when these men were informed that the king was wearing away with melancholy, and with a distemper, they dropped words to their acquaintance, how it was now a very proper time to defend the cause of God, and to pull down what had been erected contrary to the laws of their country; for it was unlawful there should be any such thing in the temple as images, or faces, or the like representation of any animal whatsoever. Now the king had put up a golden eagle over the great gate of the temple, which these learned men exhorted them to cut down; and told them, that if there should any danger arise, it was a glorious thing to die for the laws of their country; because that the soul was immortal, and that an eternal enjoyment of happiness did await such as died on that account; while the mean-spirited, and those that were not wise enough to show a right love of their souls, preferred a death by a disease, before that which is the result of a virtuous behavior.

3. At the same time that these men made this speech to their disciples, a rumor was spread abroad that the king was dying, which made the young men set about the work with greater boldness; they therefore let themselves down from the top of the temple with thick cords, and this at midday, and while a great number of people were in the temple, and cut down that golden eagle with axes. This was presently told to the king's captain of the temple, who came running with a great body of soldiers, and caught about forty of the young men, and brought them to the king. And when he asked them, first of all, whether they had been so hardy as to cut down

the golden eagle, they confessed they had done so; and when he asked them by whose command they had done it, they replied, at the command of the law of their country; and when he further asked them how they could be so joyful when they were to be put to death, they replied, because they should enjoy greater happiness after they were dead.

Josephus: Wars of the Jews, H. St. J. Thackeray, trans., Cambridge, Mass., 1928

American history glorifies Patrick Henry's plea "Give me liberty or give me death." Dying for a cause is often considered an act of supreme nobility. Does sacrificing one's life for an ideal require belief in an afterlife?

Herod was brilliant—but mad. In his thirty-three-year reign, from 37 to 4 B.C.E., he was responsible for economic prosperity and social stability, and—as almost all archeologists and students of architecture of the ancient world appreciate—he was one of the greatest builders of all human history. For these structures he might have warranted his self-proclaimed title of Herod the Great. But Herod was not only ego-maniacal. His paranoia led him to murder the wife he admittedly loved, as well as his own children and untold numbers of family and friends. The scene of his bedside as he lay near death is worthy of Greek tragedy and great theater:

Herod's Dying Wish

Josephus, *Wars of the Jews*, Book 1, Chapter 33

6. He then returned back and came to Jericho, in such a melancholy state of body as almost threatened him with present death, when he proceeded to attempt a horrid wickedness; for he got together the most illustrious men of the whole Jewish nation, out of every village, into a place called the Hippodrome, and there shut them in. He then called for his sister Salome, and her husband Alexas, and made this speech to them: "I know well enough that the Jews will keep a festival upon my death however, it is in my power to be mourned for on other accounts, and to have a splendid funeral, if you will but be subservient to my commands. Do you but take care to send soldiers to encompass these men that are now in custody, and slay them immediately upon my death, and then all Judea, and every family of them, will weep at it, whether they want to or not."

Thankfully, Herod died before the order could be carried out. After his death, Judea was put under the direct control of Roman governors. Their cruelty is exemplified by the crucifixions that were all too common—including the execution of Jesus by the order of Pontius Pilate. This, coupled with explosive tension as a result of increased taxation and corruption, led to an ill-fated Jewish revolt. Doomed from the start, a military struggle against mighty Rome was pursued by a militant sect known as the Zealots. Encouraged at first by a series of highly improbable victories, the Zealots resisted the advice of more moderate leaders counseling compromise. The Zealots' militant actions prompted Rome to respond with the full force of their best and most powerful legions, intent on making Judea as well as its capital of Jerusalem a lesson to those throughout the rest of its empire who contemplated rebellion. The result was a tragedy still mourned by Jews to this day. In the year 70 C.E., Jerusalem fell, and on the ninth day of the Hebrew month of Av—the very day on which the First Temple had been destroyed in 586 B.C.E.—the Temple was put to the torch.

The Burning of the Temple

Josephus, *Wars of the Jews,* Book 6, Chapter 5

1. While the holy house was on fire, every thing was plundered that came to hand, and ten thousand of those that were caught were slain; nor was there a commiseration of any age, or any reverence of gravity, but children, and old men, and profane persons, and priests were all slain in the same manner; so that this war went round all sorts of men, and brought them to destruction, and as well those that made supplication for their lives, as those that defended themselves by fighting. The flame was also carried a long way, and made an echo, together with the groans of those that were slain; and because this hill was high, and the works at the temple were very great, one would have thought the whole city had been on fire. Nor can one imagine any thing either greater or more terrible than this noise; for there was at once a shout of the Roman legions, who were marching all together, and a sad clamor of the seditious, who were now surrounded with fire and sword. The people also that were left above were beaten back upon the enemy, and under a great consternation, and made sad moans at the calamity they were under; the multitude also that was in the city joined in this outcry with those that were upon the hill. And besides, many of those that were worn away by the famine, and their mouths almost closed, when they saw the fire of the holy house, they exerted their utmost strength, and broke out into groans and outcries again: Pera did also return the echo, as well as the mountains round about [the city,] and augmented the force of the entire noise. Yet was the misery itself more terrible than this disorder;

for one would have thought that the hill itself, on which the temple stood, was seething hot, as full of fire on every part of it, that the blood was larger in quantity than the fire, and those that were slain more in number than those that slew them; for the ground did no where appear visible, for the dead bodies that lay on it; but the soldiers went over heaps of those bodies, as they ran upon such as fled from them. And now it was that the multitude of the robbers were thrust out [of the inner court of the temple by the Romans,] and had much ado to get into the outward court, and from thence into the city, while the remainder of the populace fled into the cloister of that outer court. As for the priests, some of them plucked up from the holy house the spikes that were upon it, with their bases, which were made of lead, and shot them at the Romans instead of darts. But then as they gained nothing by so doing, and as the fire burst out upon them, they retired to the wall that was eight cubits broad, and there they tarried; yet did two of these of eminence among them, who might have saved themselves by going over to the Romans, or have borne up with courage, and taken their fortune with the others, throw themselves into the fire, and were burnt together with the holy house; their names were Meirus the son of Belgas, and Joseph the son of Daleus.

> The moderates blamed the Zealots for their refusal to seek a peaceful solution. The Zealots blamed the Pharisees for their weakness and the Sadducees for their willingness to adopt Roman ways. The rabbis believed the underlying cause for the destruction of the Temple was "needless hatred"—the enmity and divisiveness among the Jews themselves. How much truth is there in each of these views? How may they be applied to the problems of our time?

The Siege at Masada

The last episode of the story of Jewish revolt took place in 73 C.E. at Masada, the desert fortress built years before by King Herod. It was the scene of a last stand by Jews against Rome that ended with a mass suicide in preference to slavery. Because there was one survivor, we have an eyewitness account recorded by Josephus:

Josephus, *Wars of the Jews,* Book 7, Chapter 8

6. However, neither did Eleazar once think of flying away, nor would he permit any one else to do so; but when he saw their wall burned down by the fire, and could devise no other way of escaping, or room for their

further courage, and setting before their eyes what the Romans would do to them, their children, and their wives, if they got them into their power, he consulted about having them all slain. Now as he judged this to be the best thing they could do in their present circumstances, he gathered the most courageous of his companions together, and encouraged them to take that course by a speech which he made to them in the manner following: "Since we, long ago, my generous friends, resolved never to be servants to the Romans, nor to any other than to God himself, who alone is the true and just Lord of mankind, the time is now come that obliges us to make that resolution true in practice. And let us not at this time bring a reproach upon ourselves for self-contradiction, while we formerly would not undergo slavery, though it were then without danger, but must now, together with slavery, choose such punishments also as are intolerable; I mean this, upon the supposition that the Romans once reduce us under their power while we are alive. We were the very first that revolted from them, and we are the last that fight against them; and I cannot but esteem it as a favor that God hath granted us, that it is still in our power to die bravely, and in a state of freedom, which hath not been the case of others, who were conquered unexpectedly. It is very plain that we shall be taken within a day's time; but it is still an eligible thing to die after a glorious manner, together with our dearest friends. This is what our enemies themselves cannot by any means hinder, although they be very desirous to take us alive. Nor can we propose to ourselves any more to fight them, and beat them. It had been proper indeed for us to have conjectured at the purpose of God much sooner, and at the very first, when we were so desirous of defending our liberty, and when we received such sore treatment from one another, and worse treatment from our enemies, and to have been sensible that the same God, who had of old taken the Jewish nation into his favor, had now condemned them to destruction; for had he either continued favorable, or been but in a lesser degree displeased with us, he had not overlooked the destruction of so many men, or delivered his most holy city to be burnt and demolished by our enemies. To be sure we weakly hoped to have preserved ourselves, and ourselves alone, still in a state of freedom, as if we had been guilty of no sins ourselves against God, nor been partners with those of others; we also taught other men to preserve their liberty. Wherefore, consider how God hath convinced us that our hopes were in vain, by bringing such distress upon us in the desperate state we are now in, and which is beyond all our expectations; for the nature of this fortress which was in itself unconquerable, hath not proved a means of our deliverance; and even while we have still great abundance of food, and a great quantity of arms, and other necessaries more than we want, we are openly deprived by God himself of all hope of deliverance; for that fire which was driven upon our enemies did not of its own accord turn back upon the wall which we had built; this was the effect of God's anger against us for our manifold sins, which we have been guilty of in a most insolent and extravagant manner with regard to our own country-men; the punishments of which let us not receive from the Romans, but from God himself, as executed by our own hands; for these will be more moderate than the other. Let our wives die before they are abused, and our children before they have tasted of slavery; and after we have slain them, let us bestow that glorious benefit upon one another mutually, and pre-serve ourselves in freedom, as an excellent funeral monument for us. But first let us destroy our money and the fortress by fire; for I am well assured that this will be a great grief to the Romans, that they shall not be able to seize upon our bodies, and shall fall of our wealth also; and let us spare nothing but our provisions; for they will be a testimonial when we are dead that we were not subdued for want of necessaries, but that, accord-ing to our original resolution, we have preferred death before slavery."

Josephus, *Wars of the Jews,* Book 7, Chapter 9

1. Now as Eleazar was proceeding on in this exhortation, they all cut him off short, and made haste to do the work, as full of an unconquerable ardor of mind, and moved with a demoniacal fury. So they went their ways, as one still endeavoring to be before another, and as thinking that this eagerness would be a demonstration of their courage and good con-duct, if they could avoid appearing in the last class; so great was the zeal they were in to slay their wives and children, and themselves also! Nor indeed, when they came to the work itself, did their courage fail them, as one might imagine it would have done, but they then held fast the same resolution, without wavering, which they had upon the hearing of Eleazar's speech, while yet every one of them still retained the natural pas-sion of love to themselves and their families, because the reasoning they went upon appeared to them to be very just, even with regard to those that were dearest to them; for the husbands tenderly embraced their wives, and took their children into their arms, and gave the longest parting kisses to them, with tears in their eyes. Yet at the same time did they complete what

they had resolved on, as if they had been executed by the hands of strangers; and they had nothing else for their comfort but the necessity they were in of doing this execution, to avoid that prospect they had of the miseries they were to suffer from their enemies. Nor was there at length any one of these men found that scrupled to act their part in this terrible execution, but every one of them dispatched his dearest relations. Miserable men indeed were they! Whose distress forced them to slay their own wives and children with their own hands, as the lightest of those evils that were before them. So they being not able to bear the grief they were under for what they had done any longer, and esteeming it an injury to those they had slain, to live even the shortest space of time after them, they presently laid all they had upon a heap, and set fire to it. They then chose ten men by lot out of them to slay all the rest; every one of whom laid himself down by his wife and children on the ground, and threw his arms about them, and they offered their necks to the stroke of those who by lot executed that melancholy office; and when these ten had, without fear, slain them all, they made the same rule for casting lots for themselves, that he whose lot it was should first kill the other nine, and after all should kill himself. Accordingly, all these had courage sufficient to be no way behind one another in doing or suffering; so, for a conclusion, the nine offered their necks to the executioner, and he who was the last of all took a view of all the other bodies, lest perchance some or other among so many that were slain should want his assistance to be quite dispatched, and when he perceived that they were all slain, he set fire to the palace, and with the great force of his hand ran his sword entirely through himself, and fell down dead near to his own relations. So these people died with this intention that they would not leave so much as one soul among them all alive to be subject to the Romans. Yet was there an ancient woman, and another who was of kin to Eleazar, and superior to most women in prudence and learning, with five children, who had concealed themselves in caverns under ground, and had carried water thither for their drink, and were hidden there when the rest were intent upon the slaughter of one another. Those others were nine hundred and sixty in number, the women and children being withal included in that computation. This calamitous slaughter was made on the fifteenth day of the month Xanthicus [Nisan].

In Israel today, Masada is a symbol for Jews who have chosen to die as free men rather than be enslaved or executed by the Romans. Up until recently, Israeli soldiers would go up to Masada to be sworn in. The mountain would reverberate with the echo of their oath: "Masada will never fall again!" There are those, however, who question whether a collective act of suicide, no matter the circumstances, ought to serve as a national ideal. Judaism forbids the taking of one's own life, and legal commentaries debate whether there should be any allowable exceptions. Do you think Masada should be used to commemorate heroism?

Book III

The First Millennium

70 C.E.–1000 C.E.

THE TIME FRAME

Date (C.E.)	Event
70	Fall of Jerusalem; destruction of Second Temple
73	Siege of Masada
306	Constantine the Great begins his rule. He establishes Christianity as the state religion of the Roman Empire
325	Council of Nicea: Christians begin to celebrate Sabbath on Sunday
476	Fall of Rome and beginning of Byzantine rule over Israel
500	Babylonian Talmud recorded
622	Hegira—Mohammed flees from Mecca to Medina—Islamic year 1
638	Islamic conquest of Jerusalem
711	Islamic conquest of Spain begins
c. 740	Conversion of the Khazars
767	Anan Ben David founds the Karaite sect
814	Death of Charlemagne
927	Leadership of Rav Sa'adia Gaon begins
970	Death of Hasdai Ibn Shaprut

9

Struggling to Survive

*C*an one man change history? Historians continue to debate the question. But if we reflect on the turbulent times surrounding the destruction of the Second Temple, we can't help but conclude that a critical decision by one of the rabbinic leaders of the day enabled Judaism, as well as the Jewish people, to survive. It happened just a short while before the Temple was put to the torch. An encounter between a rabbi and a Roman general created the possibility for a new kind of Judaism, a Judaism without a land or a spiritual center. Because of Rabbi Yochanan ben Zakkai, the House of God was soon replaced by the House of Study, Judaism moved its focus from the Temple to the Torah, and the Age of the Second Temple was supplanted by the Talmudic Era, a time of vibrant creativity, scholarship, and intellectual ferment that would allow Judaism to meet the challenge of the almost two thousand years of exile that followed.

The story is recorded in the Babylonian Talmud:

Rabbi Yochanan ben Zakkai and Vespasian

Babylonian Talmud, Gittin 56b

Abba Sikra the head of the *biryoni* [the Zealots who believed in military action against Rome] in Jerusalem was the son of the sister of Rabbi Yochanan b. Zakkai. [The latter] sent to him saying, Come to visit me privately. When he came he said to him, How long are you going to carry on in this way and kill all the people with starvation? Abba Sikra replied: What can I do? If I say a word to them, they will kill me. Rabbi Yochanan said: Devise some plan for me to escape. Perhaps I shall be able to save a little. He said to him: Pretend to be ill, and let everyone come to inquire about you. Bring something evil-smelling and put it by you so that they will say you are dead. Let then your disciples get under your bed, but no others, so that they shall not notice that you are still light, since they know that a living being is lighter than a corpse. He did so, and R. Eliezer went under the bier from one side and R. Joshua from the other. When they reached the door, some men wanted to put a lance through the bier. He said to them: Shall [the Romans] say, They have pierced their Master? They wanted to give it a push. He said to them: Shall they say that they pushed their Master? They opened a town gate for him and he got out.

When he reached the Romans he said, Peace to you, O king, peace to you, O king. He [Vespasian] said: Your life is forfeit on two counts, one because I am not a king and you call me king, and again, if I am a king, why did you not come to me before now? He replied: As for your saying that you are not a king, you are a king, since if you were not a king Jerusalem would not be delivered into your hand, as it is written, *And Lebanon shall fall by a mighty one* (Isaiah 10:34). "Mighty one" [is an epithet] applied only to a king, as it is written, *And their mighty one shall be of themselves* (Jeremiah 3:21); and Lebanon refers to the Sanctuary, as it says, *This goodly mountain and Lebanon* (Deuteronomy 3:25). As for your question, why if you are a king, I did not come to you till now, the answer is that the *biryoni* among us did not let me. He said to him: If there is a jar of honey round which a serpent is wound, would they not break the jar to get rid of the serpent? [You should have broken down the walls to get rid of the *biryoni*.] He could give no answer.

At this point a messenger came to him from Rome saying, Up, for the Emperor is dead, and the notables of Rome have decided to make you head [of the State]. He had just finished putting on one boot. When he tried to put on the other he could not. He tried to take off the first but it would not come off. He said: What is the meaning of this? R. Yochanan said to him: Do not worry: the good news has done it, as it says, *Good tidings make the bone fat* (Proverbs 15:30). What is the remedy? Let someone whom you dislike come and pass before you, as it is written, *A broken spirit drieth up the bones* (Proverbs 17:22). He did so, and the boot went on.

He said: I am now going, and will send someone to take my place. You can, however, make a request of me and I will grant it. He said to him: Give me Jabneh and its wise Men, [let me found an academy where scholars may pursue the study of Torah] and the family chain of Rabban Gamaliel, [that the dynasty of Rabban Gamaliel, a descendant of King David, be spared] and physicians to heal R. Zadok. R. Joseph, or some say R. Akiba, applied to him the verse, *[God] turneth wise men backward and maketh their knowledge foolish* (Isaiah 44:25). He ought to have said to him: Let them [the Jews] off this time.

(Brackets mine.—B. B.)

> Were the rabbi's critics right? What if Rabbi Yochanan ben Zakkai had asked Vespasian to spare the Temple? Is it possible that this request might have been granted—and should the rabbi be faulted for not holding out for a greater demand? And what if the Temple had been spared, thus making it unnecessary to start a school in Jabneh—would the Temple have achieved more for the survival of Judaism than the academy? How should we evaluate the separate roles of study and ritual?

Seeking a Messiah

Rome ruled with a mighty hand; the Jews sought ways to come to terms with their new reality as their God and their religion appeared to be humbled by a greater power. For some, the only possible response was a fervent belief in messianic redemption. The message of Jesus struck a responsive chord as it was preached by Paul of Tarsus. Though Jesus was crucified, his disciples affirmed that he would shortly return, resurrected. They formed the first group of Christians, made up of despairing Jews as well as newly converted Gentiles. Many others accepted their subjugation to Rome as divine punishment for their sins. They saw their tragedy as something designed to spur them to heightened religious commitment. In place of sacrifices, no longer possible without a Temple, they chose scholarship and study as practical alternatives. An intellectual renaissance would soon produce the Mishnah and the Talmud, the greatest religious literary achievements of the Jewish people.

Yet another group, still holding out hope for political independence from Rome, pushed for rebellion and warfare. Incited by a ruling of the emperor Hadrian in 130 C.E. that banned circumcision, labeling it bodily mutilation, as well as by a plan to transform Jerusalem into a pagan city-state on the Greek polis model, with a shrine to Jupiter on the site of the Jewish Temple, several hundred thousand Jews joined with Simon Bar Kochba in what would turn out to be the final ill-fated attempt to regain national freedom. Bar Kochba succeeded in throwing the Romans out of Jerusalem and Israel and establishing, if only for a very brief period, an independent Jewish state. His initial success caused many—among them Rabbi Akiva, one of the most revered of Israel's rabbis—to believe that he was the Messiah. Unfortunately, Bar Kochba turned out to be another in a long line of false messiahs. Far from bringing deliverance to the Jews, his revolt caused unparalleled death and destruction. The Roman historian Dio Cassius, writing about a hundred years later, describes the situation:

The Account of the Bar Kochba Rebellion

[The Roman general] Severus did not venture to attack his opponents in the open at any one point in view of their numbers and their desperation, but by intercepting small groups. Thanks to the numbers of soldiers and his officers, and by depriving them of food and shutting them up, he was able—rather slowly to be sure, but with comparatively little danger—to crush, exhaust and exterminate them. Very few of them in fact survived. Fifty of their most important outposts and 985 of their most famous villages were razed to the ground, and 580,000 men were slain in various raids and battles, and the number of those who perished by famine, disease and fire was past finding out.

Thus nearly the whole of Judea was made desolate, a result of which the people had had forewarning before the war. For the tomb of Solomon, which the Jews regarded as an object of veneration, fell to pieces of itself and collapsed. And many wolves and hyenas rushed howling into the cities. Many Romans, however, perished in this war. Therefore, Hadrian, in writing to the Senate, did not employ the opening phrase commonly affected by emperors: "If you and your children are in health it is well and I and my legions are in health."

Dio Cassius, Dio's Roman History, Earnest Cary, trans., Cambridge, Mass., 1916

Babylonian Talmud, Gittin 57a

They reported to Caesar that the Jews were rebelling and marched against them ... they killed [Jewish] men, women and children until their blood flowed into the Mediterranean Sea.... It was taught that for seven years the gentiles cultivated their vineyards with the blood of Israel without requiring manure for fertilization.

(Brackets mine.—B. B.)

What might have motivated prominent rabbis to assume that Bar Kochba was the long-awaited Messiah? How often has this mistake repeated itself— even in modern times? How can we distinguish between a real and a supposed messiah? How can we keep hope from coloring our perception of reality?

The Ten Martyrs

Remarkably enough, the date when the city of Betar fell, effectively ending the rebellion, was the ninth of Av of the year 135 C.E., the same day on which both the First and the Second Temple were destroyed. Many Jews saw this as not simply coincidence; clearly their rebellion was doomed more by divine decree than by the Romans. To compound the tragedy, Rome decided to make Judea an example to the rest of the empire. Jerusalem was turned into a pagan city called Aelia Capitolina, and Jews were strictly banned from entering. The corpses of those who died in the insurrection were not permitted to be buried. They lay in the fields for months, exposed to the beasts and the elements. And the worst was yet to come. Ten of the greatest religious leaders were chosen for cruel and barbaric martyrdom.

From the Jewish Prayer Book for the Ninth Day of Av

Behold the ten martyrs that were massacred by the dominion of Rome; their blood has been shed and their strength failed, O for these do I weep, and my eye gushes forth in tears. When I remember this, I cry out bitterly for the choice flower of Israel, the holy vessels, the crown, and diadem; pure in heart and holy, they died a dreadful death. They threw lots to see who should be chosen first for the sword, and when the lot fell on Rabbi Simeon Ben Gamaliel II, he bared his neck and wept when the decree was issued. When the general returned to Rabbi Simeon to kill him with crafty design, Rabbi Yishmael, the High Priest, a descendant of the seed of Aaron, craved leave to weep over the son of the princes; he took his head and laid it on his knees and cried: "O pure lamp!" He put his eyes upon his eyes, his mouth upon his mouth in perfect love, he spoke and said: "O mouth, that grew strong in the Torah! A terrible and harsh death was suddenly decreed against you!" He [the tyrant] ordered them to flay his head with a hired blade. He [R. Yishmael] gave a dread groan, making the earth quake, and the world crumbled at the time when the wicked one who flayed him reached the place of the Tefillin, the pure commandment. After him they brought Rabbi Akiva, who was unsurpassed in logical deduction of the Law and they flayed his flesh with an iron comb to shatter his faith in God; his soul expired with the recitation of the word "ONE" [as he recited the phrase *Hear O Israel, the Lord is our God, the Lord is One*] and a heavenly voice proclaimed: "Happy are you! Rabbi Akiva! Your body is pure with every kind of purity!" After him they brought in Rabbi Judah the son of Babas, humble, of heart and vigorous in his observance; he was seventy years old when he was killed by the accursed hand, while he was yet fasting; innocent he was, pious and zealous in his work. Rabbi Chananiah, the son of Teradion, who used to gather crowds at the Gates of Zion was brought in after him; he sat with a Scroll of the Law, and expounded the Torah; they wrapped him up in the Scroll, placed bundles of vine tendrils around him, and set them on fire; they then placed tufts of damp wool on his heart, so that he should not die quickly. The wicked people then killed Rabbi Yeshevav, the pious Scribe; they cast him to the dogs, and he lacked burial, whereupon a heavenly voice came forth and proclaimed that he had not left a single point of the Law of Moses unfulfilled. After him, on the same day of wrath, they slew Rabbi Chutspit, the breath of whose mouth when he expounded the Law was so fiery with his learning as to singe a passing bird. The last martyr, Rabbi Elazar the son of Shamua, was murdered by the piercing of the sword; it was the eve of Shabbat, the time of saying the Kiddush, and as he began to recite the Kiddush, they drew a sword upon him, and did not allow him to finish the Kiddush alive; his soul expired when he came to the word "which God created"—who fashioned and varied the forms of his creatures.

(Brackets mine.—B. B.)

The rabbis were condemned to death because they persisted in teaching Torah to their students despite Hadrian's decree. Why did they so blatantly endanger their lives? The Talmud records the answer given by Rabbi Akiva:

The Parable of the Fish and the Fox (Babylonian Talmud, Berakhot 61b)

Pappus, son of Judah, found Rabbi Akiva sitting in a public place, with students all about him, teaching and studying Torah in defiance of the Roman law. This was an enormously dangerous thing to do, because the penalty for violating a Roman edict was death.

Pappus was shocked that Rabbi Akiva was taking such a risk. In amazement he asked, "Akiva, aren't you afraid of the Roman government?"

Rabbi Akiva replied with a parable:

Once, a fox was walking alongside a river. He could see fish swimming in schools in the water. It appeared to him that they were swimming to and fro, as if trying to escape something or someone. The fox was very hungry and thought that a nice, fat fish would surely make a delicious lunch for a hungry fox.

The fox called out to the fish, "What are you fleeing from?" The fish replied, "We are trying to avoid the nets that fishermen cast to catch us."

Slyly, the fox said, "Would you like to come up on to the dry land so that you will be safe from the fishermen's nets?"

The fish weren't fooled by the sly fox. They replied, "Are you the one that is known as the cleverest of all the animals? You are not clever! You are foolish. If we are in danger here in the water, which is our home, how much more would we be in danger on land!"

"So it is with us," Rabbi Akiva explained. "If we are in great danger when we sit and study, teach and practice Torah, of which it is written, 'For this is your life and the length of your days' (Deuteronomy 30:20), how much worse off would we be if we neglect the Torah? It is the Torah that is our natural habitat, the only medium in which we can survive. Take us out of the waters of Torah and we will perish just as surely as fish out of water."

And with that, Rabbi Akiva returned to his studies.

> Judaism teaches the supreme value of life. Yet there have been times when rabbis have chosen martyrdom. Under what circumstances would death be a preferable alternative? How does choosing to die for a cause differ from suicide? If the ten martyrs had been offered the choice to renounce leadership and live, should they have accepted?

After Hadrian's death in 138 C.E., the persecutions ended. A new center of Torah study opened at Usha, in the northern Galilee. A proclamation went out: "Whoever has learned, let him come and teach; whoever has not learned, let him come and learn." The call was heeded. Jews continued to study their traditions. And once again they found a way to survive.

10

The Age of the Talmud

Two books serve as the major texts of the Jewish religion: the Bible and the Talmud. Together, they depict the ideal relationship between man and God. But there is an important difference between them. In the Bible, God speaks to man. In the Talmud, God speaks through man, allowing human insight and intellect to play a role in understanding divine will. Prophets simply reported what they heard from heaven; Talmudic scholars demonstrated the value of combining man's wisdom with God's.

The Talmud represents five hundred years of Jewish history. Were it not for the destruction of the Temple and the imminence of a lengthy exile, it would probably never have been written. For centuries Judaism was a tradition based on "Oral Law," a complex and detailed explanation of the Torah that would be passed on by parent to child, teacher to disciple. A caring and loving instructor accomplishes far more than an unopened book waiting to be read. But when Rabbi Judah Ha'Nassi ("The Prince"—a title given to the highest spiritual authority in Israel) realized that the oral tradition was in danger of being lost, given the absence of homeland and Temple, he wrote—in about 200 C.E.—the first collection of this Oral Law in the six volumes of the Mishnah (from the root shanah, to repeat, and, by extension, to learn). For the next three hundred years these books were discussed in numerous academies and houses of study, most of which by then were in Babylonia. Remarkably, records were kept of most of these deliberations, which became known as the Gemara (completion or conclusion). In about 500 C.E. these were then compiled and edited by Ravina and Rav Ashi into the sixty-three volumes of the *Babylonian Talmud*, which combine both the Mishnah and the Gemara.

The rabbinic leadership of the first five hundred years of the Common Era not only established the legal foundations of Jewish life for the centuries that followed but also articulated the values, the culture, and the spiritual ideals of the Jewish people.

The Talmud's eyewitness accounts of important moments in the lives of some of these major figures help us to understand the roots of modern Jewish history, as well as, perhaps, the foundations of Western civilization.

Hillel (30 B.C.E.–10 C.E.)

The Love of Study (Babylonian Talmud, Yoma 35b)

It was reported about Hillel the Elder that every day he used to work and earn one *tropaik*, half of which he would give to the guard at the House of Learning, keeping the other half for his food and family. One day he found nothing to earn and the guard at the House of Learning would not permit him to enter. He climbed up and sat upon the window, to hear the words of the Living God from the mouth of Shemayah and Abtalion. They say that day was the eve of the Sabbath in the winter solstice and snow fell down upon him from heaven. When the dawn rose, Shemayah said to Abtalion: "Brother Abtalion, on every day this house is light and today it is dark. Is it perhaps a cloudy day?" They looked up and saw the figure of a man in the window. They went up and saw him covered by three cubits of snow. They removed him, bathed and anointed him and placed him opposite the fire and they said: "This man deserves that the Sabbath be profaned on his behalf."

The Essence of Religion (Babylonian Talmud, Shabbat 31a)

It happened that a certain heathen came before Shammai and said to him, "Make me a proselyte on condition that you teach me the whole Torah while I stand on one foot." Thereupon he repulsed him with the builder's cubit which was in his hand. When he went before Hillel, he said to him, "What is hateful to you, do not do to your neighbor. That is the whole Torah; the rest is commentary. Now go and learn it."

> Stories like those of Hillel, who loved study but could not afford to pay for it, led to the institution of free public education paid for by taxation—the first system of its kind in the world.

Justice Will Prevail (Babylonian Talmud, Sukkah 53a)

Hillel saw a head floating upon the water. He addressed it as follows: "You drowned others and therefore you were drowned; but in the end your assassins will also be drowned!"

Simeon ben Shetach (circa 1st century B.C.E.)

The Donkey and the Pearl (Jerusalem Talmud, Ketubot 8:11)

Once Rabbi Simeon ben Shetach bought a donkey from an Ishmaelite. When he brought his donkey home, his disciples found a pearl in a little bag tied around the animal's neck. They said to their teacher: "God's blessing has made you rich." But Simeon answered, "I only bought the animal, not the pearl." When he returned it to the Ishmaelite, the latter exclaimed, "Blessed be Simeon ben Shetach and blessed be the God of Simeon ben Shetach."

> The rabbis defined this act as *Kiddush Hashem*, "sanctifying the name of God." They accorded it the highest rank of spiritual nobility, as it not only fulfilled the service of God but also promulgated the virtues of his ways to the world at large. Similarly, Jews who cast their religion into disrepute by acting in an improper way are guilty of *Chilul Hashem*, "Desecrating the name of God." What kinds of actions today would fall into these two categories?

Rabbis Gamaliel, Eleazar, Joshua, and Akiba

Weeping and Laughing (Babylonian Talmud, Makkot 24b)

Long ago, as Rabban Gamaliel, Rabbi Eleazar ben Azariah, Rabbi Joshua and Rabbi Akiba were walking on the road, they heard noise of the crowds at Rome traveling from Puteoli a hundred and twenty miles away. They all fell to weeping, but Rabbi Akiba seemed merry. Said they to him: "Why are you happy?" Said he to them: "Why are you weeping?" Said they: "Heathens who bow down to images and burn incense to idols live in safety and ease, whereas our Temple, the 'Footstool' of our God, is burnt down by fire, and should we then not weep?" He replied: "Therefore, am I merry. If they that offend Him fare thus, how much better shall fare they that do obey Him!"

Once again they were coming up to Jerusalem together, and just as they came to Mount Scopus they saw a fox emerging from the Holy of Holies. They fell to weeping and Rabbi Akiba seemed merry. "Why," said they to him, "are you merry?" Said he: "Why are you weeping?" Said they to him: "A place of which it was once said, *And the common man that draws nigh shall be put to death* (Numbers 1:51), has now become the haunt of foxes, and we should not weep?" Said he to them: "Therefore am I merry; for it is written, *And I will take to Me faithful witnesses to record, Uriah the priest and Zechariah the Son of Jeberechiah*"(Isaiah 8:2). Now what connection has this Uriah the priest with Zechariah? Uriah lived during the time of the first Temple, while Zechariah lived [and prophesied] during the second Temple? Yet, the Bible linked the later prophecy of Zechariah with the earlier prophecy of Uriah. In the earlier prophecy in the days of Uriah it is written, *Therefore shall Zion for your sake be ploughed as a field* (Micah 3:12). In Zechariah it is written, *Thus saith the Lord of Hosts, there shall yet sit old men and old women in the broad places of Jerusalem.* So long as Uriah's threatening prophecy had not been fulfilled, I had misgivings lest Zechariah's prophecy might not come to pass. Now that Uriah's prophecy has come true, it is quite certain that Zechariah's prophecy also will shortly be fulfilled. Said they to him: Akiba, you have comforted us! Akiba, you have comforted us!

(Brackets mine.—B. B.)

Rabbi Joshua ben Chanania (2nd century C.E.)

Debating the Emperor (Midrash, Kohelet Rabba 2:8)

The emperor Hadrian once said to Rabbi Joshua: "I am greater than your master Moses, for he is dead but I am alive." To this Rabbi Joshua responded: "Can you decree that people should not light fires in their houses for three consecutive days?" "Yes, of course, I can do so," the Emperor answered, and he immediately issued such a decree. That same evening the Emperor and Rabbi Joshua went out of the gates of the palace for a stroll and they saw smoke issuing out of a chimney. Rabbi Joshua said to him, "Look, even while you live, your commandments are ignored while our teacher Moses commanded many centuries ago that no fires be lit on the Sabbath and to this day no Jew will make a fire on the Sabbath!"

The Rabbi and the Emperor's Daughter (Midrash Eliyahu Zuta, 23)

Rabbi Joshua did not possess a pleasing appearance but he was very wise, and the Emperor's daughter, who admired knowledge, enjoyed discussing matters with him. Unable to restrain herself, she once said to him: "Is it possible that such wisdom should be contained in such an ungainly vessel?" Rabbi Joshua said to her: "Why is it that your father, who is an Emperor, keeps his wine in a clay vessel the same as all other people? Why does he not keep it in a silver or in a golden vessel?" The princess inquired of her father and he explained to her that good wine would soon spoil in a silver or golden vessel. She then understood what Rabbi Joshua had meant to tell her.

Seeing God (Babylonian Talmud, Hullin 59b)

The Emperor Hadrian once said to Rabbi Joshua, "I would believe in your God if you would only show Him to me that I might know Him better." "I can do that easily," Rabbi Joshua said. "If you want to see my God, I will show Him to you." He then led the Emperor outside on a hot summer day and told him to look at the sun, but the latter declared that he could not do so, for the sun blinds his eyes. Then Rabbi Joshua said, "If you cannot look at the face of the lowest servant of God, how can you expect to see Him?"

Rabbi Ishmael ben Elisha (1st to 2nd century C.E.)

Rabbinic Responsibility (Mekhilta Parshat Mishpatim)

It is told that when Rabbi Ishmael and Rabbi Simeon were led to execution, Rabbi Simeon said to Rabbi Ishmael: "Rabbi, my heart quivers with fear, for I do not know for what sins I am being executed." Rabbi Ishmael answered him: "Did never a man come to you to ask a question or to settle a dispute and you made him wait until you finished drinking your water, or lacing your shoe or wrapping your shawl about yourself? By doing so you have transgressed against the commandment of the Torah not to cause suffering to a widow or an orphan which is punishable by death irrespective of whether the suffering caused was great or small."

Rabbi Hanina ben Teradion (2nd century C.E.)

Eternity in an Instant (Babylonian Talmud, Avoda Zarah 17b)

Rabbi Jose b. Kisma died and all the great men of Rome went to his burial and made great lamentation for him. On their return, they found Rabbi

Hanina ben Teradion sitting and occupying himself with the Torah, gathering assemblies, and keeping a scroll of the Law in his bosom. Straightaway they took hold of him, wrapped him in the Scroll of the Law, placed bundles of branches round him and set them on fire. They then brought tufts of wool, which they had soaked in water, and placed them over his heart, so that he should not expire quickly. His daughter exclaimed, "Father, that I should see you in this state!" He replied, "If it were I alone being burnt it would have been a thing hard to bear; but now that I am burning together with the Scroll of the Law, He who will have regard for the plight of the Torah will also have regard for my plight." His disciples called out, "Rabbi, what do you see?" He answered them, "The parchments are being burnt but the letters are soaring on high." "Open then your mouth" they said, "so that the fire enter into you." He replied, "Let Him who gave me my soul take it away, but no one should cause his own death." The Executioner then said to him, "Rabbi, if I raise the flame and take away the tufts of wool from over your heart, will you cause me to enter into the life to come?" "Yes," he replied. "Then swear unto me," he urged. He swore unto him. He thereupon raised the flame and removed the tufts of wool from over his heart, and his soul departed speedily. The Executioner then jumped and threw himself into the fire. And a heavenly voice exclaimed: R. Hanina ben Teradion and the executioner both have been assigned to the world to come. When Rabbi Judah heard it he wept and said: "One may acquire eternal life in a single hour, another after many years."

Rabbi Meier and Beruriah, His Wife (2nd century C.E.)

Facing the Death of a Child (Midrash, Mishley 31)

Rabbi Meier was giving a lecture at the synagogue one Sabbath afternoon. At the very same time, unbeknown to him, his two beloved sons suddenly died. The grief-stricken mother, Beruriah, covered them with a sheet and waited until her husband came home after the Sabbath.

When Rabbi Meier arrived and asked where his sons were, his wife begged her husband to first recite the Havdalah service marking the departure of the Sabbath. Then, she said, she had a very important question to ask him. Perplexed, but nonetheless acceding to his wife's wishes, Rabbi Meier recited the prayer and then asked his wife to tell him her problem. She said: "Not long ago, some precious jewels were entrusted to my care. Now the owner of the jewels has come to reclaim them. Shall I return them to him?"

Rabbi Meier was surprised by the simplicity of the question and his wife's need to ask him for guidance. "But of course," he said, "you yourself know the law very well. An object entrusted for a time must be given back when the owner demands it."

Beruriah then took her husband by the hand, led him to where the dead children lay and drew back the sheet. Rabbi Meier began to weep uncontrollably. "My sons! My sons!" he cried.

Then Beruriah reminded him tearfully of his own words: "Didn't you say that we must restore to the owner what he entrusted to our care? Our sons were the jewels that God allowed us to have for some years. Now their Master has taken back His own gifts to us. Let us, even at this tragic moment of loss, feel gratitude for the gift God gave us in all the time we were blessed to have these jewels, our precious children."

Rabbi Simeon ben Yochai (2nd century C.E.)

Advice to the Lovelorn (Shir Hashirim Rabba 1:31)

This incident occurred while Rabbi Simeon ben Yochai was in Sidon. A married couple who lived together for ten years and had no children came to him to obtain a divorce. Rabbi Simeon said to them: "Since you do not want to part in anger you must do now as you did at the time of your wedding. At your wedding you made a feast; you must also make a feast at your parting."

The husband and wife did as Rabbi Simeon advised them. During the feast the husband became merry with drink and he said to his wife: "Choose that which is most beautiful and dearest to you in the house and take it with you when you return to your father's house." When the husband fell asleep she ordered the slaves to carry him on his bed to her father's house. When he awoke and found himself in strange surroundings he asked his wife, "Where am I?" and she replied, "You are in my father's house."

The man further asked, "What have I to do in your father's house?" and his wife replied, "You asked me to take that which I held dearest in your house and I could find nothing dearer to me than yourself." They then went to Rabbi Simeon ben Yochai a second time to ask him what to do. He advised them not to part for he was certain that God would reward such a wife with children. He also promised to pray for them.

> If a married couple has no children after ten years, the oral law taught that they should divorce and find new partners in order to fulfill the commandment to "be fruitful and multiply." The rabbis of the Talmud, while feeling bound by the ruling, found several alternative solutions. Adopting a child, they declared, makes anyone who raises it the equivalent of a parent. Alternatively, moving to Israel or changing one's life in such a way as to be more deserving of God's blessing also permits a couple to continue to live together. In many instances, rabbis found ingenious ways to combine compassion with strict religious rulings.

Christianity Gains Ascendancy

The wisdom of the Talmudic scholars didn't go unnoticed by the world around them. As we have seen, some of the rabbis had frequent conversations with Roman officers and at times even conversed with the emperor. Judaism proved appealing to a number of prominent non-Jews; several historians claim that the Roman philosopher-emperor Marcus Aurelius seriously considered conversion, and Pompeia, Nero's wife, did convert to Judaism. But in 324 C.E., during the reign of Constantine, Christianity was proclaimed the state religion of the Roman Empire. Christians were now no longer an oppressed minority. With their newfound power, they began to assert themselves with both the cross and the sword. That spelled the end of many civil rights for the Jews and the beginning of what would prove to be a long and painful relationship with the Church. Even as the rabbis were busy writing the Talmud, the newly Christianized Romans were composing laws that would subjugate Jews for centuries to come.

Laws against the Jews

III. A Law of Theodosius II, January 31, 439: Concerning Jews, Samaritans, Heretics, and Pagans

Wherefore, although according to an old saying [of the Greek Hippocrates, the father of medicine] "no cure is to be applied in desperate sicknesses," nevertheless, in order that these dangerous sects which are unmindful of our times may not spread into life the more freely, in indiscriminate disorder as it were, we ordain by this law to be valid for all time:

No Jew—or no Samaritan who subscribes to neither [the Jewish nor the Christian] religion—shall obtain offices and dignities; to none shall the administration of city service be permitted; nor shall any one exercise the office of a defender [that is, overseer] of the city. Indeed, we believe it sinful that the enemies of the heavenly majesty and of the Roman laws should become the executors of our laws—the administration of which they have slyly obtained and that they, fortified by the authority of the acquired rank, should have the power to judge or decide as they wish against Christians, yes, frequently even over bishops of our holy religion themselves, and thus, as it were, insult our faith.

Moreover, for the same reason, we forbid that any synagogue shall rise as a new building. However, the propping up of old synagogues which are now threatened with imminent ruin is permitted. To these things we add that he who misleads a slave or a freeman against his will or by punishable advice, from the service of the Christian religion to that of an abominable sect and ritual, is to be punished by loss of property and life. On the one hand, whoever has built a synagogue must realize that he has worked to the advantage of the Catholic church [which will confiscate the building]; on the other hand, whoever has already secured the badge of office shall not hold the dignities he has acquired. On the contrary, he who worms himself into office must remain, as before, in the lowest rank even though he will have already earned an honorary office. And as for him who begins the building of a synagogue and is not moved by the desire of repairing it, he shall be punished by a fine of fifty pounds gold for his daring. Moreover, if he will have prevailed with his evil teachings over the faith of another, he shall see his wealth confiscated and himself soon subjected to a death sentence.

And since it behooves the imperial majesty to consider everything with such foresight that the general welfare does not suffer in the least, we ordain that the tax-paying officeholders of all towns as well as the provincial civil servants—who are obligated to employ their wealth and to make public gifts as part of their burdensome and diverse official and military duties shall remain in their own classes, no matter what sect they belong to. Let it not appear as if we have accorded the benefit of exemption to those men, detestable in their insolent maneuvering, whom we wish to condemn by the authority of this law.

This further limitation is to be observed, namely, that these public servants from these above-mentioned sects shall never, as far as private affairs are concerned, carry out judicial sentences, nor be wardens of the jail.

Jacob Marcus, The Jew in the Medieval World: A Source Book, 315–1791,
New York, 2000.

IV. A Law of Justinian, July 28, 531: Concerning Heretics and Manichaeans and Samaritans

Since many judges, in deciding cases, have addressed us in need of our decision, asking that they be informed what ought to be done with witnesses who are heretics, whether their testimony ought to be received or rejected, we therefore ordain that no heretic, nor even they who cherish the Jewish superstition, may offer testimony against orthodox Christians who are engaged in litigation, whether one or the other of the parties is an orthodox Christian.

Jacob Marcus, The Jew in the Medieval World

11

The Challenge of Islam: Mohammed and the Caliphs

According to the French Bible critic Ernest Renan, "Only a hair's breadth prevented all Arabia from becoming Jewish." That's because the Jews who fled Rome during the early days of persecution established towns and villages throughout Arabia, often attracting many admirers and converts. There are records of entire tribes converting to Judaism. Jewish ideas about one God, about their biblical ancestors, and about prophets and prophecy gained widespread attention. The influence of Jews on the Arab world would prove to be profound and long-lasting—extending into the present day, with unforeseen consequences.

It was Jews who founded the city of Yathrib, better known by its later name of Medina, Islam's second-holiest city after Mecca. More important still, it was Jewish monotheism that first drew a young trader, Mohammed ibn Abdallah, to found a new faith, one that he acknowledged many times was revealed to him by way of "the Bible of Israel." The Koran lists twenty-five prophets, nineteen of whom are from the Jewish Scriptures. The law of circumcision and the prohibition against eating pork, as well as many other rituals, are a direct borrowing from Jewish tradition. Moses is quoted over a hundred times in the Koran (sometimes inaccurately). Mohammed constantly stressed that the Arabs, like the Jews, were also descendants of Abraham—by way of Ishmael, son of Abraham and Hagar—but that they had over the course of time forgotten the important teaching of monotheism. As Paul Johnson, in his History of the Jews, explains:

What he [Mohammed] seems to have wished to do was to destroy the polytheistic paganism of the oasis culture by giving the Arabs Jewish ethical monotheism in a language they could understand and in terms adapted to their ways. He accepted the Jewish God and their prophets, the idea of fixed law embodied in scripture—the Koran being an Arabic substitute for the Bible—and the addition of an Oral Law applied in religious courts.

In 622 C.E., *Mohammed fled from Mecca to Yathrib (Medina), a journey known as the Hegira and immortalized as marking the year 1 of the Islamic calendar. Like the early Christians before him, Mohammed assumed he would easily be able to convert the Jews to his teachings in light of their similarity to Judaism. When he was rebuffed, Mohammed—and subsequently his followers—expressed particular anger against Jewish "infidels." The following passages from the Koran reflect these feelings.*

The Koran and the Jews

A Warning to the Children of Israel

The Cow

[2.39] And (as to) those who disbelieve in and reject My communications, they are the inmates of the fire, in it they shall abide. . . .

[2.62] Surely those who believe, and those who are Jews, and the Christians, and the Sabians, whoever believes in Allah and the Last day and does good, they shall have their reward from their Lord, and there is no fear for them, nor shall they grieve.

The True Believers

[2.120] And the Jews will not be pleased with you, nor the Christians until you follow their religion. Say: Surely Allah's guidance, that is the (true) guidance. And if you follow their desires after the knowledge that has come to you, you shall have no guardian from Allah, nor any helper.

[2.121] Those to whom We have given the Book read it as it ought to be read. These believe in it; and whoever disbelieves in it, these it is that are the losers.

[2.122] O children of Israel, call to mind My favor which I bestowed on you and that I made you excel the nations.

[2.123] And be on your guard against a day when no soul shall avail another in the least neither shall any compensation be accepted from it, nor shall intercession profit it, nor shall they be helped.

The Fate of Infidels and Nonbelievers

Believers, take neither Jews nor Christians for your friends. (Koran 5:51)

Fight against such as those to whom the Scriptures were given [Jews and Christians] . . . until they pay tribute out of hand and are utterly subdued. (Koran 9:29.) (Brackets mine.—B. B.)

Prophet, make war on the unbelievers and the hypocrites and deal rigorously with them. Hell shall be their home. (Koran 9:73)

Muhammad is God's apostle. Those who follow him are ruthless to the unbelievers but merciful to one another. (Koran 48:29)

Mohammed's sayings and deeds, called sunnah, *form another body of religious literature that is studied and revered by Muslims. One of these sayings is as follows:*

The Day of Resurrection will not arrive until the Moslems make war against the Jews and kill them, and until a Jew is hiding behind a rock and tree, and the rock and tree will say: "O Moslem, O servant of Allah, there is a Jew behind me, come and kill him!" (Sahih Bukhari 004.52.176)

> Many of these quotations from Islamic religious texts are today interpreted as strict rulings that require observance by religious Muslims. They serve as a justification for jihad—a battle to the death against infidels. Can Islam redefine them in a way that will allow its followers to live in peace alongside members of other faiths?

Laws against Jews in Muslim Countries

By the time of Mohammed's death in 632 C.E., his followers had gained sufficient power to threaten the Persian and Byzantine Empires. The church began to be overshadowed by the mosque. For Jews, the transition was bittersweet. Many historians believe that the goal of the church was the total elimination of the "perfidious Jews," who rejected Jesus. In Muslim countries, Jews were classified as ahl al-dhimma— *"protected people"—who had the right of residence without being forced to convert. But that didn't prevent the passage of numerous laws that made the lives of Jews extremely difficult, if not intolerable. Typical was the legislation known as the Omar Charter, a document enacted by the caliph Omar, who succeeded Mohammed. The charter placed the following restrictions on Jews living under Islamic Arab rule:*

1. *Jews were forbidden to touch the Koran.*
2. *Jews were required to wear distinctive clothing.*
3. *Jews were required to wear a yellow piece of cloth as a badge (Christians were required to wear a blue badge).*
4. *Jews were not allowed to perform their religious practices in public.*
5. *Jews were not allowed to own a horse, a sign of a nobleman.*

6. *Jews were required to bury their dead without grieving in public.*
7. *Jews were required to pay special taxes.*
8. *Jews were not allowed to defend themselves against a Muslim.*
9. *Jews were not allowed to testify against a Muslim.*
10. *Jews were forbidden to build new synagogues.*
11. *The houses and tombs of Jews were not allowed to be higher than those of the Muslims.*
12. *The graves of Jews were required to be level so that anyone could walk over them.*

The *Omar Charter* introduced the wearing of a special badge of shame to identify Jews. In Nazi Germany, the yellow-star armband for Jews was the first step in the branding of Jews as undesirables. How significant was that development in implementing the plan for the "Final Solution" of genocide?

The Resh Galuta

It was in Babylonia that the Talmud was completed. It was in Babylonia that Jews enjoyed a thriving community for more than a thousand years under various rulers. And it was in Babylonia that Jews were allowed sufficient self-rule to be governed by a religious leader, known as the Resh Galuta ("Head of the Exile," or "Exilarch"), who, as a direct descendant of King David, was looked to for spiritual guidance and leadership by Jews around the world. With the Muslim conquest of the Middle East in the seventh century, the Persian king was replaced by the caliph, but the office of the Resh Galuta was allowed to remain. In fact, Caliph Omar was so fond of the Resh Galuta—Bustenai Ben Haninai—that when he decided to marry the daughter of the Persian king, he insisted that Bustenai marry her sister. And that's how the Resh Galuta became brother-in-law to the caliph!

Nathan the Babylonian, the Ceremony of Installation of the Exilarch

When there was a communal consensus on the appointment, the two Heads of the Academies (the major schools of Torah study) together with their students, all the leaders of the congregation, and the elders, would gather in some prominent individual's house in Baghdad. He would be one of the greatest of that generation, such as Netira or the like. The man in whose home they gather is singled out for honor by this and receives much praise. His standing is enhanced by this meeting of the leaders and elders in his home.

The community would gather in the main synagogue on Thursday. The Exilarch would be installed by the laying of hands. The shofar was sounded to let all the people know from the youngest to the eldest. And when everyone heard it, each of them would send him a gift—each according to his means. All the leaders of the congregation and the wealthy would send him fine clothes, jewelry, and gold and silver vessels—each as he saw fit. . . .

. . . From that time [the installation] on, he does not leave his house. People gather and pray with him there, be it on secular days, Sabbaths, or holidays. If he does have to go out on some business, he rides in the litter of an official similar to that of the Caliph's ministers. He would be beautifully attired. Behind him would walk a train of as many as fifteen men. His servant would run after him. Should he happen to pass any Israelites, they would run up to him, touch his hands, and greet him. As many as fifty or sixty people might do this both on his way to his destination and upon his return home. This is the custom. He would never go out without his entourage, just like any of the Caliph's ministers. Whenever the Exilarch wishes to appear before the Caliph either to request something or simply to wait upon him, he asks the Caliph's viziers and servants who have regular entry to his court to speak to the Caliph, so that he may grant him the permission to come into his presence. The Caliph then grants the permission and orders the guards at the palace gate to admit him. When the Exilarch enters, the Caliph's slaves would run before him. He comes prepared with *dinars* and *dirhams* in his pocket to distribute to all those slaves who usher him in. He would continually be putting his hand into his bosom pocket and giving each and every one whatever God had ordained for him. They in turn treat him with honor and touch his hand until he comes into the presence of the Caliph and bows to him. The Caliph signals to one of his retainers who takes the Exilarch by the hand and seats him in the spot which the Caliph has indicated. The Exilarch then converses with the Caliph. The latter would ask after his health and his affairs, and the purpose of the visit. The Exilarch then requests permission to address him, which is immediately granted. He then begins with praises and blessings formally prepared beforehand in which he eulogizes the Caliph's ancestors. He conciliates him with kind words until his request is granted and he is given what he has asked. The Caliph then commands that a decree be written to that effect, and the Exilarch retires, happily taking his leave.

Norman Stillman, *The Jews of Arab Lands,* New York, 1979. (Brackets mine.—B. B.)

Can the position of the Resh Galuta serve as the model for a corresponding leadership role today for Jews in the Diaspora, outside of Israel? Is it wise to vest one person with spiritual authority over all Jews? Which aspects of the position of Resh Galuta might be useful for today's Jewish leaders?

12

Different Kinds of Jews: The Karaites and the Khazars

T he eighth century saw the beginnings of two different groups of Jews. It was during the 700s that the Karaites broke with traditional rabbinic Judaism and founded a sect that, although few in numbers, would survive to this day. And it was in the 700s that an entire country converted to Judaism, as the kingdom of the Khazars opted to accept the faith of the Jews—a decision that may have significantly influenced the genetic makeup of European Jewry. Their stories are fascinating examples of two concurrent trends throughout history: Judaism loses adherents in one way and gains them in another.

The Birth of the Karaites

From the Karaite Elijah ben Abraham

Anan had a younger brother named Hananiah. Although Anan exceeded this brother in both learning and age, the contemporary Rabbinic scholars refused to appoint him exilarch (*Resh Galuta*), because of his great lawlessness and lack of piety. They therefore turned to his brother Hananiah, for the sake of the latter's great modesty, retiring disposition, and fear of Heaven, and they set him up as exilarch. Thereupon Anan was seized with a wicked zeal—he and with him all manner of evil and worthless men set up a dissident sect—in secret, for fear of the Moslem government which was then in power—and they appointed Anan their own exilarch.

On a certain Sunday, however, the affair was discovered by the government, and the order was given that Anan be imprisoned until the following Friday, when he was to be hanged on the gallows as a political rebel. In prison Anan came upon a Moslem scholar who was also confined there and was likewise to be hung on the same Friday, as a violator of the Mohammedan faith. This scholar advised Anan, saying, "Are there not in the Law ordinances admitting of two contradictory interpretations?" "Indeed there are," answered Anan. "Observe then," said the Moslem scholar, "the interpretation accepted in the teaching of those who follow your brother and take the other interpretation for yourself providing that those who follow you will back you up in it. Then give a bribe to the viceroy so that you might perchance be permitted to speak in your defense, after which prostrate yourself before the caliph and say: 'O my Lord the King! Did you set up my brother to rule over one religion or over two?' Upon his replying: 'Over one religion only,' say to him further: 'But I and my brother belong to two different religions!' Of a certainty you will save yourself, providing you explain to him the difference between your religion and that of your brother, and providing your followers back you up. Say these things, and when the king hears them he will say nothing further about your execution."

Anan undertook also to deceive his own followers and said to them: "Last night Elijah the prophet appeared before me in a dream and said to me, 'You deserve to be put to death for violating that which is written in the Law.'" [Anan convinced his followers that Rabbinic Judaism falsified the true intent of the Bible by interpreting it according to the Oral Law as clarified in the Talmud.] He spoke thus to them in order to entice them with his crafty argumentation and out of fear for his life so that he might save himself from a cruel death and might perpetuate his name in eternity. He also expended a great sum of money in bribes, until the king gave him permission to speak, whereupon he said, "The religion of my brother employs a calendar based upon calculation of the time of the new moon and intercalation of leap years by cycles, whereas mine depends upon actual observation of the new moon and intercalation regulated by the ripening of new grain." Since the king's religion likewise employed the latter method, Anan thus gained his favor and good will.

Leon Nemoy, ed., *The Karaite Anthology*, New Haven, Conn., 1987

The Karaites get their name from the Hebrew word for scripture (mikra). They accepted the authority of the Hebrew Bible alone, and they were characterized by asceticism and rigid adherence to the literal interpretation of biblical laws. The literal text of the Bible forbade fire on the Sabbath day. The Talmud clarified that its use was not forbidden; only setting a fire on Sabbath was not permitted. The Karaites sat in darkness all of the seventh day. In order to demonstrate their error, Rabbinic Judaism insisted that the Sabbath be ushered in by the lighting of candles.

Karaites didn't follow many of the most universally accepted practices of Rabbinic Judaism, such as the use of phylacteries (tefillin) in prayer, the prohibition of eating meat with milk, and the celebration of the festival of Hanukkah. Intermarriage with non-Karaite Jews was forbidden. Their influence grew considerably, and they might have had even more were it not for the efforts of Saadiah Gaon (882–942), who spearheaded a major offensive against their views with his classic work The Book of Beliefs and Opinions. The Karaites had communities throughout Byzantium and Asia Minor, Spain, and, from the twelfth century on, Russia and Lithuania. Remarkably, Hitler added his voice to the question of this sect's legitimacy as Jews. In 1939 the Nazis ruled that the Karaites were not to be considered Jews under the German program of genocide. Today, there are estimated to be 1,500 Karaites in the United States, about a hundred Karaite families in Istanbul, and about twelve thousand Karaites in Israel, most of them living near the town of Ramleh.

About the year 740, the Khazars, a powerful Turkish tribe occupying the steppes of southern Russia, became converts to Judaism. More than two centuries later, the report of the existence of this Jewish kingdom aroused the curiosity of Hasdai ibn Shaprut (about 915–970). Ibn Shaprut was not only the personal physician of the Spanish califs Abd-al-Rahman III (912–961) and his son Hakam II (961–976) but was also inspector-general of customs and an adviser in foreign affairs. To learn more, Hasdai wrote to the ruler of the Khazars in about 960 and some time later received an answer from Joseph, the reigning king. The exchange of letters between Hasdai and Joseph, both originally written in Hebrew, reveal a fascinating story of a people's desire to embrace the faith of the Jews.

The Conversion of the Khazars

Hasdai ibn Shaprut's Letter to the King of the Khazars

I, Hasdai, son of Isaac, son of Ezra, belonging to the exiled Jews of Jerusalem, in Spain, a servant of my Lord the King, bow to the earth before him and prostrate myself towards the abode of your Majesty, from a distant land. I rejoice in your tranquillity and magnificence, and stretch forth my hands to God in Heaven that He may prolong your reign in Israel. But who am I . . . ?

Praise be to the beneficent God for his mercy towards me! Kings of the earth, to whom His magnificence and power are known, bring gifts to him [the king of Spain]. . . . All their gifts pass through my hands and I am charged with making gifts in return. . . . I always ask the ambassadors of these monarchs about our brethren the Israelites, the remnant of the captivity, whether they have heard anything concerning the deliverance of those who have pined in bondage and had found no rest. At length mercantile emissaries of Khorasan told me that there is a kingdom of Jews who are called Khozars and between Constantineh (Constantinople) and that country is a sea voyage of fifteen days, by land many nations dwell between us and them. But I did not believe these words, for I thought that they told me such things to procure my goodwill and favour. I was, therefore, hesitating and doubtful till the ambassadors of Constantineh came. . . . They answered me, "It is quite true; there is in that place a kingdom, Alcusari, distant from Constantineh a fifteen days' journey by sea; . . . the name of the king now reigning is Joseph: ships sometimes come from their country bringing fish, skins, and wares of every kind; the men are our brethren and are honored by us; there is frequent communication between us by embassies and mutual gifts; they are very powerful; they maintain numerous armies. . . ." This account inspired me with hope, wherefore I bowed down and adored the God of Heaven.

I now looked about for a faithful messenger whom I might send into your country. . . . The thing seemed impossible to me, owing to the very great distance of the locality, but at length by the will and favor of God, a man presented himself to me named Mar Isaac, the son of Nathan. He put his life into his hand and willingly offered to take my letter to my Lord the King. I gave him a large reward, supplying him with gold and silver . . . and with everything necessary. Moreover, I sent out of my own resources a magnificent present to the king of Constantineh, requesting him to aid this my messenger in every possible way.

Accordingly this messenger set out, went to the king and showed him my letter and presents. The king, on his part, treated him honorably, and detained him there for six months. . . . One day he told my messenger to return, giving him a letter in which he wrote that the way was dangerous, that the peoples through whom he must pass were engaged in warfare, that the sea was stormy. . . . When I heard this I was grieved even to death, and took it very ill.

Afterwards I wished to send my letter by way of Jerusalem, because persons there guaranteed that my letter should be dispatched from thence to Nisibis, thence to Armenia, from Armenia to Berdaa, and thence to your country. While in this state of suspense, behold ambassadors of the king of Gebalim [the Slavonians], arrived, and with them two Israelites; the name of one was Mar Saul, of the other Mar Joseph. These persons comforted me, saying, "Give us your letter, and we will take care it be carried to the king of the Gebalim, who for your sake send it to the Israelites dwelling in the land of the Hungarians, they will send it to Russ, thence to Bulgar, till at last . . . its destination."

I did none of these things for the sake of mine own honour, but only to know the truth, whether the Israelitish exiles anywhere form one independent kingdom and are not subject to a foreign ruler. If, indeed, I could learn that this was the case, then, despising all my glory, abandoning my high estate, leaving family, I would go over mountains and hills, through seas and lands, till I should arrive at the place where my Lord the King resides, that I might see not only his glory and magnificence but also the tranquillity of the Israelites. On beholding this my lips would pour forth praises to God, who has not withdrawn his favor from his afflicted ones.

Now, therefore, let it please your Majesty, I beseech you to send back a reply . . . to inform me fully concerning the condition of the Israelites, and how they came to dwell there. . . .

One thing more I ask of my Lord . . . whether there is among you any computation concerning the final redemption which we have been awaiting so many years, whilst we went from one captivity to another, from one exile to another. . . . And oh! How can I hold my peace and be restful in the face of the desolation of the house of our glory and remembering those who, escaping the sword, have passed through fire and water, so that the remnant is but small. We have been cast down from our glory, so that we have nothing to reply when they say daily unto us, "Every other people has its kingdom, but of yours there is no memorial on the earth." Hearing, therefore, the fame of my Lord the King, as well as the power of his dominions, . . . we lifted up our head, our spirit revived. . . . Blessed be the Lord of Israel who has not left us without a kinsman as defender nor suffered the tribes of Israel to be without an independent kingdom. May my Lord the King prosper for ever.

Jacob Marcus, *The Jew in the Medieval World: A Source Book,* 315–1791, New York, 2000

King Joseph's Reply to Hasdai ibn Shaprut

We are of the posterity of Japhet and the descendants of his son Togarma. We read in the genealogic books of our forefathers that Togarma had ten sons; we are the issue of Khozar, the seventh. It is set down in our chronicles that from his days onward our ancestors had to fight against peoples more numerous and more powerful than they. . . . Some centuries later there came a descendant of Khozar, King Bulan, a wise man and God-fearing. . . . The kings of Edom [Christians] and of Ishmael [Mohammedans] sent their ambassadors to him with great treasures, and also sent their learned men to convert them to their religions. But the king, in his wisdom, also sent for a learned Israelite . . . and he then had them as it were compete, so that each one expounded with fire the principles of his own religion and sought to refute the arguments of his antagonists. Then the king said to the monk: "Of the two religions, that of the Israelite and that of the Ishmaelite, which is to be preferred?" The priest replied: "That of the Israelite." Then he asked the cadi: "Between the faith of the Israelite and the faith of the Edomite, which is to be preferred?" The cadi replied: "The religion of the Israelite is much to be preferred to the religion of the Nazarenes." To this the prince answered: "You both acknowledge that the faith of the Israelites is the wiser and the better; I therefore choose that religion, the religion of Abraham." From that time on God always helped him and strengthened him, and he and his people were all circumcised. . . . From that time on we have followed this religion: God be praised for it eternally. . . .

With reference to your question concerning the marvelous end [the restoration to former glory by the Messiah] our eyes are turned to the Lord our God and to the wise men of Israel who dwell in Jerusalem and Babylon. Though we are far from Zion, we have heard that because of our iniquities the computations are erroneous. . . . But, if it please the Lord, He will do it for the sake of His great name; nor will . . . all the troubles which have come upon us be lightly esteemed in His sight. He will fulfill His promise, and "the Lord whom ye seek shall suddenly come to His temple, the messenger of the covenant whom ye delight in: behold he shall come, saith the Lord of Hosts." [Malachi 3:1] Besides this we have only the prophecy of Daniel. May God hasten the redemption of Israel, gather together the captives and dispersed, you and I, and all Israel that love His name, in the lifetime of us all. Finally, you mention that you desire to see my face. I also long, and desire to see your honored face, to behold your wisdom and magnificence. Would that it were according to your word, and, that it were granted me to be united with you, so that you might be my father and I your son. All my people would pay homage to you: according to your word and righteous counsel we should go out and come in. Farewell.

Jacob Marcus, *The Jew in the Medieval World: A Source Book, 315–1791,* New York, 2000

The Khazars in Contemporary Chronicles

Some intriguing contemporary reports of the Khazars have been found in historical documents. (The selections below appear online at www.khazaria.com.)

At the present time we know of no nation in the world where Christians do not live. For in the lands of Gog and Magog who are a Hunnish race and call themselves Gazari there is one tribe, a very belligerent one— Alexander enclosed them and they escaped—and all of them profess the Jewish faith. The Bulgars, however, who are of the same race, are now becoming Christians.

Christian of Stavelot, in *Expositio in Matthaeum Evangelistam,* composed circa 864

All of the Khazars are Jews. But they have been Judaized recently.

Ibn al-Faqih, a tenth-century author

One of the Jews undertook the conversion of the Khazars, who are composed of many peoples, and they were converted by him and joined his religion. This happened recently in the days of the Abbasids. . . . For this was a man who came single-handedly to a king of great rank and to a very spirited people, and they were converted by him without any recourse to violence and the sword. And they took upon themselves the difficult obligations enjoined by the law of the Torah, such as circumcision, the ritual ablutions, washing after a discharge of the semen, the prohibition of work on the Sabbath and during the feasts, the prohibition of eating the flesh of forbidden animals according to this religion, and so on.

Abd al-Jabbar ibn Muhammad al-Hamdani, in his early-eleventh-century work *The Establishment of Proofs for the Prophethood of Our Master Muhammad*

The Khazars write Hebrew [letters].

Muhammad ibn Ishaq an-Nadim of Baghdad, in his late-tenth-century *Kitab al-Fihrist*

The Khazar Jews came to the court of Prince Vladimir and said: "We have heard that Bulgarians (Muslims) and Christians came to teach you their religion. . . . We, however, believe in the one God of Abraham, Isaac, and Jacob." Vladimir asked them: "What kind of law do you have?" They answered: "We are required to be circumcized, we may not eat pork or hare meat, and we must observe the Sabbath." And he asked: "Where is your land?" They answered: "In Jerusalem." And again he asked: "It is really there?" They answered: "God got angry with our fathers and therefore scattered us all over the world and gave our land to the Christians." Vladimir asked: "How is it that you can teach people Jewish law even while God rejected you and scattered you. If God had loved you and your law, you would not be scattered throughout foreign lands. Or do you wish us Russians to suffer the same fate?"

The Russian Chronicle, describing a visit of Khazar missionaries to Kiev in the year 986

A number of significant relics of the Khazars have been found, and some historians have concluded, as Abba Eban put it in his book *My People: The Story of the Jews,* that "it is likely . . . that some Khazar progeny reached the various Slavic lands where they helped to build the great Jewish centers of Eastern Europe." In his highly controversial book *The Thirteenth Tribe: The Khazar Empire and Its Heritage,* Arthur Koestler maintains that the Khazars migrated to Poland and formed the cradle of Western Jewry. That would make a major portion of today's Jews of non-Semitic origin, descended from converts, rather than the biological offspring of Abraham, Isaac, and Jacob. If true, how would that affect our understanding of Jews and of Judaism?

Book IV

Late Medieval Times: 1000–1700s

THE TIME FRAME

Date (C.E.)	Event
1055	Death of Samuel Ha-Nagid
1066	William of Normandy conquers England
1096	First Crusade
1130	Birth of Maimonides
1144	First blood libel against the Jews (England)
1204	Death of Maimonides (Egypt)
1215	Fourth Lateran Council (Badge of Shame instituted); Magna Carta
1242	Burning of the Talmud in Paris
1244	Tartars capture Jerusalem
1260	Mongols under Hulagu devastate Jerusalem
1290	Expulsion of all Jews from England
1291	Acre captured by Muslims; end of the Latin Kingdom of Jerusalem
1337	Beginning of the Hundred Years' War
1348	The Black Death

Date (C.E.)	Event
1394	Expulsion of all Jews from France
1480	Inquisition established in Spain
1492	Expulsion of all Jews from Spain; Columbus discovers America
1516	Ottoman Turks conquer Palestine
1544	Martin Luther (Protestant Reformation) turns against the Jews
1569	Rabbi Issac Luria ("Ari") comes to Safed to teach Jewish mysticism (Kaballah)
1580	First legislation of the "Council of the Four Lands" in Poland
1582	Gregorian calendar established
1588	Destruction of Spanish Armada
1593	First Marrano settlement established in Holland
1620	*Mayflower* arrives at Plymouth Rock
1648	Chmielnicki massacres; end of Thirty Years' War
1650	Menasseh Ben Israel publishes *The Hope of Israel*
1654	First Jewish settlement established in North America (New Amsterdam)
1676	Death of Sabbatai Zevi, false messiah
c. 1706	Congregation Shearith Israel of New York organized
1760	Death of Baal Shem Tov, founder of Hasidic movement
1772	Rabbinic ban against followers of Hasidic movement
1776	American Revolution

13

"It Was the Best of Times": The Golden Age of Spain

T here have been times in Jewish history when the sun has shone. True, the Dark Ages still define much of what was happening in the world during the first centuries of the second millennium. There are more than enough tales of suffering, of Jew-hatred, of unbearable cruelty and oppression. We'll get to the bad news in the next chapter. But let's take a break from tragedy to take note of the good news: for a while at least, Jews found acceptance, respect, and positions of great prominence in one country to such a degree that we still call it the Golden Age of Spain.

We've already met one of Spanish Jewry's great figures, Hasdai ibn Shaprut, in his role as correspondent with Joseph, king of the Khazars. Hasdai served under two caliphs of Cordova in the tenth century, as both physician and inspector-general of customs. His many talents—including medicine, finance, mastery of languages, broad scholarship, and love of learning—allowed him great influence at the palace, which he skillfully used in the interests of his people.

Following in his footsteps soon after was Samuel ibn Naghrela (933–1055), better known by the title Ha-Nagid, "The Prince," which he immodestly assumed for himself. Literally rising from rags to riches, Samuel became vizier of the state—a climb comparable in our times to the Jewish Henry Kissinger becoming America's secretary of state. More incredible still, and emblematic of the elimination of the "glass ceiling" for Jewish people, Samuel rose to become the leader of an army of Muslims. To commemorate an impressive victory over the forces of the kingdom of Seville in 1040, he wrote a military song of victory echoing the words of Moses and the Jews at the Red Sea after the drowning of the Egyptians:

Samuel Ha-Nagid, "Song of Victory"

As my enemies drew near to eat my flesh
I rose up while they fell down enfeebled.
They brought pain to my heart but God
Sent healing balm at the time of suffering and anguish.
He commanded the ministering angels and they were
My help from the heavens, descending and ascending;
Even to the nation which thought to divide
The booty of his people, He allotted ruin in his wrath.
We will build the *succot* with joy
While they lament in their shame.

. . . .

Children of my people, join me in this praise.
Put it at the head of all laudations.
Set its words in proper order
In the mouths of old and young.
For when in future times your sons will ask:
"What is this?" You will then to the questioner reply:
"A song of praise it is to God who redeemed his beloved,
Who composed it for the redeemed to recite.
It is a song of praise, great and glorious
To the glory of God and his mighty works."

Leon J. Weinberger, *Jewish Prince in Moslem Spain: Selected Poems
of Samuel Ibn Nagrela*, Tuscaloosa, Ala., 2001

The Last Will and Testament of a Cultured Spanish Jew

*We can learn a lot about the lives and interests of cultured Spanish Jews from this
ethical will left by Judah ibn Tibbon (circa 1120–1190) to his son Samuel. Judah ibn
Tibbon was born in Granada and eventually migrated to southern France. He is
known as the father of translators from Arabic into Hebrew.*

From the Ethical Will of Judah ibn Tibbon

My son, listen to my precepts, neglect none of my injunctions. Set my
admonition before your eyes; thus shall you prosper and prolong your
days in pleasantness! . . .

You know, my son, how I swaddled you and brought you up, how I led you in the paths of wisdom and virtue. I fed and clothed you; I spent myself in educating and protecting you. I sacrificed my sleep to make you wise beyond your fellows and to raise you to the highest degree of science and morals. These twelve years I have denied myself the usual pleasures and relaxations of men for your sake, and I still toil for your inheritance.

I have honored you by providing an extensive library for your use, and have thus relieved you of the necessity to borrow books. Most students must bustle about to seek books, often without finding them. But you, thanks be to God, lend and borrow not. Many books, indeed, you own two or three copies. I have besides made for you books on all sciences, hoping that your hand might find them all as a nest.

Seeing that your Creator had graced you with a wise and understanding heart, I journeyed to the ends of the earth and fetched for you a teacher in secular sciences. I minded neither the expense nor the danger of the ways. Untold evil might have befallen me and you on those travels, had not the Lord been with us!

But you, my son did deceive my hopes. You did not choose to employ your abilities, hiding yourself from all your books, not caring to know them or even their titles. Had you seen your own books in the hand of others, you would not have recognized them; had you needed one of them, you would not have known whether it was with you or not, without asking me; you did not even consult the catalogue of your library. . . .

Therefore, my son! Stay not your hand when I have left you, but devote yourself to the study of the Torah and to the science of medicine. But chiefly occupy yourself with the Torah, for you have a wise and understanding heart, and all that is needful on your part is ambition and application. I know that you will repent of the past, as many have repented before you of their youthful indolence. . . .

Let your countenance shine upon the sons of men; tend their sick and may your advice cure them. Though you take fees from the rich, heal the poor gratuitously; the Lord will requite you. Thereby shall you find favor and good understanding in the sight of God and man. Thus will you win the respect of high and low among Jews and non-Jews, and your good name will go forth far and wide. You will rejoice your friends and make your foes envious. For remember what is written in the *Choice of Pearls* [53:617, of Ibn Gabirol]: "How shall one take vengeance on an enemy? By increasing one's own good qualities." . . .

My son! Examine regularly, once a week, your drugs and medicinal herbs, and do not employ an ingredient whose properties are unknown to you. I have often impressed this on you in vain. . . .

My son! I command you to honor your wife to your utmost capacity. She is intelligent and modest, a daughter of a distinguished and educated family. She is a good housewife and mother, and no spendthrift. Her tastes are simple, whether in food or dress. Remember her assiduous attendance of you in your illness, though she had been brought up in elegance and luxury. Remember how she afterwards reared your son without man or woman to help her. Were she a hired nurse, she would have earned your esteem and forbearance; how much the more, since she is the wife of your bosom, the daughter of the great, art you bound to treat her with consideration and respect. To act otherwise is the way of the contemptible. The Arab philosopher [Al Ghazali, 1058–1112] says of women: "None but the honorable honors them, none but the despicable despises them." . . .

If you would acquire my love, honor her with all your might; do not exercise too severe an authority over her; our Sages [Gittin 6b] have expressly warned men against this. If you give orders or reprove, let your words be gentle. Enough is it if your displeasure is visible in your look; let it not be vented in actual rage. Let your expenditure be well ordered. It is remarked in the *Choice of Pearls* [1:3] "Expenditure properly managed makes half an income." And there is an olden proverb: "Go to bed without supper and rise without debt." Defile not the honor of your countenance by borrowing; may the Creator save your from that habit! . . .

Examine your Hebrew books at every New Moon, the Arabic volumes once in two months, and the bound codices once every quarter. Arrange your library in fair orders so as to avoid wearying yourself in searching for the book you need. Always know the case and the chest where the book should be. A good plan would be to set in each compartment a written list of the books therein contained. If, then, you are looking for a book, you can see from the list the exact shelf it occupies without disarranging all the books in the search for one. Examine the leaves in the volumes and bundles, and preserve them. These fragments contain very important matters, which I collected and copied out. Do not destroy any writing or letter of all that I have left. And cast your eyes frequently over the catalogue so as to remember what books are in your library.

Never intermit your regular readings with your teacher; study in the college of your master on certain evenings before sitting down to read with the young. Whatever you have learned from me or from your teachers, impart it again regularly to worthy pupils, so that you may retain it, for by teaching it to others you will know it by heart, and their questions will compel your to precision, and remove any doubts from your own mind.

Never refuse to lend books to anyone who has not the means to purchase books for himself, but only act thus to those who can be trusted to return the volumes. You know what our sages said in the Talmud, on the text: "Wealth and riches are in his house; and his merit endures for ever." [Ketubot 50a applies this verse, Psalm 112:3, to one who lends his copies of the Bible.] But, [Proverbs 3:27] "Withhold not good from him to whom it is due," and take particular care of your books. Cover the bookcases with rugs of fine quality, and preserve them from damp and mice, and from all manner of injury, for your books are your good treasure. If you lend a volume, make a memorandum before it leaves your house, and when it is returned, draw your pen over the entry. Every Passover and Sukkot call in all books out on loan.

I enjoin on you, my son, to read this, my testament, once daily, at morn or at eve. Apply your heart to the fulfillment of its behests, and to the performance of all therein written. Then will you make your ways prosperous, then shall you have good success.

Israel Abrahams, ed., Hebrew Ethical Wills, New York, 1976

> Ethical wills have often proven extremely effective. In this instance, Samuel became even more famous as a translator than his father was. His most valuable work was his translation from Arabic into Hebrew of Maimonides' classic work of philosophy, *The Guide for the Perplexed.* The power of ethical wills obviously resides in their role as dying requests. They allow people to sum up their philosophy of life and transmit it to their descendants. What would you advise your children in a final testament?

From Moses to Moses—There Was No One like Moses

In 1985, to commemorate the 850th anniversary of the birth of Maimonides, Moses ben Maimon (1135–1204) (also known by the acronym RAMBAM, for Rabbi Moses Ben Maimon), a UNESCO conference was held in Paris, and a Maimonidean scholar, Shlomo Pines, confidently asserted that "Maimonides is the most influential Jewish thinker of the Middle Ages, and quite possibly of all times." A Soviet scholar, Vitaly Naunkin, said at the same gathering, "Maimonides is perhaps the only philosopher in the Middle Ages, perhaps even now, who symbolizes a confluence of four cultures: Greco-Roman, Arab, Jewish, and Western."

Born in Cordova, Maimonides eventually settled in Cairo, where he was appointed house physician to the vizier of Egypt. His life encapsulates the contributions of Jews to the world when their talents were permitted to flower in medicine and science, in philosophy, in law, and in theology. How one man was able to accomplish all that he did is a mystery. Some insight, however, can be found in this fascinating letter he wrote to Samuel ibn Tibbon.

The Schedule of Maimonides

Only the Heavenly Creator of the World knows under what conditions I am writing this letter to you! I have had to flee my colleagues and take refuge in a hidden spot. I am so weak that I must occasionally prop myself up against the wall or write while lying down.

Regarding your wish to visit me, I can only tell you how much pleasure that would give me for I would truly like to discuss this question with you. I would have been even happier than you about our meeting were it not for the worry created by such a long and dangerous trip. I am also obliged to dissuade you from taking such a perilous journey, all the more so since we would only see each other for the few moments that I would consider it my duty to devote to welcoming you. Otherwise, this visit would not be particularly useful for you. We would be unable to speak about anything for even an hour, a day, or an evening. I submit my schedule to you so that you yourself can see how busy I am.

I live in Fostat and the sultan lives in Cairo; the two cities are a Shabbat's distance from one another, or some four thousand cubits. My obligations insofar as the monarch is concerned are the most time consuming. I must visit him daily and when he, one of his children, or one of the harem dwellers is ill, I spend most of the day at the palace. Moreover, one or two of the dignitaries visiting the court are often ill, in which case I spend the entire day attending to them. In general this means that I go to Cairo very early in the morning and even when nothing in particular happens, I do not return to Fostat until the afternoon, by which time I am dying of hunger. All of the waiting rooms are full of Jews and Gentiles alike, important and humble people, theologians, bailiffs, friends and enemies, all sorts of people await my return. I leave my horse, wash my hands, and ask those who are waiting to grant me a few moments during which I can eat something light, my sole meal of the day. Then I begin the consultations, write out prescriptions and prescribe diets. The flow of patients continues until nightfall and can on occasion, I swear to you, continue until eight o'clock or even later. I receive them lying on my back, overwhelmed by weariness, and when night has fallen, I am so exhausted that I can barely speak.

Given this schedule, I never have a free moment during the week to meet the Jews who would like to discuss the affairs of the community or private matters with me. I therefore devote my Shabbat to this. The congregation, at least the majority of its members, meets at my home after morning services and it is only at that point that I give my instructions for the week. Then we study until noon. Some return after *minha* (afternoon service), and we spend our time reading until *ma'ariv* (evening prayer). And I am only relating one part of what you would see if, despite everything, you were to persist in wanting to visit me, with God's help. . . .

I pray for your health and happiness my dear son and disciple, and for the deliverance of our unfortunate people. Written by Moses, son of Maimon, the 8 Tishri 1511 of the Seleucid era (Sept. 30, 1199). Peace.

Franz Kobler, Letters of Jews: Through the Ages, London, 1953

Of his many thousands of legal rulings, the letter of Maimonides to a Muslim convert to Judaism is especially noteworthy. It highlights a number of all-important ideas: that Judaism is not a race, but rather a religion; that Jews are not so much a "chosen people" as they are a "choosing people" who opt to accept God, a choice open to all believers whether they are descendants of Abraham or not; and that Jews dare not look down upon converts because of their origins—rather, these converts are to be admired for their courage and newfound conviction.

Letter of Maimonides to Obadiah the Convert

Thus says Moses the son of Rabbi Maimon, one of the exiles from Jerusalem, who lived in Spain:

I received the question of the master Obadiah, the wise and learned proselyte, may the Lord reward him for his work, may a perfect recompense be bestowed upon him by the Lord of Israel, under whose wings he has sought cover.

You ask me if you, too, are allowed to say in the blessings and prayers you offer alone or in the congregation: "Our God" and "God of *our* Fathers," "Thou who hast sanctified *us* through Thy commandments," "Thou who hast who hast separated *us*," "Thou who hast chosen *us*," "Thou who hast inherited *us*," "Thou who hast brought *us* out of the land of Egypt," "Thou who hast worked miracles to *our* fathers," and more of this kind.

Yes, you may say all this in the prescribed order and not change it in the least. In the same way as every Jew by birth says his blessing and prayer, you, too, shall bless and pray alike, whether you are alone or pray in the congregation. The reason for this is, that Abraham, our father, taught the people, opened their minds, and revealed to them the true faith and the unity of God; he rejected the idols and abolished their adoration; he brought many children under the wings of the Divine Presence; he gave them counsel and advice, and ordered his sons and the members of his household after him to keep the ways of the Lord forever, as it is written, "For I have known him, to the end that he may command his children and his household after him, that they may keep the way of the Lord, to do righteousness and justice." Ever since then whoever adopts Judaism and confesses the unity of the Divine Name, as it is prescribed in the Torah, is counted among the disciples of Abraham, our father, peace be with him. These men are Abraham's household, and he it is who converted them to righteousness.

In the same way as he converted his contemporaries through his words and teaching, he converts future generations through the testament he left to his children and household after him. Thus Abraham, our father, peace be with him, is the father of his pious posterity who keep his ways, and the father of his disciples and of all proselytes who adopt Judaism.

Therefore you shall pray, "Our God" and "God of our fathers," because Abraham, peace be with him, is *your* father. And you shall pray, "Thou who hast taken for his own our fathers," for the land has been given to Abraham, as it is said, "Arise, walk through the land in the length of it and in the breadth of it; for I will give it unto thee." As to the words, "Thou who hast brought us out of the land of Egypt" or "Thou who hast done miracles to our fathers"—these you may change, if you will, and say, "Thou who hast brought Israel out of the land of Egypt" and "Thou who hast done miracles to Israel." If, however, you do not change them, it is no transgression, because since you have come under the wings of the Divine Presence and accepted the Lord, no difference exists between you and us, and all miracles done to us have been done as it were us and to you. Thus it is said in the book of Isaiah, "Neither let the son of the stranger, that hath joined himself to the Lord, speak, saying, 'The Lord hath utterly separated me from His people.'" There is no difference whatever between you and us. You shall certainly say the blessing, "Who hast chosen us," "Who hast given us," "Who hast taken us for Thine own" and "Who hast separated us": for the Creator, may He be extolled, has indeed chosen you and separated you from the nations and given you the Torah. For the Torah has been given to us *and* to the proselytes, as it is said, "One ordinance shall be both for you of the congregation, and also for the stranger that sojourneth with you, an ordinance for ever in your generations; as you are, so shall the stranger be before the Lord." Know that our fathers, when they came out of Egypt, were mostly idolaters; they had mingled with the pagans in Egypt and imitated their way of life, until the Holy One, may He be blessed, sent Moses, our teacher, the master of all prophets, who separated us from the nations and brought us under the wings of the Divine Presence, us and all proselytes, and gave to all of us one Law.

Do not consider your origin as inferior. While we are the descendants of Abraham, Isaac and Jacob, you derive from Him through whose word the world was created. As it is said by Isaiah: "One shall say, I am the Lord's, and another shall call himself by the name of Jacob."

Franz Kobler, Letters of Jews: Through the Ages, London, 1953

Contrast this ruling with laws passed in Nazi Germany to define who is a Jew.

Benjamin of Tudela: The Marco Polo of the Jews

Rabbi Benjamin, the son of Jonah of Tudela in the kingdom of Navarre, took it upon himself to travel the known world and record his impressions. In 1173 he returned with a fascinating account that tells us a great deal about both the Jews and the Gentiles of his day. Here is his account of his visit to Rome.

From "The Travels of Benjamin of Tudela"

A journey of six days from thence brings you to the large city of Rome, the metropolis of all Christendom. Two hundred Jews live there, who are very much respected, and pay tribute to no one. Some of them are officers in the service of pope Alexander (Alexander III, who held the papacy from 1159 to 1181), the chief ecclesiastic and head of the Christian church. The principals of the many eminent Jews resident here are R. Daniel and R. Jechiel. The latter is one of the pope's officers, a handsome, prudent, and wise man, who frequents the pope's palace, being the steward of his household and minister of his private property. R. Jechiel is a descendant of R. Nathan, the author of the book Aruch, and its comments. . . .

The city of Rome is divided into two parts by the river Tiber, which runs through it. In the first of these divisions you see the large place of worship called St. Peter of Rome, on the site of the extensive palace of Julius Caesar.

The city contains numerous buildings and structures entirely different from all other buildings upon the face of the earth. The extent of ground covered by the ruined and inhabited parts of Rome amounts to four-and-twenty miles. You there find eighty halls of the eighty eminent kings who were all called Imperator, from King Tarquin to King Pepin, the father of Charles (Charlemagne), who first conquered Spain and wrested it from the Mohammedans. In the outskirts of Rome is the palace of Titus, who was rejected by three hundred senators in consequence of his having wasted three years in the conquest of Jerusalem, which, according to their will, he ought to have accomplished in two years. There is likewise the hall of the palace of King Vespasianus, a very large and strong building; also the hall of King Galba, containing 360 windows, equal in number to the days of the year. The circumference of this palace is nearly three miles. A battle was fought here in times of yore, and in the palace fell more than a hundred thousand, whose bones are hung up there even to the present day. The King caused a representation of the battle to be drawn, army against army, the men, the horses, and all their accoutrements being sculptured in marble, in order to preserve a memorial of the wars of antiquity. You there find also a cave under ground containing the King and his Queen upon their thrones, surrounded by about one hundred nobles of their court, all embalmed by physicians and in good preservation to this day.

Another remarkable object is St. Giovanni *in porta Latina,* in which place of worship there are two copper pillars constructed by King Solomon, of blessed memory, whose name, "Solomon, son of David," is engraved upon each. The Jews in Rome told me that every year, about the time of the 9th of Ab, these pillars sweat so much that the water runs down from them. You there see also the cave in which Titus, the son of Vespasian, hid the vessels of the temple, which he brought from Jerusalem; and in another cave on the banks of the Tiber, you find the sepulchers of those holy men of blessed memory, the ten martyrs of the kingdom. Opposite St. Giovanni de Laterano, there is a statue of Samson, with a lance of stone in his hand; also that of Absalom, the son of David, and of King Constantine, who built Constantinople, which city is called after his name; his statue is cast in copper, the man and horse being gilt. Rome contains many other remarkable buildings and works, the whole of which nobody can enumerate.

Benjamin of Tudela, in *Early Travels in Palestine,* Thomas Wright, ed., London, 1848

14

"It Was the Worst of Times": The Church and the Jews

I n the latter half of the twentieth century, a major event took place within the Catholic Church. Pope John XXIII convened Vatican II and called for aggiornamento, *the internal reconstruction of the church's doctrine and liturgy toward Jews and Judaism. Thus began a process to overcome two thousand years of the Church's hostility to the Jews. It marked a profound attempt at repentance and reconciliation in which the present pope, John Paul II, begged for forgiveness for the many sins of the Church against Jews throughout the past centuries. Whether Jews of this generation may grant forgiveness for sins committed against their ancestors is theologically and morally debatable. What is certainly true, though, is that we owe it to the past to record and to remember. Recognizing the blessing of reconciliation, we nevertheless need to reflect on a relationship between Christians and Jews that witnessed unspeakable crimes made all the more unimaginable because they were committed in the name of God and religion.*

The Crusades

In 1095 Pope Urban II called for a "holy Crusade" to drive the infidel Turks out of Jerusalem. This unleashed a series of violent and barbaric marches through Europe, characterized by mob brutality, rape, and pillage, with Jews—identified as the killers of Christ—most often the victims. In the course of the ten Crusades, lasting from 1095 through 1291, it's estimated that from 30 to 50 percent of European Jews were slaughtered. Crusaders were encouraged to take part in this "holy mission" in order to "save" the Jews—while at the same time they were released from any debts they might owe to Jews who had been forced into moneylending as one of the very few livelihoods legally available to them.

The York Massacre As Described by Ephraim of Bonn (1189–1190)

Afterwards, in the Hebrew year 4551 (1190 C.E.) the Wanders came upon the people of the Lord in the city of Evoric (York) in England, on the Great Sabbath [before Passover] and the season of the miracle was changed to disaster and punishment. All fled to the house of prayer. Here Rabbi Yom-Tob stood and slaughtered sixty souls, and others also slaughtered. Some there were who commanded that they should slaughter their only sons, whose foot could not tread upon the ground from their delicacy and tender breeding. Some, moreover, were burned for the Unity of their Creator. The number of those slain and burned was one hundred and fifty souls, men and women, all holy bodies. Their houses moreover they destroyed, and they despoiled their gold and silver and the splendid books which they had written in great number, precious as gold and as much fine gold, there being none like them for their beauty and splendour. These they brought to Cologne and to other places, where they sold them to the Jews.

Joseph Ha Cohen's sixteenth-century chronicle "Valley of Tears," in Cecil Roth,
A History of the Jews in England, Oxford, England, 1985

> Jews who knew they were going to be slaughtered often opted to follow in the footsteps of their ancestors at Masada and took their own lives as an act of "sanctification of the Divine Name." They also killed their own children rather than allowing them to be taken to be forcibly baptized. Scholars have debated this issue at great length. During the time of the Holocaust, it was almost universally agreed that the most powerful response to those who sought Jewish annihilation was for the Jews to do everything in their power to survive.

The Crusaders in Mainz

It was on the third of Sivan at noon that Emico the wicked, the enemy of the Jews, came with his whole army against the city gate, and the citizens opened it up for him. Emico a German noble, led a band of plundering German and French crusaders. Then the enemies of the Lord said to each other: "Look! They have opened up the gate for us. Now let us avenge the blood of 'the hanged one' [Jesus]."

The children of the holy covenant who were there, martyrs who feared the Most High, although they saw the great multitude, an army numerous as the sand on the shore of the sea, still clung to their Creator. Then young and old donned their armor and girded on their weapons and at their head was Rabbi Kalonymus ben Meshullam, the chief of the community. Yet because of the many troubles and the fasts which they had observed they had no strength to stand up against the enemy. [They had fasted to avert the impending evils.] Then came gangs and bands, sweeping through like a flood until Mayence was filled from end to end. . . .

. . . The bishop's men, who had promised to help them, were the very first to flee, thus delivering the Jews into the hands of the enemy. . . .

When the children of the covenant saw that the heavenly decree of death had been issued and that the enemy had conquered them and had entered the courtyard, then all of them—old men and young, virgins and children, servants and maids, cried out together to their Father in heaven and, weeping for themselves and for their lives, accepted as just the sentence of God. One to another they said: "Let us be strong and let us bear the yoke of the holy religion, for only in this world can the enemy kill us—and the easiest of the four deaths is by the sword. But we, our souls in paradise, shall continue to live eternally, in the great shining reflection [of the divine glory]." . . .

As soon as the enemy came into the courtyard they found some of the very pious there with our brilliant master, Isaac ben Moses. He stretched out his neck, and his head they cut off first. The others, wrapped by their fringed praying shawls, sat by themselves in the courtyard, eager to do the will of their Creator. They did not care to flee into the chamber to save themselves for this temporal life, but out of love they received upon themselves the sentence of God. The enemy showered stones and arrows upon them, but they did not care to flee, and [Esther 9:5] "with the stroke of the sword, and with slaughter, and destruction" the foe killed all of those whom they found there. . . .

. . . Why did the heavens not grow dark and the stars not withdraw their brightness? Why did not the moon and the sun grow dark in their heavens when on one day, on the third of Sivan, on a Tuesday, eleven hundred souls were killed and slaughtered, among them many infants and sucklings who had not transgressed nor sinned, among them many poor, innocent souls?

Soloman bar Samson, May 27, 1096, in Jacob Marcus, *The Jew in the Medieval World: A Source Book*, 315–1791, New York, 2000

Libels against the Jews

From *A Book of Historical Records*, circa 1200

In the year 4931 [1171], evil appeared in France, too, and great destruction in the city of Blois, in which at that time there lived about forty Jews. It happened on that evil day, Thursday, toward evening, that the terror came upon us. A Jew [Isaac bar Eleazar] rode up to water his horse; a common soldier—may he be blotted out of the book of life—was also there watering the horse of his master. The Jew bore on his chest an untanned hide, but one of the corners had become loose and was sticking out of his coat. When, in the gloom, the soldier's horse saw the white side of the hide, it was frightened and sprang back, and it could not be brought to water.

The Christian servant hastened back to his master and said "Hear, my lord, what a certain Jew did. As I rode behind him toward the river in order to give your horses a drink, I saw him throw a little Christian child, whom the Jews have killed, into the water. When I saw this, I was horrified and hastened back quickly for fear he might kill me too. Even the horse under me was so frightened by the splash of the water when he threw the child in that it would not drink." The soldier knew that his master would rejoice at the fall of the Jews, because he hated a certain Jewess influential in the city. He as much as put the following words into his master's mouth: "Now I can wreak my vengeance on that person, on that woman Pulcelina."

The next morning the master rode to the ruler of the city, to the cruel Theobald, son of Theobald—may his unrighteousness and bitter, evil curses fall upon his head. [Theobald V was Count of Blois, 1152–1191. He was called "the Good."]

When he heard this he became enraged and had all the Jews of Blois seized and thrown into prison. But Dame Pulcelina encouraged them all, for she trusted in the affection of the ruler who up to now had been very attached to her. However, his cruel wife, a Jezebel, swayed him, for she also hated Dame Pulcelina. [Theobald's wife was Alix, the daughter of King Louis VII of France.] All the Jews had been put into iron chains except Pulcelina, but the servants of the ruler who watched her would not allow her to speak to him at all, for fear she might get him to change his mind.

The ruler was revolving in his mind all sorts of plans to condemn the Jews, but he did not know how. He had no evidence against them until a priest appeared—may he be destroyed and may his memory be uprooted from the land of the living—who said to the ruler: "Come, I'll advise you how you can condemn them. Command that the servant who saw the Jew throw the child into the river be brought here, and let him be tested by the ordeal in a tank of water to discover if he has told the truth."

The ruler commanded and they brought him, took off his clothes, and put him into a tank filled with holy water to see what would happen. If he floated, his words were true; if he sank, he had lied. Such are the laws of the Christians who judge by ordeals—bad laws and customs by which one cannot live! The Christians arranged it in accordance with their wish so that the servant floated, and they took him out and thus they declared the wicked innocent and the righteous guilty.

The ruler had started negotiations for a money settlement before the coming of the priest who incited the ruler not to accept any ransom for the dead child. He had sent a Jew to the Jews of the other communities and had asked how much they would give him. The Jews consulted with their Christian friends and also with the Jews in the dungeon, and these latter advised offering only one hundred pounds and in addition their uncollected debts amounting to the sum of one hundred eighty pounds.

In the meantime the priest arrived on the scene, and from this time on the ruler paid no attention to the Jews and did not listen to them, but only to the instruction of the priest. In the day of wrath money could not help them. At the wicked ruler's command they were taken and put into a wooden house around which were placed thornbushes and faggots. As they were led forth they were told: "Save your lives. Leave your religion and turn to us." They mistreated them, beat them, and tortured them, hoping that they would exchange their glorious religion for something worthless, but they refused. Rather did they encourage each other and say to one another: "Persist in the religion of the Almighty!"

At the command of the oppressor they then took the two Jewish priests, the pious Rabbi Jehiel, the son of Rabbi David HaKohen, and the just Rabbi Jekutiel HaKohen, the son of Rabbi Judah, and tied them to a single stake in the house where they were to be burned. They were both men of valor, disciples of Rabbi Samuel and Rabbi Jacob. They also tied the hands of Rabbi Judah, the son of Aaron, and then set fire to the faggots. The fire spread to the cords on their hands so that they snapped, and all three came out and spoke to the servants of the oppressor: "The fire has no power over us. Why should we not go free?" The enemy answered: "By our lives! You shall not get out." They kept on struggling to get out but they were pushed back into the house. They came out again and seized hold of a Christian to drag him along with them back onto the pyre. When they were right at the fire the Christians pulled themselves together, rescued the Christian from their hands, killed them with their swords, and then threw them into the fire. Nevertheless they were not burnt, neither they nor all those thirty-one persons. Only their souls were released by the fire; their bodies remained intact. When the Christians saw it, they were amazed and said to one another: "Truly these are saints."

It was also reported that as the flames mounted high, the martyrs began to sing in unison a melody that began softly but ended with a full voice. The Christian people came and asked us, "What kind of a song is this for we have never heard such a sweet melody?" We knew it well for it was the song: "It is incumbent upon us to praise the Lord of all." [This prayer, the *Alenu*, or Adoration, is now recited daily; it was then a New Year's prayer with a special melody.]

Of their own free will all the communities of France, England, and the Rhineland observed Wednesday, the 20th of Sivan, 4931, as a day of mourning and fasting. This was also the command of the great teacher Jacob, the son of Rabbi Meir, who wrote letters to them informing them that it was proper to fix this day as a fast for all our people, and that it must be greater even than the Fast of Gedaliah ben Ahikam; it was to be like the Day of Atonement [a twenty-hour fast].

A Book of Historical Records, a Hebrew historical work of Ephraim Ben Jacob (1132–circa 1200), a German Jewish Talmudist and poet of note, in Jacob Marcus, *The Jew in the Medieval World: A Source Book, 315–1791*, New York, 2000

Among the most outrageous of the libels used against Jews was the claim that Jews were required by their religious law to kill Christian babies in order to use their blood for the baking of matzo for Passover. The first time this allegation was made was in Norwich, England, in 1144. It continues to find expression to this day. In a recent article in the Cairo daily *Al Akhbar,* the contemporary Egyptian intellectual and journalist Anis Mansour assured his readers that "They [the Jews] have what they call the Easter Feast, the feast of the unleavened bread, which is celebrated by bleeding a non-Jew. Then they take a piece of flesh and mix it with the Matzo. The Rabbi himself does the butcher's work. This is the nature of our enemy." How is it possible for a lie of such gross proportions to have found—and to continue to find— believers, especially amongst supposed "intellectuals"?

The Inquisition

During the 1200s, the hunt for heretics led to establishment of the Inquisition, which spread throughout Europe. Pope Innocent IV authorized torture. Under interrogation by Dominican priests, screaming victims were stretched, burned, pierced, and broken on fiendish pain machines to make them confess to disbelief and to identify fellow transgressors. Jews who had been forcibly baptized but were suspected of secretly continuing to practice their former faith (known as Marranos) were frequent victims of this diabolical system that elicited confessions of heresy as a result of torture, only to be rewarded by execution. A sickening sample, from the official records of the Holy Office of the Inquisition, follows:

"Confessions" under Torture

She was carried to the torture chamber and told to tell the truth, when she said that she had nothing to say. She was ordered to be stripped and again admonished, but was silent. When stripped, she said "Señores, I have done all that is said of me and I bear false-witness against myself, for I do not want to see myself in such trouble; please God, I have done nothing." She was told not to bring false testimony against herself but to tell the truth. The tying of the arms commenced; she said, "I have told the truth; what have I to tell?" She was told to tell the truth and replied, "I have told the truth and have nothing to tell." One cord was applied to the arms and twisted and she was admonished to tell the truth but said she had nothing to tell. Then she screamed and said, "I have done all they say." Told to tell in detail what she had done she replied, "I have already told the truth." Then she screamed and said, "Tell me what you want for I don't know what to say." She was told to tell what she had done, for she was tortured because she had not done so, and another turn of the cord was ordered. She cried: "Loosen me, Señores, and tell me what I have to say: I do not know what I have done, O Lord have mercy on me, a sinner!" Another turn was given and she said, "Loosen me a little that I may remember what I have to tell; I don't know what I have done; I did not eat pork, for it made me sick; I have done everything; loosen me and I will tell the truth." . . . She was told to tell what she had done contrary to our holy Catholic faith. . . . She was told to tell in detail truly what she did. She said, "What am I wanted to tell? I did everything—loosen me for I don't remember what I have to tell—don't you see what a weak woman I am? Oh! Oh! My arms are breaking." More turns were ordered and as they were given she cried, "Oh . . . Oh, my arms! I don't know what I have to say—If I did I would tell it." The cords were ordered to be tightened when she said, "Señores, have you no pity on a sinful woman?"

She was told, yes, if she would tell the truth. She said, "Señor tell me, tell me it." The cords were tightened again, and she was ordered to tell in detail, to which she said, "I don't know how to tell it, señor, I don't know." Then the cords were separated and counted, and there were sixteen turns, and in giving the last turn the cord broke.

She was then ordered to be placed on the *potro* [frame]. She said: "Señores, why will you not tell me what I have to say? Señor, put me on the ground—have I not said that I did it all? I have said I did all that the witnesses say. Señores release me, for I do not remember it." She was told to tell it. She said, "I do not know it. Oh, Oh, they are tearing me to pieces—I have said that I did it—let me go." She was told to tell it. She said: "Señores, it does not help me to say that I did it, and I have admitted that what I have done has brought me to this suffering—Señor, you know the truth—Señores, for God's sake have mercy on me. Oh Señor, take these things from my arms—Señor, release me, they are killing me." . . . The garrotes were ordered to be tightened. She said, "Señor, do you not *see* how these people are killing me? Señor, I did it—for God's sake let me go." She was told to tell it. She said, "Señor, remind me of what I did not know." . . . She was told to tell the truth or the cords would be tightened. She said, "Remind me of what I have to say for I don't know it—I said that I did not want to eat it—I know only that I did not want to eat it," and this she repeated many times. She was told to tell why she did not want to eat it. She said, "For the reason that the witnesses say—I don't know how to tell it—miserable that I am that I don't know how to tell it. I say I did it, and my God how can I tell it?" Then she said that, as she did not do it, how could she tell it—"They will not listen to me—these people want to kill me. Release me and I will tell the truth." . . . She was told to declare it. She said, "I don't know how to say it—I have no memory—Lord, you are witness that if I knew how to say anything else I would say it. I know nothing more to say than that I did it and God knows it." She said many times, "Señores, Señores, nothing helps me. You, Lord, hear that I tell the truth and can say no more. They are tearing out my soul—order them to loosen me." Then she said, "I do not say that I did it—I said no more." Then she said, "Señor, I did it to observe that law." She was asked what law. She said, "The law that the witnesses say—I declare it all Señor, and don't remember what law it was—O, wretched was the mother that bore me." She was asked what was the law she meant and what was the law she said the witnesses say. This was asked repeatedly, but she was silent and at last said that she did not know. She was told to tell the truth or the garrotes would be tightened but she did not answer. Another turn was ordered on the garrotes and she was admonished to say what law it was. She said, "If I knew what to say I would say it. Oh Señor, I don't know what I have to say—Oh, Oh, they are killing me—if they would tell me what—Oh, Señores! Oh, my heart!" Then she asked why they wished her to tell what she could not tell and cried repeatedly "O, miserable me!" Then she said, "Lord, bear witness that they are killing me without my being able to confess." She was told that if she wished to tell the truth before the water was poured she should do so and discharge her conscience. She said that she could not speak and that she was a sinner. Then the linen *toea* [funnel] was placed [in her throat] and she said "Take it away, I am strangling and am sick in the stomach." A jar of water was then poured down, after which she was told to tell the truth. She clamored for confession, saying that she was dying. She was told that the torture would be continued till she told the truth and was admonished to tell it, but though she was questioned repeatedly she remained silent.

Then the inquisitor, seeing her exhausted by the torture, ordered it to be suspended.

Cecil Roth, A History of the Marranos, New York, 1992

15

"Get Out and Stay Out": The Decrees of Expulsion

W here can a Jew feel he has found a home? Exiled from their ances-
tral land, Jews found many different places of temporary repose. In
none of them, no matter how seemingly secure, how comfortable, or how wealthy,
would they find permanent dwelling. The script was usually the same wherever they
went: Against almost impossible odds, they prospered; their success produced envy;
they were expelled "on religious grounds," with all of their property confiscated and
given to the crown and all the debts owed to them by the populace canceled.
Sometimes this profitable scheme was replayed several times in the same place.
Expulsion was often followed not too much later by a "compassionate reprieve," so
that the lucrative cycle could be started all over again.

Here's just a small list of instances in which a country played the "let's kick out
the Jews for profit" game:

- The Jews were expelled from France in 1182
- The Jews were expelled from England in 1290
- The Jews were expelled from France in 1306 and 1394
- The Jews were expelled from Hungary in 1349 and 1360
- The Jews were expelled from Germany in 1348 and 1498
- The Jews were expelled from Austria in 1421
- The Jews were expelled from Lithuania in 1445 and 1495
- The Jews were expelled from Spain in 1492
- The Jews were expelled from Portugal in 1497

You would think that after a while a decree of expulsion would no longer come as *a shock to Jews. But one eviction notice came as the cruelest and most incomprehensible blow. Spain, after all, was the country where Jews had risen to the very highest positions of government. Spain was the land to which Jews made outstanding contributions in every field—science, medicine, literature, and the arts. Spain was where Jews had enjoyed a Golden Age. It was almost too much to bear when Spain joined the Jew-haters and callously kicked them out as well. The year was 1492—and Jews could only pray that as one door was being closed to them God would see to it that another would open for them. God—and Columbus—would not disappoint them.*

The Expulsion from France: 1182

From *Gesta Philippi Augusti,* a Contemporary Latin History by the Monk Rigord

At this time [1180–1181] a great multitude of Jews had been dwelling in France for a long time past [over 1,000 years], for they had flocked thither from diverse parts of the world, because peace abode among the French, and liberality; for the Jews had heard how the kings of the French were prompt to act against their enemies, and were very merciful toward their subjects. And therefore their elders and men wise in the Law of Moses, who were called by the Jews *didascali* [teachers], made resolve to come to Paris.

When they had made a long sojourn there, they grew so rich that they claimed as their own almost half of the whole city, and had Christians in their houses as menservants and maidservants, who were open backsliders from the faith of Jesus Christ, and *judaized* with the Jews. And this was contrary to the decree of God and the law of the Church. And whereas the Lord had said by the mouth of Moses in Deuteronomy [23:20–21], "Thou shalt not lend upon usury to thy brother," but "to a stranger," the Jews in their wickedness understood by "stranger" every Christian, and they took from the Christians their money at usury. And so heavily burdened in this wise were citizens and soldiers and peasants in the suburbs, and in the various towns and villages, that many of them were constrained to part with their possessions. Others were bound under oath in houses of the Jews in Paris, held as if captives in prison. [Germanic law permitted a creditor to hold a debtor prisoner.]

The most Christian King Philip heard of these things, and compassion was stirred within him. He took counsel with a certain hermit, Bernard by name, a holy and religious man, who at that time dwelt in the forest of Vincennes, and asked him what he should do. By his advice the King released all Christians of his kingdom from their debts to the Jews, and kept a fifth part of the whole amount for himself.

Finally came the culmination of their wickedness. Certain ecclesiastical vessels consecrated to God—the chalices and crosses of gold and silver bearing the image of our Lord Jesus Christ crucified—had been pledged to the Jews by way of security when the need of the churches was pressing. These they used so vilely, in their impiety and scorn of the Christian religion, that from the cups in which the body and blood of our Lord Jesus Christ was consecrated they gave their children cakes soaked in wine. . . .

In the year of our Lord's Incarnation 1182, in the month of April, which is called by the Jews Nisan, an edict went forth from the most serene king, Philip Augustus, that all the Jews of his kingdom should be prepared to go forth by the coming feast of St. John the Baptist [June 24]. And then the King gave them leave to sell each his movable goods before the time fixed, that is, the feast of St. John the Baptist. But their real estate, that is, houses, fields, vineyards, barns, winepresses, and such like, he reserved for himself and his successors, the kings of the French.

When the faithless Jews heard this edict some of them were born again of water and the Holy Spirit and converted to the Lord, remaining steadfast in the faith of our Lord Jesus Christ. To them the King, out of regard for the Christian religion, restored all their possessions in their entirety, and gave them perpetual liberty.

Others were blinded by their ancient error and persisted in their perfidy; and they sought to win with gifts and golden promises the great of the land—counts, barons, archbishops, bishops—that through their influence and advice, and through the promise of infinite wealth, they might turn the King's mind from his firm intention. But the merciful and compassionate God, who does not forsake those who put their hope in Him and who doth humble those who glory in their strength so fortified the illustrious King that he could not be moved by prayers nor promises of temporal things. . . .

The infidel Jews, perceiving that the great of the land, through whom they had been accustomed easily to bend the King's predecessors to their will, had suffered repulse, and astonished and stupefied by the strength of mind of Philip the King and his constancy in the Lord, exclaimed with a certain admiration: "*Shema Israel!*" [that is, "Hear O Israel"] and prepared to sell all their household goods. The time was now at hand when the King had ordered them to leave France altogether, and it could not be in any way prolonged. Then did the Jews sell all their movable possessions in great haste, while their landed property reverted to the crown. Thus the Jews, having sold their goods and taken the price for the expenses of their journey, departed with their wives and children and all their households in the aforesaid year of the Lord 1182.

Jacob Marcus, *The Jew in the Medieval World: A Source Book, 315–1791,*
New York, 2000

> Many historians believe that a portion of the monies taken from the evicted Jews was used to build the Louvre Museum in Paris. Even in their absence, it seems, Jews continued to play a major role in enhancing the cultural life of France!

The Expulsion from England: 1290

In addition to banishing the Jews from England, King Edward I, in the following decree, relieves their Christian debtors from any interest owing on loans and orders the debtors to pay the principal—to him.

The Royal Decree

We, in requital for their crimes and for the honor of the Crucified, have banished them from our realm as traitors. We, being minded in nowise to swerve from our former intent, but rather to follow it, do hereby make totally null and void all penalties and usuries and whatsoever else in those kinds may be claimed on account of the Jewry by actions at what time so ever arising against any subjects of our realm. Being minded that nothing may in any wise be claimed from the said Christians on account of the said debts except only the principal sums which they have received from the said Jews, we decree that the said Christians do verify the amount before you by the oath of three true and lawful men, by whom the truth of the matter may the better be known, and thereafter pay the amount to us at such convenient times as may be determined by you. And to that intent we command you that you cause this our grace so benevolently granted to be read, and to be enrolled in the said Exchequer, and to be strictly observed, according to the form above indicated.

B. Lionel Abrahams, "The Expulsion of the Jews from England in 1290,"
in the *Jewish Quarterly Review,* 1895

The Expulsion from Spain: 1492

In the name of Ferdinand and Isabella of Spain, the following proclamation, dated March 30, 1492, banished the Jews from Spain.

The Royal Decree

We who rule by God's grace, Ferdinand and Isabella, rulers of Castile and Aragon, rulers of Leon and Murcia, rulers of Majorca and Sardinia, rulers of Granada and Navarra, etc.: The cries of the Marranos have come up to us, upon some of whom we have decreed burning and upon others to be imprisoned forever, for they have been found wayward in our religion, while some of those who have remained free of these punishments, have done so because they have repented their ways completely.

Yet the hands of the inquisitors are still stretched forth to investigate the evil of their deeds, and they cried out to us bitterly that it is the Jew who to this day have been the reason for their rebellion and their forsaking of the Christian religion, by teaching them their ways, their laws and their beliefs, as well as the laws of their feasts and festivals, and as long as Jews are to be found among them in Spain, it will be impossible for them to be complete and true Christians. We have therefore seen fit to totally banish the Jews from all places in our kingdom, even though they deserve a greater punishment than this for what they have done.

However, we have had mercy on them, and we are content to limit ourselves to this punishment. We therefore decree and command that every male and female, young and old, who is a Jew and who lives in our kingdom is to be banished and is to leave all those places where they live and to go outside the provinces of our kingdom to another land within the coming three months, starting with 1 May and ending on the last day of July. And whoever disobeys us and does not leave will be sentenced to death by hanging or to convert to Christianity.

E. H. Lindo, *The History of the Jews of Spain and Portugal*, London, 1848

The passage that follows was written by Don Isaac Abravanel (1437–1508), the most powerful Jew in Spain. Abravanel first served as treasurer to Alfonso V of Portugal, but he was forced to flee when he was falsely implicated in a plot by his enemies. When he arrived in Spain, his talents were soon recognized by Ferdinand and Isabella, who appointed him treasurer of all of Spain. Abravanel is recognized to this day not only for his financial acumen, diplomatic skills, and political genius but also for his contributions as a foremost biblical commentator and scholar. He helped finance Columbus's journey but was unable to greet him upon his successful return because Abravanel was a Jew, and the royal reward for his manifold contributions turned out to be expulsion. Here is his description of the calamitous event.

Abravanel's Account of the Expulsion

In the year of 5252, or 1492, the king of Spain seized the entire kingdom of Granada and the great city of Granada, one with a large populace and an important city. Esau [the Spanish king], then said in his heart: "How can I repay God who has enabled me to emerge victorious in battle? How can I greet my Maker who gave this city into my hands, if not by having enter into His fold the nation which walks in darkness, the scattered lamb of Israel, and have the wayward daughter return to my faith? Failing that, I will send them forth to another land before me, so that they will no longer live in my land and will no longer be before my eyes."

He therefore issued a proclamation which stated: "I say to all the families of the house of Israel, that if you are baptized and pray and worship to the god of the other nations, you will eat of the best of the land as I do today, and you will dwell in the land and trade in it. However, if you refuse and rebel and do not wish to make mention of my god, you are to go out from the midst of my people, from the lands of Spain, Seville, Majorca and Sardinia which are under my rule, and within three months there is not to remain a single Jew in my realm!"

At the time I was in the king's court, I was exhausted from calling unto him until my throat became hoarse. I met with the King three times, begging him: "Save us, O king. Why do you do thus to your servants? Impose a large payment on us, one of gold and silver, and every Jew will give for his land." I called upon all my friends who were close to the king, asking them to intercede before him with all their might, so that the decree to destroy all the Jews might be rescinded. But he remained completely deaf to my entreaties and did not respond to my plea. All this time, it was the queen who stood behind him and hardened his resolve to carry out the decree. We labored, but were not granted that which we sought. I did not rest and did not remain silent and did not let up, but the decree remained.

As for the Jews, when they heard the decree they all mourned, and wherever the news of the king's word and order was heard, the Jews despaired, and all feared greatly, a fear unequaled since the exile of Judah from its land to a foreign land. Each said to the other, "Let us strengthen one another in our faith and the Torah of our God, against the enemy who blasphemes and wishes to destroy us. If he lets us live, we shall live, and if he kills us, we shall die, but we will not desecrate our covenant and we will not retreat. We will go in the ways of the Lord our God." In the end there left, without strength, three hundred thousand people on foot, from the youngest to the oldest, all at one time, from all the provinces of the king, to wherever they were able to go. Their King went before them, God at their helm. Each pledged himself to God anew. Some went to Portugal and Navarre, which are close, but all they found were troubles and darkness, looting, starvation and pestilence. Some traveled through the perilous ocean, and here, too, God's hand was against them, and many were seized and sold as slaves, while many others drowned in the sea. Others again, were burned alive, as the ships on which they were traveling were engulfed by flames.

In the end, all suffered: some by the sword and some by captivity and some by disease, until but a few remained of the many. In the words of our fathers (Num. 17:28), "Behold we perish, we die, we all perish," may the name of the Lord be blessed. I, too, chose the way of the sea, and I arrived here in the famed Naples, a city whose kings are merciful.

Isaac Abravanel, Commentary to the Prophets, author's translation from Hebrew

The Aftermath of the Spanish Exile

From *Shevet Yehuda* (The Staff of Judah)

Those who went to Fez endured a great deal from God, may He be blessed, and especially terrible hunger. The local inhabitants refused to allow them to enter the cities lest the price of food increase, and they were therefore forced to live in the fields and in tents. They grazed for grass but found none, because the climate was so dry that there was nothing, except for a few isolated clumps. A large number of them died there, and there was none to bury them. Those who remained alive simply did not have the strength because they, too, were starving. On the Sabbath, they would graze with their mouths, because one is forbidden to uproot anything with one's hands [on the Sabbath].

At that time, an event occurred, the like of which is unheard. An Arab came, and saw a beautiful young Jewish woman, and in front of her parents he violated her. About half an hour later he returned with a spear and stabbed the young woman through her belly. They said to him: "O cruel one! Why did you do this?" He answered: "I was afraid that she might become pregnant, and her child would be raised as a Jew." Hear and see! Has such a thing happened in the world, or did one hear of such? . . .

I have also heard from various elders who left Spain that a certain ship was struck by an epidemic. The captain thereupon threw the people onto the land, in a place where there was no human settlement, and there most died of starvation. A few managed to find the strength to walk until they found a settlement.

One Jew, along with his wife and two sons, decided to walk, and as the wife was unaccustomed to the exertion, she fainted and died. The man then carried his two sons, until he and his two sons also fainted from hunger. When he awoke from his faint he saw that his two sons were dead. In his despair, he got to his feet and said: "Lord of the Universe! You have done much to have me abandon my religion. I want you to know clearly that, in spite of the forces of Heaven, I am a Jew and I will remain a Jew, and whatever you have brought or will yet bring against me will be to no avail!" He then took some earth and buried his sons, and went on to look for a settlement.

Solomon Ibn Verga (circa 1450–1520), author's translation from Hebrew

Sailing with Columbus

From the Diary of Luis De Torres, a Marrano Jew

The fateful day, the day of our expulsion from Spain, was Tisha b'Av on the Jewish calendar in the year 5252/1492. That day marked the tragedy of the destruction of both holy temples many centuries before, and now, one more tragic event was added to that mournful day. Three hundred thousand people, half the amount that were redeemed from Egyptian slavery, descended to the Mediterranean shore, searching for passage to a new land, to a land where they could openly practice Judaism. I was among them.

However, I was not a refugee; I had been commissioned to join Christopher Columbus's voyage of discovery. I agreed to accompany him because I hoped that if we found Jewish brethren, I would be able to live my life in peace and in freedom. Don Rodriguez, his uncle Don Gabriel Sanchez, Alonso de Loquir, Rodrigo de Triana, Chon Kabrera, Doctor Briena and Doctor Marco, all agreed with my reasoning and joined, but except for Rodrigo, they sailed on the other ships. We were a large group of *conversos* (Morranos), living in perpetual fear of the Inquistion, hoping that we would find a way out of the precarious situation we were in. . . .

Columbus thought that when he would reach China and the Far East, he would locate the exiled Jews from the Ten Lost Tribes, and he wanted me [with a knowledge of Hebrew] to be able to communicate with them.

"The Diary of Luis De Torres," in the *Los Angeles Jewish Times,* Dec. 24, 1999.
(Brackets mine.—B. B.)

Is it possible that Columbus himself had a motive similar to that of Luis de Torres? There is considerable speculation that Columbus may have shared Jewish ancestry with the Marranos on board. *Christopher Columbus's Jewish Connection,* by Jane Frances Amler, offers some fascinating hints to lend credence to this possibility. Most intriguing is the link between the journey of discovery and the fate of the Jews that serves as the very first entry in Columbus's diary:

In the same month in which their Majesties issued the edict that all Jews should be driven out of the kingdom and its territories, in the same month, they gave me the order to undertake with sufficient men my expedition of discovery of the Indies.

That's why some historians claim it was not Ferdinand and Isabella's jewels, but rather their Jews, that were most responsible for the discovery of the New World.

16

The Renaissance: New Beginnings

The sultan of the Turkish Ottoman Empire, Bayezid II, realized something the rulers of those countries that expelled the Jews didn't: "They tell me that Ferdinand of Spain is a wise man but he is a fool. For he takes his treasure and sends it all to me." As Jews sought new havens, there were a few places like Turkey that recognized their talents and invited them in. History records that as a result these countries then prospered. The Ottoman Empire, led by Sultans Selim I and Suleiman I, soon became one of the greatest world powers. Conversely, the lands that expelled their Jews quickly paid a heavy price. The rapid decline of Spain is inextricably tied to the year 1492. Rulers with vision saw the folly of this policy and extended invitations to the fleeing exiles. So begins the Jewish Renaissance—rebirth in new lands where they could start over again. Remarkably, one of the warmest and most enticing welcome mats was put out by a country that would centuries later house Auschwitz and most of the other concentration camps of the Holocaust whose function was annihilation.

Poland and the Support of Torah Study

In 1567 Sigismund II Augustus, the king of Poland and grand duke of Lithuania, as part of an effort to stimulate the immigration of Jews to Poland, issued an edict granting the Jews permission to establish a yeshiva in Lublin, Poland.

The Edict of Sigismund II Augustus

As a result of the efforts of our advisors and in keeping with the request of the Jews of Lublin we do hereby grant permission to erect a Yeshiva and a synagogue by its side . . . and to outfit the said Yeshiva with all that is required to advance learning. The administration of the Yeshiva is to be vested in a person who will be accorded authority and influence by the teachers and who will be capable of maintaining order and discipline among the students.

All the learned men and rabbis of Lublin shall come together and from among their number choose one to serve as the head of the Yeshiva. Let their choice be of a man who will magnify the Torah and bring it glory! To him shall be granted the right of supervision over teachers and students alike.

We hereby grant him the honorary title of Rosh Yeshiva and assert that he shall not be subject to the authority of the present rabbi of Lublin nor to that of those who hold that position in the future. Not only that, we do here affirm that the Rosh Yeshiva shall be the superior of all the rabbis and learned men of the city.

And inasmuch as instruction in the said Yeshiva is to be given without charge and at no cost to the student, we declare the Rosh Yeshiva to be exempt from all taxes and duties due our treasury and the treasury of the State.

Rabbi Ken Spiro, "Crash Course in Jewish History Part 49—The Jews of Poland,"
at www.aish.com

Jewish Life in Poland

Poland's efforts were clearly successful. In 1500 there were about fifty thousand Jews in Poland; by 1650 there were half a million. It's estimated that by the middle of the seventeenth century, over 30 percent of world Jewry was living in Poland. The very name Poland, Jews liked to pun, sounded like the Hebrew words po lin, *meaning "Here you shall live." In Poland Jews developed the lifestyle of the* shtetl *that would later be immortalized in* Fiddler on the Roof. *Here they created their own communities, developed their own language of Yiddish that was a mishmash of Hebrew and the many tongues of their former places of exile (especially German), and were permitted to govern themselves under a council known as the* Va'ad Arba Artzot— *the Council of the Four Lands, presided over by their own elected rabbis. To many, this period was a successor to their glorious Spanish past, and they called it the Golden Age of Poland.*

From *Yeven Mezulah* (The Abyss of Despair)

And now I will begin to describe the practices of the Jews in the Kingdom of Poland, which were founded on principles of righteousness and steadfastness.

It is said in Tractate Aboth: Simon the Just was one of the last survivors of the Great Synagogue. He used to say: "Upon three things the world is based: Upon the Torah, upon divine service, and upon the practice of charity." Rabban Simeon, the son of Gamaliel said: "By three things is the world preserved: by truth, by judgment and by peace." All the six pillars upon which the world rests were in existence in the Kingdom of Poland.

The Pillar of the Torah: Matters that are well known need no proof, for throughout the dispersions of Israel there was nowhere so much learning as in the Kingdom of Poland. Each community maintained academies, and the head of each academy was given an ample salary so that he could maintain his school without worry, and that the study of the Torah might be his sole occupation. The head of the academy did not leave his house the whole year except to go from the house of study to the synagogue. Thus he was engaged in the study of the Torah day and night. Each community maintained young men and provided for them a weekly allowance of money that they might study with the head of the academy. And for each young man they also maintained two boys to study under his guidance, so that he would orally discuss the Gemara (Talmud), the commentaries of Rashi, and the Tosafoth, which he had learned, and thus he would gain experience in the subtlety of Talmudic argumentation. The boys were provided with food from the community benevolent fund or from the public kitchen. If the community consisted of fifty householders it supported not less than thirty young men and boys. One young man and two boys would be assigned to one householder. And the young man ate at his table as one of his sons. Although the young man received a stipend from the community, the householder provided him with all the food and drink that he needed. Some of the more charitable householders also allowed the boys to eat at their table, thus three persons would be provided with food and drink by one householder the entire year.

There was scarcely a house in all the Kingdom of Poland where its members did not occupy themselves with the study of the Torah. . . .

Pillar of Charity: There was no measure for the dispensation of charity in Kingdom of Poland, especially as regards hospitality. If a scholar or preacher visited a community, even one which had a system of issuing communal tickets [meal tickets] to be offered hospitality by a householder, he did not have to humiliate himself to obtain a ticket, but went to some community leader and stayed wherever he pleased. The community beadle then came and took his credentials to collect funds to show it to the synagogue official or the community leader for the month, and they gave an appropriate gift which was delivered by the beadle in dignified manner. He was then the guest of the householder for as many days as he desired. Similarly all other transients who received tickets, would be the guests of a householder, whose turn it was by lot, for as many days as he wished. A ticket was good for at least three days. The guest was given food and drink, morning, noon and evening. If they wished to depart they would be given provisions for the road, and they would be conveyed by horse and carriage from one community to another. . . .

The Pillar of Justice was in the Kingdom of Poland as it was in Jerusalem before the destruction of the Temple, when courts were set up in every city, and if one refused to be judged by the court of his city he went to the nearest court, and if he refused to be judged by the nearest court, he went before the great court. For in every province there was a great court. Thus in the capital city of Ostrog there was the great court for Volhynia and the Ukraine, and in the capital city of Lwow there was the great court for [Little] Russia. There were thus many communities each of which had a great court for its own province. . . .

The Pillar of Truth: Every community appointed men in charge of weights and measures, and of other business dealings, so that everything would be conducted according to truth and trustworthiness.

The Pillar of Peace: For it is said: "The Lord will give strength unto His people; the Lord will bless His people with peace." There was in Poland so much interest in learning that no three people sat down to a meal without discussing the words of Torah, for throughout the repast everyone indulged in debating matters of the Law and puzzling passages in the Midrashim, in order to observe: "Thy law is in my inmost parts." And the Holy One blessed be He, recompensed them so that even when they were in the land of their enemies, He did not despise them and did not break his covenant with them. And wherever their feet trod the ground among our brothers of the House of Israel they were treated with great generosity, above all, our brethren of the House of Israel who were in distress and in captivity among the Tartars. For the Tartars led them to Constantinople, a city that was a mother in Israel, and to the famed city of Salonica, and to other communities in Turkey and Egypt, and in Barbary and other provinces of Jewish dispersion where they were ransomed for much money, as mentioned above. To this day they have not ceased to ransom prisoners that are brought to them each day. The Lord recompense them.

Those who escaped the sword of the enemy in every land where their feet trod, such as Moravia, Austria, Bohemia, Germany, Italy, were treated with kindness and were given food and drink and lodging and garments and many gifts, each according to his importance, and they also favored them with other things. Especially in Germany did they do more than they could. May their justice appear before God to shield them and all Israel wherever they are congregated, so that Israel may dwell in peace and tranquility in their habitations. May their merit be counted for us and for our children, that the Lord should hearken to our cries and gather our dispersed from the four corners of the earth, and send us our righteous Messiah, speedily in our day.

Nathan Hanover, in Jacob Marcus, The Jew in the Medieval World: A Source Book,
315–1791, New York, 2000

In 1648 the Golden Age came to a crashing halt as the Ukrainian Cossacks succeeded in freeing the Ukraine from Polish rule. The Cossack leader, Bogdan Chmielnicki, took special delight in venting his rage against the Jews who had served Polish landowners as rent and tax collectors. The Chmielnicki massacre is remembered in Jewish prayers to this day as an act of genocide on a par with the most horrendous in history. An estimated one hundred thousand Jews were brutally murdered and three hundred Jewish communities destroyed. What set this apart from other uprisings against the Jews was that its cruelty was rooted in sadism rather than an attempt at religious conversion or economic gain.

From *Yeven Mezulah* (The Abyss of Despair)

Some of them [the Jews] had their skins flayed off them and their flesh was flung to the dogs. The hands and feet of others were cut off and they [their bodies] were flung onto the roadway where carts ran over them and they were trodden underfoot by horse. . . . And many were buried alive. Children were slaughtered at their mother's bosoms and many children were torn apart like fish. They ripped up the bellies of pregnant women, took out the unborn children, and flung them in their faces. They tore open the bellies of some of them and placed a living cat within the belly and they left them alive thus, first cutting off their hands so that they should not be able to take the living cat out of the belly . . . and there was never an unnatural death in the world that they did not inflict upon them.

Hanover, in Marcus, *The Jew in the Medieval World*

> Chmielnicki is today considered a national hero in Ukraine. In Kiev there is a big statue in the square erected in his honor. What does a country's choice of national heroes tell us about the values of its people?

Martin Luther and the Jews

Pogroms, officially sanctioned mob murder and violence against Jews, would become a fairly regular feature of Eastern European life. Yet Jews remained and somehow survived. Being welcomed at first and then cruelly mistreated was something they had long learned to live with.

In the interim, Europe was beginning a religious transformation with profound implications for the Jews. The Protestant Reformation was born when, in 1517, Martin Luther posted his "95 Academic Theses on the Power of Indulgences" and dared to publicly attack the Church. Guided by the theory that "the enemy of my enemy is my friend," Luther at first shocked his contemporaries with the startling essay he wrote in 1523 to show his sympathy toward Jews in their long struggle with the Church and the papacy:

From "That Jesus Christ Was Born a Jew"

For our fools, the popes, bishops, sophists and monks—the gross asses' heads—have treated the Jews to date in such fashion that he who would be a good Christian might almost have to become a Jew. And if I had been a Jew and had seen such oafs and numbskulls governing and teaching the Christian faith, I would have rather become a sow than a Christian.

For they have dealt with the Jews as if they were dogs and not men. They were able to do nothing but curse them and take their goods. When they were baptized, no Christian teaching or life was demonstrated to them, rather they were only subjected to papistry and monkery. When they then saw that Judaism had such strong scriptural support and that Christianity was nothing but twaddle *without* any scriptural support, how could they quiet their hearts and become true *good* Christians? I myself have heard from pious baptized Jews that if they had not in our time heard the gospel, they would have remained life-long Jews under the Christian exterior. For they confess that they never yet have heard anything about Christ from their baptizers and masters. . . .

Therefore, I would request and advise that one manage them decently and instruct them from the Scripture so that some of them might be brought along. But since we now drive them with force and slander them, accuse them of having Christian blood if they don't stink, and who knows what other foolishness, so that they are regarded just as dogs—what good can we expect to accomplish with them? Similarly, that we forbid them to work, do business, and have other human association with us, so that we drive them to usury—how does that help them?

If we wish to help them, we must practice on them not the papal law but rather the Christian law of love, and accept them in a friendly fashion, allowing them to work and make a living, so that they gain the reason and opportunity to be with and among us [and] to see and to hear our Christian teaching and life.

If some are obstinate, what does it matter? After all, we too are not all good Christians. Here I will let matters rest until I see what I have accomplished.

Martin Luther, in Jacob Marcus, *The Jew in the Medieval World: A Source Book, 315–1791*, New York, 2000

With the passage of time, Luther's love for the Jews underwent an almost inexplicable reversal. The man who had preached compassion and understanding became the spokesman for the most extreme expressions of cruelty and organized violence against the people "who rejected Jesus." Perhaps the only way to explain his altered behavior is, as many theologians have suggested, to recognize that Luther truly believed that Jews would embrace his version of Christianity and renounce their own faith. When that didn't happen, Luther, like a spurned lover, turned into one of history's greatest Jew haters. Some have also suggested that Luther subconsciously felt that Lutheranism, like Catholicism before it, needed Jewish conversion as proof of its ultimate truth, and when that conversion was not forthcoming, the only solution seemed to be the annihilation of the Jews, as he outlined in this essay in 1543.

From "On the Jews and Their Lies"

What shall we do with this rejected and condemned people, the Jews? Since they live among us, we dare not tolerate their conduct, now that we are aware of their lying and reviling and blaspheming. If we do, we become sharers in their lies, cursing, and blasphemy. Thus we cannot extinguish the unquenchable fire of divine wrath, of which the prophets speak, nor

can we convert the Jews. With prayer and the fear of God we must practice a sharp mercy to see whether we might save at least a few from the
glowing flames. We dare not avenge ourselves. Vengeance a thousand
times worse than we could wish them already has them by the throat.

First, their synagogues or churches should be set on fire, and whatever
does not burn up should be covered or spread over with dirt so that no
one may ever be able to see a cinder or stone of it. . . .

Secondly, their homes should likewise be broken down and destroyed.
For they perpetrate the same things there that they do in their synagogues.
For this reason they ought to be put under one roof or in a stable, like gyp-
sies, in order that they may realize that they are not master in our land, as
they boast, but miserable captives, as they complain of us incessantly
before God with bitter wailing.

Thirdly, they should be deprived of their prayer-books and Talmuds in
which such idolatry, lies, cursing, and blasphemy are taught.

Fourthly, their rabbis must be forbidden under threat of death to teach
any more. . . .

Fifthly, passport and traveling privileges should be absolutely forbidden to the Jews. . . .

Sixthly, they ought to be stopped from usury. All their cash and valu-
ables of silver and gold ought to be taken from them and put aside for
safekeeping. For this reason, as said before, everything that they possess
they stole and robbed from us. . . .

Seventhly, let the young and strong Jews and Jewesses be given the flail,
the ax, the hoe, the spade, the distaff, and spindle, and let them earn their
bread by the sweat of their noses as is enjoined upon Adam's children. . . .

If, however, we are afraid that they might harm us personally, or our
wives, children, servants, cattle, etc. when they serve us or work for us . . .
let us drive them out of the country for all time. For, as has been said,
God's rage is so great against them that they only become worse and worse
through mild mercy, and not much better through severe mercy.
Therefore away with them. . . .

I wish and ask that our rulers who have Jewish subjects exercise a sharp
mercy toward these wretched people, as suggested above, to see whether
this might not help (though it is doubtful). . . . If this does not help we
must drive them out like mad dogs, so that we do not become partakers of
their abominable blasphemy and all their other vices and thus merit God's

wrath and be damned with them. I have done my duty. Now let everyone see to his. I am exonerated.

Martin Luther, in Marcus, *The Jew in the Medieval World*

The Reformation and the Jews

The Reformation led to bloody wars between Catholics and Protestants. Among the consequences with special implications for Jews were the decentralization of Christian leadership and control, which made it more difficult to attack Jews. In addition, the spirit of the Reformation led people to question authority and to think for themselves. Eventually that would lead to greater toleration of different faiths and bring about the Age of Enlightenment.

During the seventeenth century, Jews, as a result of the efforts of Rabbi Menasseh ben Israel (famed as the rabbi painted by Rembrandt), were readmitted to England. Other communities once again sprang up in Germany, France, and elsewhere in Western Europe. We have a fascinating eyewitness account of Jewish life in those days in the memoirs of Glückel of Hameln (1646–1724) written to "her dear beloved children."

From the Introduction to the Diary of Glückel of Hameln

With the help of God, I began writing this, my dear children, upon the death of your good father in the hope of distracting my soul from the burdens laid upon it, and the bitter thought that we have lost our faithful shepherd. In this way I have managed to live through many wakeful nights, and springing from my bed have shortened the sleepless hours.

I do not intend, my dear children, to compose and write for you a book of morals. Such I could not write, and our wise men have already written many. Moreover, we have our holy Torah in which we may find and learn all that we need for our journey through this world to the world to come. Of our beloved Torah we may seize hold. . . . We sinful men are in the world as if swimming in the sea and in danger of being drowned. But our great, merciful and kind God, in his great mercy, has thrown ropes into the sea that we may take hold of them and be saved. These are our holy Torah where is written what are the rewards and punishments for good and evil deeds. . . .

Dear children, I do not want to speak at length upon this, for if I would penetrate too deeply into this matter ten books were not sufficient. Read in the German "Brandspiegel", in "Leb Tob" [both are moralistic books], or, for those who can study, in [other] books of morals; there you will find everything.

I pray you this, my children: be patient, when the Lord, may He be praised, sends you a punishment, accept it with patience and do not cease to pray to Him; perhaps He will have mercy upon you. . . . Therefore, my dear children, whatever you lose, have patience, for nothing is our own, everything is only a loan. . . . We men have been created for nothing else but to serve God and to keep His commandments and to obey the Torah, for "He is thy life, and the length of thy life."

The kernel of the Torah is: "Thou shalt love thy neighbor as thyself." But in our days we seldom find it so, and few are they who love their fellow-men with all their heart. On the contrary, if a man can contrive to ruin his neighbor nothing pleases him more. . . .

The best thing for you, my children, is to serve God from your heart without falsehood or deception, not giving out to people that you are one thing while, God forbid, in your heart you are another. Say your prayers with awe and devotion.

During the time for prayers do not stand about and talk of other things. While prayers are being offered to the Creator of the world, hold it a great sin to engage another man in talk about an entirely different matter—shall God Almighty be kept waiting until you have finished your business?

Moreover, set aside a fixed time for the study of the Torah, as best you know how. Then diligently go about your business, for providing your wife and children with a decent livelihood is likewise a mitzvah—the command of God and the duty of man. We should, I say, put ourselves to great pains for our children, for on this the world is built, yet we must bear in mind that if children did as much for their parents, the children would quickly tire of it. . . .

Above all, my children, be honest in money matters, with both Jews and Gentiles, lest the name of Heaven be profaned. If you have in hand money or goods belonging to other people, give more care to them than if they were your own, so that, please God, you do no one a wrong. The first question put to a man in the next world is, whether he was faithful in his business dealings. Let a man work ever so hard amassing great wealth dishonestly, let him during his lifetime provide his children fat dowries and upon his death a rich heritage—yet woe, I say, and woe again to the wicked man who for the sake of enriching his children has lost his share in the world to come! For the fleeting moment he has sold Eternity.

When God sends evil days upon us, we shall do well to remember the remedy contrived by the physician in the story told by Rabbi Abraham ben Sabbatai haLevi. A great king, he tells us, once imprisoned his physician, and had him bound hand and foot with chains, and fed on a small dole of barley-bread and water. After months of this treatment, the king dispatched relatives of the physician to visit the prison and learn what the unhappy man had to say. To their astonishment he looked as hale and hearty as on the day he entered his cell. He told his relatives he owed his strength and well-being to a brew of seven herbs he had taken the precaution to prepare before he went to prison, and of which he drank a few drops every day. "What magic herbs are these?" they asked; and he answered: "The first is trust in God, the second is hope, and the others are patience, recognition of my sins, joy that in suffering now I shall not suffer in the world to come, contentment that my punishment is not worse, as well it could be, and, lastly, knowledge that God who thrust me into prison can, if He will, at any moment set me free."

However, I am not writing this book in order to preach to you, but, as I have already said, to drive away the melancholy that comes with the long nights. So far as my memory and the subject permit, I shall try to tell everything that has happened to me from my youth upward. Not that I wish to put on airs or pose as a good and pious woman. No, dear children, I am a sinner. Every day, every hour, and every moment of my life I have sinned, nearly all manner of sins. God grant that I may find the means and occasion for repentance. But, alas, the care of providing for my orphaned children, and the ways of the world, have kept me far from that state.

If God will that I may live to finish them, I shall leave you my Memoirs in seven little books. And so, as it seems best, I shall now begin with my birth.

The Memoirs of Glückel of Hameln, Marvin Lowenthal, trans., New York, 1988

In Glückel's "seven little books" we learn the beauty of a Jewish life lived in accord with the values of the Torah. Nevertheless, Glückel considered herself a sinner. Should a pious person always live with a feeling of imperfection?

17

The Three Spiritual Revolutions

Revolutions don't come about only by way of the sword. Some of the most dramatic changes in history occurred as a result of clashes of the mind and the spirit. As we look back at the sixteenth, seventeenth, and eighteenth centuries, we should note the lasting impact of three major spiritual revolutions that marked this period, one in each century. Two of them were successful and left us with living legacies. The other resulted in a collective despair that continues to haunt the Jewish people with its stern warning against any repeat of its sordid aspects.

The Sixteenth Century: The "Ari" and the Kabbalah

Kabbalah *comes from the Hebrew word for "received." It is the part of Jewish tradition that remains forever unwritten, only to be "received" by the most qualified people whom a master teacher finds worthy. The Kabbalah deals with secrets—the mysteries of the universe, the presence of God, death and the afterlife, reincarnation, and Messianic redemption. Although rooted in ancient tradition, its teachings flowered in the sixteenth century in the city of Safed in Israel as a result of the "Ari"—an acronym for the Hebrew spelling of* Elohi Rabbi Yitzhak—*the godly Rabbi Isaac Luria (1534–1572). In his short life of thirty-eight years, the Ari transformed an almost unknown branch of Jewish study into a school of thought that would play a vital role in defining Jewish life and would manifest itself in many aspects of mainstream Judaism for generations to come. His uniqueness was described by his most famous disciple, Rabbi Chaim Vital.*

From the Introduction to *Shaar HaHakdamot* (Gate of the Emanations)

The Ari overflowed with Torah. He was thoroughly expert in Scripture, Mishnah, Talmud, Pilpul, Midrash, Agadah, Ma'aseh Bereishit and Ma'aseh Merkavah. He was expert in the language of trees, the language of birds, and the speech of angels. He could read faces in the manner outlined in the Zohar (vol. II, p. 74b). He could discern all that any individual had done, and could see what they would do in the future. He could read people's thoughts, often before the thought even entered their mind. He knew future events, was aware of everything happening here on earth, and what was decreed in heaven.

He knew the mysteries of gilgul [reincarnation], who had been born previously, and who was here for the first time. He could look at a person and tell him how he was connected to higher spiritual levels, and his original root in Adam. The Ari could read wondrous things [about people] in the light of a candle or in the flame of a fire. With his eyes he gazed and was able to see the souls of the righteous, both those who had died recently and those who had lived in ancient times. With these departed souls, he studied the true mysteries.

From a person's scent, he was able to know all that he had done. (See Zohar, Yenuka vol. III, p. 188a.) It was as if the answers to all these mysteries were lying dormant within him, waiting to be activated whenever he desired. He did not have to seclude himself to seek them out.

All this we saw with our own eyes. These are not things that we heard from others. They were wondrous things that had not been seen on earth since the time of Rabbi Shimon bar Yochai. None of this was attained through magic, heaven forbid. There is a strong prohibition against these arts. Instead, it came automatically, as a result of his saintliness and asceticism, after many years of study in both the ancient and the newer Kabbalistic texts. He then increased his piety, asceticism, purity and holiness until he reached a level where Elijah would constantly reveal himself to him, speaking to him "mouth to mouth," teaching him these mysteries and secrets.

Rabbi Chaim Vital, in Jacob Marcus, *The Jew in the Medieval World: A Source Book, 315–1791*, New York, 2000

From *Hemdat Yamim* (Desire of Days)

He who fears the word of the Lord will take care to see that his business is carried on honestly in order that he shall not sin through false representation or through theft. He should at all times renounce his own in favor of his neighbor and in this way he can be sure that that which belongs to his neighbor will not come into his possession. It is impossible to do business so as to be exactly correct and to stick to the middle of the road and not to take something from your neighbor or he from you. Therefore, he who fears the word of God and who dreads divine punishment for theft will renounce a little of what he really has coming to him, for if he does not it is inevitable that he will take something, if only a trifle, of what he comes across.

In the days of Luria—of blessed memory—the late Rabbi Abraham Galante had asked the Master to give an "improvement" to his soul. [Galante, who died at Safed in 1588, was a wealthy Italian cabalist.] The Master was very timid about doing so because of Galante's outstanding position, until finally the latter said to him: "If you do not declare unto me everything that you see on my forehead then I will adjure you by God to inform me!" Luria then turned to look at his forehead and said: "There is a possibility, my lord and teacher, that you are guilty of theft." [The mystics believed that sin leaves its mark on the forehead.]

Galante was immediately terribly frightened and cried out: "Whither shall I carry my shame since I am guilty of the crime of theft," and went home out of sorts and displeased and put on sackcloth and ashes. He then sent and summoned all the garment workers in his employ [he was a manufacturing weaver], and when they came to him they found their employer clad in sackcloth sitting on the earth, and they were very much distressed.

"Can you not realize and understand that I am only a human being and have no desire to go to Gehenna [hell] because of you," he said to them. "Now if you will examine most carefully the accounts of your wages for the work you have done for me, I will appreciate it. If there is nothing due you, then leave me."

"What demands can we make of you for payment?" they responded. "Ever since we have been in your employ we have lacked nothing and do not expect to lack anything. God's blessing has rested upon us; we have had more than enough to eat, and there is no one of us who keeps accounts."

"Nevertheless," he then replied, "it is obvious that I am guilty of the crime of theft since you refuse to make your just demands for moneys due from me. Now I am therefore going to put some money before you and I want every one of you to take whatever you want and to forgive me for all that I have taken that belongs to you, and I, in turn, will forgive you."

He put the money before them, but they were not willing to stretch out their hands to take even a single penny. One woman, however, did put out her hand and take two pennies, and then altogether they called out and said: "We completely forgive you, down to the last penny, etc."

Galante then arose and went to the synagogue of the Master—may his memory endure in the world to come—who hurried out to meet him and said to him: "Why, my lord, were you so exceedingly fearful?" To which Galante answered: "Is it a small matter to feel that I may possibly be guilty of theft? Now if I have found favor in your sight take a look at my forehead and see whether it carries the sign of anything."

"There is no sign of sin," responded the Master and then revealed to Galante the mystery of how it came about that there was a suspicion of theft, by informing him that it was because of that woman who stretched out her hand and took the two pennies. The error arose out of the fact that that woman did the finest work and was superior to the other weavers and should have received more, but was *only* paid the same wages as the other craftsmen. "But in the heavens above," said Luria, "where they are very particular about such things, they held it against you and stamped the account in writing on your forehead!"

Nathan Benjamin Ghazzati, in Marcus, The Jew in the Medieval World

What is important is not so much whether these things were true but that they were believed to be so. That allowed for the teachings of the Ari to gain a wide following. The pendulum of intellectual thought constantly moves back and forth between the rational and the mystical. What accounts for the movement from one to the other? Where are we today? Is the mystical way of looking at the world once again fashionable and the Kabbalistic view of reincarnation the wave of the future?

The Seventeenth Century: Sabbatai Zevi, the False Messiah

The Kabbalistic concern with the coming of the Messiah would play a major role in one of the most fascinating stories in the century that followed. Imagine the Jewish world so captivated by the imminence of final redemption that hundreds of thousands were misled to follow a pretender to the title of Messiah. In 1666, a year that Kabbalistic predictions had endowed with eschatological significance, mass hysteria spread unchecked as countless people gave up their jobs and their worldly possessions in the belief that they no longer had any need for them. The story of Sabbatai Zevi

(1626–1676) is a made-for-movies script that would probably be rejected for being too far-fetched—but of course truth is often stranger than fiction.

How could it have happened? How were so many people fooled for so long? I guess you had to be there. Read what Rabbi Leib ben Ozer, a seventeenth-century chronicler of the Sabbatian Sect, had to say about Sabbatai Zevi:

You must believe that this was how it was. . . . I spoke with people who ate and drank and were near him . . . who were not proponents [of Sabbatai Zevi's] and they told me that there was none like him in stature and in the way his face looked, like that of one of God's angels. . . . And they testified that when he sang Sabbath hymns to God, which he did several times a day . . . it was not possible to look into his face, for one who looked at it, it was as if he looked into fire. . . . And this is one of the greatest occurrences, clearly supernatural, that came to pass in those days and a reason for the great belief in Shabtai Zvi, for in the year five thousand four hundred and twenty-six of creation [1665], in the month of Tevet, it happened in many places, in Izmir and in Constantinople and in Adrianople and in Salonika, that prophets arose in hundreds and thousands, women and men, boys and girls and even little children; all of them prophesied in the holy tongue [Hebrew] and in the language of the Zohar as well, and none of them knew a letter of Hebrew and all the less so the [idiosyncratic] language of the Zohar.

Leib ben Ozer, The Story of Shabbetai Zevi, Jerusalem, 1978

According to the Kabbalah, the Messiah is supposed to be born on the ninth day of Av. Sabbatai Zevi, as it happens, was born on that day. Jews had suffered horrendously from the Chmielnicki massacres in Eastern Europe. Tradition has it that the Messiah will come in the wake of terrible tragedies. Small wonder that Jews were prepared to believe this charismatic figure. Remarkably, Sabbatai Zevi had as followers not only most of the Jewish world but many Christians and Muslims as well. Sir Paul Rycaut (1628–1700), secretary at the British embassy to the Ottoman court and consul at Smyrna, birthplace of Zevi, gave the following eyewitness account.

Sir Paul Rycaut's Report on the Sabbatai Zevi Affair

Anno 1666

We shall begin this year with the strange rumor and disturbance of the Jews, concerning Sabbatai Zevi, their pretended Messiah which, for being most principally acted in Turkey, may properly belong to the history of this time and place. . . .

According to the predictions of several Christian writers, especially of such who comment upon the *Apocalypse* or *Revelations*, this year of 1666 was to prove a year of wonders, of strange revolutions in the world, and particularly, of blessing to the Jews. . . .

Strange reports flew from place to place of the march of multitudes of people from unknown parts into the remote deserts of Arabia, supposed to be the ten tribes and a half, lost for so many ages. That a ship was arrived in the northern parts of Scotland, with her sails and cordage of silk, navigated by mariners who spoke nothing but Hebrew, and with this motto on their sails, "The Twelve Tribes of Israel." . . .

In this manner millions of people were possessed when Sabbatai Zevi first appeared at Smyrna, and published himself to the Jews for their Messiah, relating the greatness of their approaching kingdom, the strong hand whereby God was about to deliver them from bondage, and gather them from all parts of the world. It was strange to see how this fancy took and how fast the report of Sabbatai and his doctrine flew through all parts where Jews inhabited, and so deeply possessed them with a belief of their new kingdom and riches, and many of them with promotion to offices of government, renown, and greatness; that in all places from Constantinople to Buda (which it was my fortune that year to travel) I perceived a strange transport in the Jews, none of them attending to any business, unless to wind up former negotiations, and to prepare themselves and families for a journey to Jerusalem. All their discourses, their dreams, and disposal of their affairs tended to no other design but a reestablishment in the Land of Promise, to greatness and glory, wisdom and doctrine of the Messiah [Sabbatai], whose origin, birth, and education are first to be recounted.

Sabbatai Zevi was son of Mordecai Zevi, an inhabitant and natural of Smyrna who gained his livelihood by being broker to an English merchant in that place; a person who before his death was very decrepit in his body, and full of the gout and other infirmities. But his son Sabbatai Zevi, addicting himself to study and learning, became a notable proficient in the Hebrew and Arabic languages. And especially in divinity and metaphysics he was so cunning a sophister that he vented [expressed] a new doctrine in their Law, and drew to the profession of it so many disciples as raised one day a tumult in the synagogue; for which afterwards he was, by censure of the Hakams (who are the expounders of the Law), banished out of the city.

During the time of his exile he traveled to Thessalonica, now called Salonica. . . . And being now free from the encumbrances of a family, his wandering head moved him to travel through the Morea [southern Greece], then to Tripoli in Syria, Gaza, and Jerusalem . . . and meeting there with a certain Jew called Nathan, a proper instrument to promote his design, he communicated to him his condition, his course of life, and intentions to declare himself the Messiah of the world, so long expected and desired by the Jews.

This design took wonderfully with Nathan; and because it was thought necessary, according to Scripture and ancient prophecies, that Elijah was to precede the Messiah, as St. John Baptist was the forerunner of Christ, Nathan thought no man so proper to act the part of the prophet as himself. And so no sooner had Sabbatai declared himself the Messiah, but Nathan discovers himself to be his prophet, forbidding all the fasts of the Jews in Jerusalem, and declaring that the Bridegroom [the Messiah] being come, nothing but joy and triumph ought to dwell in their habitations; writing to all the assemblies of the Jews to persuade them to the same belief. And now the schism being begun, and many Jews really believing what they so much desired, Nathan took the courage and boldness to prophesy that [in 1666] one year from the 27th of Kislev . . . the Messiah was to appear before the Grand Signior [the Sultan of Turkey], and to take from him his crown, and lead him in chains like a captive. . . .

And now all the cities of Turkey, where the Jews inhabited, were full of the expectation of the Messiah; no trade or course of gain was followed. Every one imagined that daily provisions, riches, honors, and government were to descend upon him by some unknown and miraculous manner. An example of which is most observable in the Jews at Thessalonica, who now full of assurance that the restoration of their kingdom and the accomplishment of the times for the coming of the Messiah was at hand . . . applied themselves immediately to fastings; and some in that manner beyond the abilities of nature, that having for the space of seven days taken no sustenance, were famished.

Others buried themselves in their gardens, covering their naked bodies with earth, their heads only excepted, remained in those beds of dirt, until their bodies were stiffened with the cold and moisture. Others would endure to have melted wax dropt upon their shoulders; others to roll themselves in snow and throw their bodies in the coldest season of the winter into the sea, or frozen waters. But the most common manner of mortification was first to prick their backs and sides with thorns and then to give themselves thirty-nine lashes. All business was laid aside; none worked or opened shop, unless to clear his warehouse of merchandise at any price. Who[ever] had superfluity in household stuff sold it for what he could. . . .

The Grand Signior, having by this time received diverse information of the madness of the Jews and the pretenses of Sabbatai, grew big with desire and expectation to see him; so that he no sooner arrived at Adrianople, but the same hour he was brought before the Grand Signior. . . . The Grand Signior . . . declared that, having given public scandal to the professors of the Mahometan religion and done dishonor to his sovereign authority by pretending to withdraw from him so considerable a portion as the land of Palestine, his treason and crime could not be expiated without becoming a Mahometan convert: which if he refused to do, the stake was ready at the gate of the seraglio to impale him.

Sabbatai, being now reduced to his last game and extremity (not being in the least doubtful what to do, for to die for what he was assured was false was against nature and the death of a mad man), replied with much cheerfulness that he was contented to turn Turk and that it was not of force, but of choice; having been a long time desirous of so glorious a profession, he esteemed himself much honored that he had an opportunity to own it first in the presence of the Grand Signior [September 1666]. . . .

The news of Sabbatai turning Turk and of the Messiah to a Mahometan quickly filled all parts of Turkey. The Jews were strangely surprised at it, and ashamed of their easiness of belief, of the arguments with which they had persuaded others, and of the proselytes they had made in their own families. Abroad they became the common derision of the towns where they inhabited. The boys hooted after them, coining a new word at Smyrna (poustai!) which every one seeing a Jew, with a finger pointed out, would pronounce with scorn and contempt; so that this deceived people for a long time after remained with confusion, silence, and dejection of spirit.

And yet most of them affirm that Sabbatai is not turned Turk, but his shadow only remains on earth, and walks with a white head, and in the habit of Mahometan; but that his body and soul are taken into heaven, there to reside until the time appointed for accomplishment of these wonders. And this opinion began so commonly to take place, as if this people resolved never to be undeceived, using the forms and rules for devotion prescribed them by their Mahometan Messiah. Insomuch that the Hakams of Constantinople, fearing the danger of this error might creep up and equal the former, condemned the belief of Sabbatai being Messiah as damnable, and enjoined them to return to the ancient method and service of God, upon pain of excommunication. . . .

And thus the . . . Jews [returned] again to their wits, following their trade and profession of brokage as formerly, with more quiet and advantage than the means of regaining their possessions in the Land of Promise. And thus ended this mad frenzy amongst the Jews, which might have cost them dear, had not Sabbatai renounced his Messiahship at the feet of Mahomet [IV, sultan, 1648–1687].

> Jacob Marcus, *The Jew in the Medieval World: A Source Book*,
> *315–1791*, New York, 2000

You would think that with Zevi's conversion to Islam the story would be over. Everyone would have to admit that they had been fooled by a master con man. Yet so great is the desire to believe that Zevi retained many followers. Well into the nineteenth century there were still those who claimed Zevi was in fact the true Messiah and that he adopted conversion as a mere ruse until he returns to reveal himself. A few Jews who converted to Islam along with him, the Doenmeh, continued as a Muslim sect within Turkey until World War I, when the Ottoman Empire fell. What is there in the human psyche that allows people to disregard reality when it conflicts with hope?

The Eighteenth Century: The Baal Shem Tov and Hasidism

When the Messiah didn't come, the mystical spirit sought another outlet. To avoid total despair, Hasidism was born. In Podolia Province, now in Ukraine, the Baal Shem Tov (literally "Master of the Good Name"), Israel the son of Eliezer (1698–1760), created a movement that would eventually spread around the world and, although steeped in the past, redefine much of the Jewish religion. Hasidism accomplished many things. It brought the uneducated Jew back to a place of honor at the table of God. It stressed spirituality over scholarship; it emphasized feeling over force-of-habit religious compliance; it spoke to the heart more than the head; and it taught that God wants most of all to be served with joy in appreciation for the world he created and about which he proclaimed, "And behold it is very good."

The Teaching of the *Besht* (Baal Shem Tov), Recorded by His Grandson

Commenting on Psalm 107:18: "Their soul abhorred all manner of food," Baruch of Miedzyboz [a grandson of the Besht] said that they once asked the Good Master of the Name: "What is the essence of religious service? Do we not know and have not our fathers told us that in ancient days pious men used to fast from one Sabbath to another? But now you have stopped this sort of thing for you have said that every man who fasts will some day have to justify himself and that he will be considered a sinner inasmuch as he has plagued his soul. Now, therefore, tell us what is the essence of religious service."

Thereupon the Good Master of the Name answered them: "I have come to this world to point out another way whereby man may attract to himself these three things, namely, love of God, love of Israel, and love of Torah. And there is no need to practice asceticism!"

Another story: On a frigid winter day, the Baal Shem Tov passed near a stream, on whose banks some people had carved idols out of ice. "How remarkable," he said to his followers. "Water has the ability to purify. We immerse ourselves and become holy. And yet, even water, when it is frozen, turns into an idol. So, too, Jews who allow their spirits and fervor to freeze, end up with pagan worship."

And one more tale that was oft told by the Baal Shem Tov:

Two Jews lived next door to each other. One was a scholar, the other a poor laborer. The scholar would rise every day at the break of dawn, go to the synagogue, study a page of Talmud, and say the morning prayers quietly and slowly until almost midday. His neighbor, the poor laborer, also rose early and went to work in order to feed his family, having no time to go to the synagogue to pray with the congregation at the proper hour. Precisely at midday, the scholar left the synagogue to return home, filled with a sense of satisfaction. He would invariably meet his neighbor, the poor laborer, hurrying to the house of worship with great anguish and regret for his tardiness. The laborer would utter a mournful groan, bemoaning his inability to have fulfilled his religious obligations properly. At the same time, the scholar would look with scorn at his simple, working neighbor, and a smirk would form on his lips as he considered his superiority.

For many years it was so, until both of them eventually passed on to be judged by the Heavenly Court. For the scholar, they brought forth the scales and on one side put all of his good deeds, all of his study of Torah, and all of his brilliance. On the other they placed the smirk of contempt he had for a fellow Jew. Behold, the weight of the smirk turned the scale to guilty! For the poor laborer, they put his few failings on one side: coming late to the synagogue, not studying enough Torah. But on the other, they put the groan that issued from the depths of his soul, a groan that showed how much more he wanted to do had his poverty not prevented him. And the weight of the groan of the poor worker turned the scale to innocent!

The Baal Shem Tov Foundation, Cleveland, Ohio

There were scholars who furiously rejected the teachings of the Baal Shem Tov and his disciples. They were called *Mitnagdim*—"Opponents"—and they stressed the supremacy of study over prayer and the service of the mind over the soul. The dispute raged for many years and, on some level, still exists to this day. Who is right? Almost certainly the answer lies in a blend of both. There is a traditional belief that when Hasidim and Mitnagdim come together and create a Judaism that encompasses both their teachings, the Messiah will come!

Book V

The Age of Emancipation: 1700s–1800s

THE TIME FRAME

Date (C.E.)	Event
1790	Letter of George Washington to Newport Synagogue
1791	Napoleon establishes Sanhedrin for Jews of France
1827	Czar Nicholas issues Cantonist Decrees
1835	Moses Montefiore knighted by queen of England
1845	Reform Rabbinical Conference at Frankfurt
1858	Baron Lionel Rothschild inducted into House of Commons
1860	United States Civil War
1895	Dreyfus trial in France
1896	Theodor Herzl publishes *The Jewish State*
1897	First World Zionist Congress in Basel
1898	Emile Zola secures pardon for Dreyfus

18

America the Beautiful

The Renaissance gave way to the Age of Reason, a time that historians call the Enlightenment. Secularism began to replace piety as the spirit of science fostered critical thinking and rationalism. Religious extremism and fundamentalism were slowly replaced by an atmosphere of open-mindedness and tolerance. As the Church lost its power, it became more acceptable for faith to assume different forms. The Enlightenment preached the sacredness of every individual—a principle that would become the cornerstone of the American democratic ideal that "all men are created equal, with liberty and justice for all." Civil rights for all people was a concept that slowly began to make headway in the civilized Western world. In most of Europe, the impact of this novel way of thinking would not affect Jews until the late nineteenth century. But there was now a New World—and America at its very inception pioneered the approach to religious freedom that was so elegantly expressed in the following exchange of letters between George Washington and Moses Seixas, warden of the Newport Synagogue in Rhode Island.

Letter of Newport Synagogue to George Washington, August 17, 1790

Sir: Permit the children of the stock of Abraham to approach you with the most cordial affection and esteem for your person and merit, and to join with our fellow-citizens in welcoming you to Newport.

With pleasure we reflect on those days of difficulty and danger when the God of Israel, who delivered David from the peril of the sword, shielded your head in the day of battle; and we rejoice to think that the same spirit which rested in the bosom of the greatly beloved Daniel, enabling him to preside over the provinces of the Babylonian Empire, rests and ever will rest upon you, enabling you to discharge the arduous duties of the Chief Magistrate of these States.

Deprived as we hitherto have been of the invaluable rights of free citizens, we now—with a deep sense of gratitude to the Almighty Disposer of all events—behold a government erected by the majesty of the people—a government which to bigotry gives no sanction, to persecution no assistance, but generously affording to all liberty of conscience and immunities of citizenship, deeming every one of whatever nation, tongue or language, equal parts of the great governmental machine.

This so ample and extensive Federal Union, whose base is philanthropy, mutual confidence and public virtue, we cannot but acknowledge to be the work of the great God who rules in the armies of the heavens and among the inhabitants of the earth, doing whatever seemeth to Him good.

For all the blessings of civil and religious liberty which we enjoy under an equal and benign administration, we desire to send up our thanks to the Ancient of days, the great Preserver of men, beseeching Him that the angels who conducted our forefathers through the wilderness into the promised land may graciously conduct you through all the difficulties and dangers of this mortal life; and when, like Joshua, full of days and full of honors, you are gathered to your fathers, may you be admitted into the heavenly paradise to partake of the water of life and the tree of immortality.

Done and signed by order of the Hebrew Congregation in Newport, Rhode Island.

Moses Seixas, *Warden*
The Touro Synagogue Foundation, Newport, R.I.

George Washington's Reply

Gentlemen: While I received with much satisfaction your address replete with expressions of esteem, I rejoice in the opportunity of assuring you that I shall always retain grateful remembrance of the cordial welcome I experienced on my visit to Newport from all classes of citizens.

The reflection on the days of difficulty and danger which are past is rendered the more sweet from a consciousness that they are succeeded by days of uncommon prosperity and security.

If we have wisdom to make the best use of the advantages with which we are now favored, we cannot fail, under the just administration of a good government, to become a great and happy people.

The citizens of the United States of America have a right to applaud themselves for having given to mankind examples of an enlarged and liberal policy—a policy worthy of imitation. All possess alike liberty of conscience and immunities of citizenship.

It is now no more that toleration is spoken of as if it were the indulgence of one class of people that another enjoyed the exercise of their inherent natural rights, for, happily, the Government of the United States, which gives to bigotry no sanctions, to persecution no assistance, requires only that they who live under its protection should demean themselves as good citizens in giving it on all occasions their effectual support.

It would be inconsistent with the frankness of my character not to avow that I am pleased with your favorable opinion of my administration and fervent wishes for my felicity.

May the children of the stock of Abraham who dwell in this land continue to merit and enjoy the good will of the other inhabitants—while every one shall sit in safety under his own vine and fig tree and there shall be none to make him afraid.

May the father of all mercies scatter light, and not darkness, upon our paths, and make us all in our several vocations useful here, and in His own due time and way everlastingly happy.

G. Washington

The Touro Synagogue Foundation, Newport, R.I.

The synagogue in Newport, known as the Touro Synagogue to commemorate the philanthropic contributions of Abraham Touro, is the oldest Jewish house of worship in the United States. Built between 1759 and 1763, it was declared a National Historic Site by President Harry Truman on March 5, 1946. Perhaps the most interesting architectural feature of the synagogue is a trapdoor and ladder located directly beneath the cantor's platform and leading to a hidden room—a remnant of Spanish and Portuguese tradition in which synagogues were built with secret rooms where Jews could hide from the agents of the Inquisition. Thankfully, American Jews would never need this kind of protection.

Jews in America

The story of Jews in America begins with the arrival of twenty-three refugees to New Amsterdam fleeing from the Portuguese who had conquered Recife, Brazil. By the time the colonies fought the War of Independence in 1776, there were about two thousand Jews living in America. Though minimal in numbers, they played a major role in the founding of the new government. Francis Salvador, a Jew, was the first patriot to be killed in Georgia. Haym Salomon (1740–1785), honored by the U.S. Postal Service with a stamp that hails him as the "Financial Hero of the American Revolution," is acknowledged as the one man whose financial support made possible the victory of Washington's forces. Salomon negotiated many loans for the Colonies from France and Holland, but he never took a commission for himself. According to legend, General Washington's appeal for funds with which to maintain his ragged army came to Salomon on Yom Kippur, the holiest day of the Jewish calendar. Devoutly religious, Salomon recognized that love of country was an aspect of his religion. So he turned to the congregation and suspended services to secure pledges. Only after he obtained the necessary amount did he proceed with the solemn holiday observances. Toward the close of the Revolutionary War, Salomon personally lent several hundreds of thousand of dollars to the Continental Congress—a sum he was never repaid, leaving him to die bankrupt and penniless.

By 1820 there were still only about six thousand Jews in America. It would not be until the mid- to late nineteenth century that heavy waves of migration would come from Europe, both to escape persecution and to make a new life for themselves in a land where, as rumor had it, the streets were paved with gold and with just a little bit of mazel *(good luck) anyone could become a millionaire. The truth for most would turn out to be far different. Life would be hard; not every pushcart vendor would be as fortunate as Lazarus Straus, whose family founded Abraham & Straus and Macy's. Far more representative was this German-Jewish merchant's account of his efforts to survive in a strange land.*

From the Diary of Abraham Kohn (1842 and 1843)

Peddling in New England

Last week in the vicinity of Plymouth I met two peddlers, Lehman and Marx. Marx knew me from Furth, and that night we stayed together at a farmer's house. After supper we started singing, and I sat at the fireplace, thinking of all my past and of my family. . . .

Today, Sunday, October 16th, we are here in North Bridgewater, and I am not so downcast as I was two weeks ago. The devil has settled 20,000 shoemakers here, who do not have a cent of money. Suppose, after all, I were a soldier in Bavaria; that would have been a bad lot. I will accept three years in America instead. But I could not stand it any longer.

As far as the language is concerned, I am getting along pretty well. But I don't like to be alone. The Americans are funny people. Although they sit together by the dozen in taverns, they turn their backs to each other, and no one talks to anybody else. Is this supposed to be the custom of a republic? I don't like it. Is this supposed to be the fashion of the nineteenth century? I don't like it either. "Wait a little! There will be more things you won't like." Thus I can hear my brother talking.

The week from the 16th to the 22nd of October found me feeling pretty cheerful, for I expected to meet my brother. Ah, it is wonderful to have a brother in this land of hypocrisy, guile, and fraud! How glad I was to meet my two brothers in Boston on Saturday, the 22nd! Now I was not alone in this strange country.

How much more could I write about this queer land! It likes comfort extremely. The German, by comparison, hardly knows the meaning of the word. The wife of an American farmer can consider herself more important than the wife of a Bavarian judge. For hours she can sit in her rocking chair shaking back and forth as she thinks of nothing but beautiful clothes and fine hairdo. The farmer, himself, unlike the German farmer who works every minute, is able to sit down for a few hours every day, reading his paper and smoking his cigar. . . .

This week I went, together with my brother Juda, from Boston to Worcester. We were both delighted, for the trip was a welcome change from our daily heavy work. Together we sat in the grass for hours, recalling the wonderful years of our youth. And in bed, too, we spent many hours in talking.

Today, the 30th of October, we are here in Northborough, and I feel happier than I have for a fortnight. Moses is in New York, and we will meet him, God willing, at Worcester on Tuesday. The sky is clear and cloudless, and nature is so lovely and romantic, the air so fresh and wholesome, that I praise God, who has created this beautiful country.

Yet, at the same time, I regret that the people here are so cold and that their watchword seems to be "Help yourself: that's the best help." I cannot believe that a man who adapts himself to the language, customs, and character of America can ever quite forget his home in the European countries. Having been here so short a time, I should be very arrogant if I were to set down at this time my judgments on America. The whole country, however, with its extensive domestic and foreign trade, its railroads, canals and factories, looks to me like an adolescent youth. He is a part of society, talking like a man and pretending to be a man. Yet he is truly only a boy. That is America! Although she appears to know everything, her knowledge of religion, history, and human nature is, in truth, very elementary. . . . American history is composed of Independence and Washington: that is all! On Sunday the American dresses up and goes to church, but he thinks of God no more than does the horse that carries him there.

It seems impossible that this nation can remain a republic for many years. Millions and millions of dollars go each year to Europe, but only for the purchase of luxuries. Athens and Rome fell at the very moment of their flowering, for though commerce, art, and science had reached their highest level, luxury—vases of gold and silver, garments of purple and silk—caused their downfall. The merchant who seeks to expand too rapidly in his first years, whose expenses are not balanced by his income, is bound to become a bankrupt. America consumes too much, produces too little. Her inhabitants are lazy and too much accustomed to providing for their own comforts to create a land which will provide for their real and their spiritual needs. . . .

O youth of Bavaria, if you long for freedom, if you dream of life here, beware for you shall rue the hour you embarked for a country and a life far different from what you dream of. This land—and particularly this calling—offers harsh, cold air, great masses of snow, and people who are credulous, filled with silly pride, cold toward foreigners and toward all who do not speak the language perfectly. And though "money is beauty, scarce everywhere," yet there is still plenty of it in the country. The Whig government, the new bankruptcy law, the high tariff bill all combine to create a scarcity of ready cash the like of which I have never seen nor the oldest inhabitants of the land ever experienced.

Kohn, Abraham, "A Jewish Peddler's Diary," Abram Vossen Goodman,
trans., American Jewish Archives, III, 1951

Jewish Soldiers during the Civil War

From 1850 to 1880, the Jewish population in America soared from 17,000 to 270,000. But even when their numbers were small, Jews played a role in the major events of American history. Anxious to serve their newfound land, they volunteered for battle during the Civil War. At the same time they struggled to maintain the right to their own religious beliefs. A fascinating example of this struggle is this letter written by the father of a Union soldier during the Civil War to President Abraham Lincoln:

A Letter to President Lincoln

To His Excellency the President of the United States.

By your order of the 16th day of November, 1862, you recommend that the officers and men of the army shall observe the Sabbath and do no work on Sunday, because we are a Christian people. But according to the Declaration of Independence and according to the constitution of the United States, the people of the United States is not a Christian people, but a free, sovereign people with equal rights, and each and every citizen of the United States has the right and liberty to live according to his own consciousness in religious matters, and no one religious denomination, be it a majority or minority of the people, can have a privilege before the other under this our beloved constitution.

Now by the order of your Excellency you give the privilege to those officers and men in the army who by their religious creed do observe the Sunday as a holy day and a day of rest; but you make no provision for those officers and men in the army who do not want to observe the Sunday as a holy day, (as for instance those Christians called the Seventh-day Baptists and the Jews, who observe the Saturday as a holy day and a day of rest,) that they may enjoy the same privilege as those who observe the Sunday as a holy day, as well as for the heathen or the so called infidels, who do not want to celebrate either the Sunday or the Saturday as a Sabbath, but choose perhaps some other day as a day of rest.

Now I stand before you as your namesake Abraham stood before God Almighty in days of yore, and asked, "Shall not the Judge of all earth do justice?" So I ask your Excellency, the first man and President of all the United States, shall you not do justice? Shall you not give the same privilege to a minority of the army that you give to the majority of it? I beseech you to make provision, and to proclaim in another order, that also all those in the army who celebrate another day as the Sunday may be allowed to celebrate that day which they think is the right day according to their own conscience; and this will be exactly lawful, as the Constitution of the United States ordains it, and at the same time it will be exactly according to the teaching of the Bible, as recorded in Leviticus xix. 18: "Thou shalt love thy neighbor as thyself."

I gave my consent to my son, who was yet a minor that he should enlist in the United States army; I thought it was his duty, and I gave him my advice to fulfill his duty as a good citizen, and he has done so. At the same time I taught him also to observe the Sabbath on Saturday, when it would not hinder him from fulfilling his duty in the army. Now I do not want that he shall be dragged either to the stake or the church to observe the Sunday as a Sabbath. Your Excellency will observe in this my writing that I am not very well versed in the English language, and if there should be found a word which is not right, pardon it, and never such a word shall be construed so as if I would offend your Excellency or the people; for I love my country, the Constitution, and the Union, and I try to be always a loyal citizen.

I remain, respectfully, your most obedient servant and fellow citizen,

B. Behrend

The Occident and American Jewish Advocate, Philadelphia, December 4, 1862

Beginning in November 1861, The Jewish Messenger, *a New York weekly newspaper, printed a series of letters entitled "Sketches from the Seat of War," signed by "a Jewish Soldier." This anonymous recruit, stationed in the Washington, D.C., area, reported on his surroundings and his experiences from a Jewish point of view and for a Jewish audience. The letters ceased after the* Jewish Messenger *reported that he had "left Washington for the South."*

From "Sketches from the Seat of War"

Jews in the Union Army

Mr. Russell, L.L.D., in one of his letters to the London Times, speaks of the Jewish element in the federal army, as consisting of a "slight sprinkling of Jews in the Cameron Dragoons," and adds that their application for a Jewish Chaplain was nothing but "a hoax of imperceptible fun and tendency." . . .

A friend of mine, who has special facilities for ascertaining the extent of the Jewish element in the army and has devoted considerable time to that inquiry informs me, that, although it is extremely difficult to obtain correct statistics, yet he believes that there are no less than five thousand Jews in our army. He attempted, by a twofold process, to arrive at a correct estimate of their number, first by requesting the Quartermasters of each regiment, to ascertain how many Jews there were in each company, and secondly, by calling upon the Jewish soldiers in general to send in their names to his address, in both of which, he signally failed. This want of success on his part may be traced to various causes, but principally to the fact that few people feel disposed to give an account of their religious principles, when no practical object is to be attained, and inquiries of this nature are generally regarded as unbecoming, and even insulting. As a general rule, the Jews do not care to make their religion a matter of notoriety, as it would at once involve them in an intricate controversial disquisition with the Christian Chaplains, for which they do not always feel themselves qualified, and which, of course can, under no circumstance, afford them any thing but annoyance. Some of our brethren fear that, were they known as Hebrews, it would expose them to the taunts and sneers of those among their comrades who have been in the habit of associating with the name of Jew, everything that is mean and contemptible; but I must say, and it redounds much to the credit of the army, that in the course of my experience in the camps, which has been considerable, I have heard but of a single instance in which a Jew was wantonly insulted on account of his religion, and that was by a drunken Scotchman, who commences damning in every variety of language and motion, when he learned that he was addressing an Israelite, declaring them all to be cheats and thieves. His wrath was, however, of short duration, for the soldiers who were present, finding him incorrigible, after having repeatedly warned him to desist, as last resolved to inflict summary punishment, and collectively flung him into a certain capacious receptacle for liquid matter, from which, let us hope, he emerged a wiser and a cooler man.

My friend found his estimate of the number of Jewish soldiers on the fact, that according to his observation, at least, one in every hundred soldiers is a Jew, and supposing the army to consist of half a million of men, the Jews must number at least five thousand. This estimate, he believes to be supported by other calculation, for, supposing the Jews to have enlisted in the same proportion as the rest of the population, which is two and a half per cent, this would make them reach the above figure, as it is generally supposed that there are two hundred thousand Jews in this country. Without, however, insisting on the accuracy of this estimate, we may safely assert, that they are largely represented in the army, not only among the privates, but also among the commissioned officers. There are at least five Jewish colonels, as many lieutenant colonels and majors, and quite a host of captains, lieutenants, and quartermasters among the volunteer regiments, but in the regular army I know of no Jew holding a higher rank than that of captain. Some of the Jewish officers and privates told me that they had taken part in the Crimean, Hungarian and Italian wars, and that they followed the profession of arms from inclination, but not liking the dull routine of a soldier's life in times of peace, they eagerly avail themselves of every opportunity to return to their tents and the battlefield. This was the first time I had ever heard of the existence of such a class of military adventurers among our people.

Most people take it for granted, that every soldier is an infidel, and that no sooner does he enter on active duty, than he banishes all idea of religion from his mind. This is a great mistake, at least as far as the Jews are concerned. My own observation has convinced me that military life does not injuriously affect their ideas of duty and devotion, but that, on the contrary, in well-disciplined minds it evokes religious feelings of the most sterling character. It is quite common for Jewish soldiers belonging to the same company, to meet together for worship on Sabbath, in some secluded spot, and I know a young soldier, who was on Yom Kippur morning, ordered to take part in a skirmish, near Harper's Ferry, which he had to go through, without having tasted food, and as soon as the enemy retreated, he retired to the woods, where he remained until sunset, reading his prayers. The character of these devotions is not the less interesting from the fact, that they are always performed in solemn silence, and in some secluded spot, where the noise of the camp cannot penetrate. When looking on those groups, I cannot help reflecting on the remarkable history of our race. Here are the descendants of the Hebrew patriarch who smote the confederated kings near Damascus, the descendants of those who overthrew the colossal hosts of proud Egypt, and conquered the powerful nations of Philistea, who, under the Maccabees, triumphed over the Syrian despot, the survivors of all ancient dynasties; the participants in every remarkable event of history, behold them now in the New World, shedding their blood for the maintenance of the liberties secured to them by this Republic. Whilst thus reflecting, I feel most solemnly impressed by hearing in these Virginian forests my brethren, utter the *Shema Yisrael* [*Hear O Israel, the Lord is our God, the Lord is One*], which first our great lawgiver proclaimed in the plains of Arabia.

It is with no little satisfaction that I hear from all quarters, the most favorable accounts of their conduct, and, in fact, not a single instance has come to my knowledge of neglect of duty or insubordination on their part. Not only do the military authorities speak well of their conduct in camp, but also in the performance of active duty, many of our brethren have evinced, on various occasions, great bravery, and I am quite sure, that when we move forward, our people at home will have no occasion to be ashamed of us. In promising as much, I do not claim any special merit for ourselves, since bravery is to be found among all nations that have a glorious history to sustain, much more so among ancient nations, and therefore especially among the Hebrews, who have a history of more than three thousand years to back them.

A few months since, some Jewish soldiers suggested the idea of organizing all the Jewish soldiers in the army, into distinct regiments, with Hebrew banners, etc., so that both our food and religious services may be more consonant with our habits and ideas, and we may have the pleasure of associating with our own brethren. I was further informed that such was actually the custom among the Dutch Jews when they entered on active duty, and many curious stories were told of the orders being given in Hebrew, of prayers before the battle, and of Tephillin [phylacteries—ritual items used during prayer] in the knapsacks. One of these soldiers, related my informant, was very religious, and whenever he fired off his gun, he cried out *Shema Yisrael*. This was at the battle of Waterloo. On being asked, why he said it so often, he replied that "it may be some Yehudee [Jew] gets killed by him, and he could never pardon himself, if any one of his brethren should, through him, go out of the world without *Shema Yisrael*." I well remember, having read in one of the English Cyclopedias, that a Jewish regiment was among those who most distinguished themselves at the battle of Waterloo. General Chasse, on being asked his opinion about Jewish soldiers, replied, that "were he to go again on active duty he would wish nothing better than to have an army of such Jews as fought under him in Antwerp." The suggestion of my friends to form themselves into separate regiments was, however, disapproved of by wiser heads, which was altogether unnecessary, as it is at present impracticable, and we are quite satisfied to fight with our Christian comrades for one cause, one country, and THE UNION.

It may be interesting to you to learn, that the great stronghold behind which the enemy is entrenched in front of us, derives its name from a Jew. In these mountain passes there once stood a small lodging house, where the travelers used to pass some hours, or tarry over night on their journey to Richmond, or to Winchester, and as its location was central it became quite a famous place in the days of stage coaches. The proprietor was called Manasseh, hence, on inquiring whether there was a place halfway to stop at, you would be told: "Yes, at Manasseh's." Thence the junction has retained that name, though it is now spelled Manassas. I say, old Manasseh, you can get a million of dollars and more, if you would just admit us to your place this evening. At all events, old boy, immortality has been thrust upon thee!

The Jewish Messenger, New York, Nov. 1861–March 1862

> Just as there were Jews serving in the Union Army, there were Jews from the South in the Confederate forces. Inevitably, there were moments when, in serving the cause they believed in, Jews may have been responsible for the death of fellow Jews. That points out so powerfully the truth of Abraham Lincoln's prayer: "Pray not that God is on our side but that we are on the side of God."

Jewish Immigration

In the mid-1800s, anti-Jewish riots took place in much of Europe. Hearing that America offered safety, Jews heeded the call that the German writer Leopold Kompert (1822–1886) published in An Austrian Journal for Jewish Religious Freedom, Culture, History and Literature *in May 1848.*

From "Off to America" by Leopold Kompert

For we shall go to America! Those among you who do not understand the essence of history, should take this as an indication of it—that four centuries ago, at a time when the Jews were persecuted most cruelly, it was a man from Genoa who was haunted by the idea of discovering a new world and did not find peace until Queen Isabella of Spain—whose husband had evoked the dark figure of Torquemada and his thousands of bloodstained Dominican brethren—allowed him [Christopher Columbus] to discover America. It is for this America that we are yearning, thither you shall move! "Off to America!"

We know all your objections and all your answers! . . . Do you not have any other advice for us, you ask, but to take up once again the wanderer's staff and with wife and child seek a far and foreign land? Shall we leave the native soil which has born and fed us, and in which we have buried our dead? I sense in these words something of Egypt's fleshpots; yes, I, too, smell the flavor of the golden soups and juicy roast—but I also see the people who are stirring the flames and who are extracting their daily bread from the fires of hatred, of prejudice, and of narrow-mindedness. By God, may he who has a penchant for these things stay behind and feed himself!

In our time, two sentences may serve us as points of departure. The first one was said by Moses: "Stand fast and still." The second one was said by Jeremiah: "The harvest is past, the summer is ended, and we are not saved." Which of the two sentences do you prefer? To stand still and to wait, to wait patiently, until all who are now opposed to us will make peace with us, until the spirit of humanity is victorious? Or, since "we are not saved," to seek salvation elsewhere and to move to America?

I think the two sentences can be reconciled easily! May those in our fatherland who wish to "stand fast and still" build their homes upon the sands of the future! We do not want to prevent them from doing so; on the contrary, we shall gladly provide them with bricks for their endeavor. But to all the others, the oppressed and persecuted, those who have been driven from their homes and plundered in the notorious communities, all those who have gained nothing but calamity from this "freedom," all those who feel in their hearts that it will take a long time before there is peace for them in the fatherland . . . to all those we say: we are not saved. Salvation can only be sought in America!

The idea is not new. This we know; but it is practical. . . . The purpose of emigration is the finding of a new fatherland and the gain of immediate freedom! . . .

Thousands before you have taken this step and are still taking it! And only a disproportionate few have regretted it. The God of your forefathers will watch over you. He will guide you safely across the sea and through the first difficulties of your new life! I am not afraid for you! You have all the necessary qualities and virtues: circumspection, sobriety, frugality, discipline and faith; they will help you in the building of a new life and wealth. Others have perished there, but you will prosper and grow; the God of freedom will be with you.

In my spirit I already greet your children there, the children of those who have *become* free. *Shalom aleikhem!* Greetings!

A bright glow fills me as I think of the children *born* free, and of their mothers. Therefore, in light of the horrors of the past weeks . . . I call to you: "Off to America!"

In Paul R. Mendes Flohr and Jehuda Reinharz, eds., *The Jew in the Modern World: A Documentary History,* New York, 1995

Kompert gave this advice to Jews in Vienna. Consider how prescient the words were in light of events almost a century later! Yet, remarkably enough, Kompert did not heed his own advice—he never emigrated. How can we explain this? Why would Jews remain in Germany in the 1930s even as it became clear beyond doubt that their lives were imperiled?

The Life of the Immigrants in "the Golden Land"

From a trickle to a tidal wave, Jews came to America in successive floods of immigration. They flocked primarily to New York City and tried to eke out a living in overcrowded, unsanitary tenements where unscrupulous employers, unfettered by unions, took unconscionable advantage of these "greenhorns."

In 1890, Jacob Riis (1849–1914), a journalist and reformer, published a study of the dreadful living conditions of the poor in New York City that had an immediate and profound effect, resulting in widespread reforms and social programs.

From *How the Other Half Lives* by Jacob Riis

The Home—a Workshop

The homes of the Hebrew quarter are its workshops also. . . . You are made fully aware of it before you have traveled the length of a single block in any of these East Side streets, by the whir of a thousand sewing machines, worked at high pressure from earliest dawn till mind and muscle give out together. Every member of the family, from the youngest to the oldest, bears a hand, shut in the qualmy rooms, where meals are cooked and clothing washed and dried besides, the livelong day. It is not unusual to find a dozen persons—men, women, and children—at work in a single small room. . . .

When, in the midnight hour, the noise of the sewing-machine was stilled at last, I have gone the rounds of Ludlow and Hester and Essex streets among the poorest of the Russian Jews, with the sanitary police, and counted often four, five, and even six of the little ones in a single bed, sometimes a shake-down on the hard floor, often a pile of half-finished clothing brought home from the sweater, in the stuffy rooms of their tenements. In one I visited very lately, the only bed was occupied by the entire family lying lengthwise and crosswise, literally in layers, three children at the feet, all except a boy of ten or twelve, for whom there was no room. He slept with his clothes on to keep him warm, in a pile of rags just inside the door. It seemed to me impossible that families of children could be raised at all in such dens as I had my daily and nightly walks in. And yet the vital statistics and all close observation agree in allotting to these Jews even an unusual degree of good health. The records of the Sanitary Bureau show that while the Italians have the highest death rate, the mortality in the lower part of the Tenth Ward, of which Ludlow Street is the heart and type, is the lowest in the city. Even the baby death rate is very low. But for the fact that the ravages of diphtheria, croup, and measles run up the record in the houses occupied entirely by tailors—in other words, in the sweater district, where contagion always runs riot—the Tenth Ward would seem to be the healthiest spot in the city, as well as the dirtiest and the most crowded. The temperate habits of the Jew and his freedom from enfeebling vices generally must account for this, along with his marvelous vitality. I cannot now recall ever having known a Jewish drunkard. On the other hand, I have never come across a Prohibitionist among them. The absence of the one renders the other superfluous.

Morals and Family Life

Whatever the effect upon the physical health of the children, it cannot be otherwise, of course, than that such conditions should corrupt their morals. I have the authority of a distinguished rabbi, whose field and daily walk are among the poorest of his people, to support me in the statement that the moral tone of the young girls is distinctly lower than it was. The entire absence of privacy in their homes and the foul contact of the sweaters' shops, where men and women work side by side from morning till night, scarcely half clad in the hot summer weather, does for the girls what the street completes in the boy. But for the patriarchal family life of the Jew that is his strongest virtue, their ruin would long since have been complete. It is that which pilots him safely through shoals upon which the Gentile would have been inevitably wrecked. It is that which keeps the almshouse from casting its shadow over Ludlow Street to add to its gloom. It is the one quality which redeems, and on the Sabbath eve when he gathers his household about his board, scant though the fare be, dignifies the darkest slum of Jewtown.

How strong is this attachment to home and kindred that makes the Jew cling to the humblest hearth and gather his children and his children's children about it, though grinding poverty leave them only a bare crust to share, I saw in the case of little Jette Brodsky, who strayed away from her own door, looking for her papa. They were strangers and ignorant and poor, so that weeks went by before they could make their loss known and get a hearing, and meanwhile Jette, who had been picked up and taken to Police Headquarters, had been hidden away in an asylum, given another name when nobody came to claim her, and had been quite forgotten. But in the two years that passed before she was found at last, her empty chair stood ever by her father's, at the family board, and no Sabbath eve but heard his prayer for the restoration of their lost one. It happened once that I came in on a Friday evening at the breaking of bread, just as the four candles upon the table had been lit with the Sabbath blessing upon the home and all it sheltered. Their light fell on little else than empty plates and anxious faces; but in the patriarchal host who arose and bade the guest welcome with a dignity a king might have envied I recognized with difficulty the humble peddler I had known only from the street and from the police office, where he hardly ventured beyond the door.

Jacob Riis, *How the Other Half Lives: Studies among the Tenements of New York*, New York, 1957

19

"Liberté, Egalité, Fraternité": The Winds of Change Buffet Western Europe

The Emancipation of the Jews of France

America proved that it was possible to replace the power of the king with a democratic form of government. That message was soon exported back to the European continent. The Marquis de Lafayette, a soldier and statesman who fought with the colonists during the American Revolution, wrote the Declaration of the Rights of Man and Citizen, which was adopted by the French National Assembly on August 16, 1789—a document that would serve as the key philosophic underpinning of the French Revolution. Drawing on the American Declaration of Independence, it declared "All men are born, and remain, free and equal in rights: social distinctions cannot be found but on common utility."

On September 28, 1791, France ushered in a new era for European Jewry.

Resolution of the French National Assembly

The National Assembly, considering that the conditions requisite to be a French citizen, and to become an active citizen, are fixed by the constitution, and that every man who, being duly qualified, takes the civic oath, and engages to fulfill all the duties prescribed by the constitution, has a right to all the advantages it insures; . . .

Annuls all adjournments, restrictions and exceptions contained in the preceding decrees, affecting individuals of the Jewish persuasion, who shall take the civic oath, which shall be considered as a renunciation of all privileges in their favor.

Paul R. Mendes Flohr and Jehuda Reinharz, eds., *The Jew in the Modern World: A Documentary History*, New York, 1995

The unthinkable had happened! A people condemned for centuries as Christ-killers doomed to eternal wandering and damnation were now admitted into society as equal citizens. Political emancipation was the product of the profound changes that had taken place during the Age of the Enlightenment: the world had moved away from religion and unquestioning obedience to the Church. Secularism, humanism, individualism, rationalism, and nationalism were the new reigning gods to be worshipped. Jews were no longer undesirables because of their beliefs. Their rejection of Jesus was no longer the unforgivable sin; what mattered most to nineteenth-century Europe, steeped in nationalistic fervor, was the question of Jewish patriotism to their homelands. Could Jews be good citizens even as they prayed for a Messiah to return them to their Promised Land?

Napoleon had to be reassured. In 1806 he convened the leading rabbis of France to take part in a modern-day Sanhedrin, the Supreme Court of the Jewish people during the days of the Temple. He submitted twelve questions to them that sought clarification of Jewish views.

Napoleon's Questions to the Sanhedrin

Individuals of your religion have been different in the several parts of the world: often they have been dictated by the interest of the day. But, as an assembly like the present, has no precedent in the annals of Christianity, so will you be judged, for the first time, with justice, and you will see your fate irrevocably fixed by a Christian Prince. The wish of His Majesty is, that you should be Frenchmen; it remains with you to accept the proffered title, without forgetting that, to prove unworthy of it, would be renouncing it altogether.

You will hear the questions submitted to you, your duty is to answer the whole truth on every one of them. Attend, and never lose sight of that which we are going to tell you; that, when a monarch equally firm and just, who knows every thing, and who punishes or recompenses every action, puts questions to his subjects, these would be equally guilty and blind to their true interests, if they were to disguise the truth in the least.

The intention of His Majesty is, Gentlemen, that you should enjoy the greatest freedom in your deliberations; your answers will be transmitted to us by your President, when they have been put in regular form.

As to us, our most ardent wish is to be able to report to the Emperor, that, among individuals of the Jewish persuasion, he can reckon as many faithful subjects, determined to conform in every thing to the laws and to the morality, which ought to regulate the conduct of all Frenchmen.

- Is it lawful for Jews to marry more than one wife?
- Is divorce allowed by the Jewish religion? Is divorce valid, when not pronounced by courts of justice, and by virtue of laws in contradiction with the French code?
- Can a Jewess marry a Christian, or a Jew a Christian woman? Or has the law ordered that the Jews should only intermarry among themselves?
- In the eyes of Jews are Frenchmen considered as brethren or as strangers?
- In either case what conduct does their law prescribe towards Frenchmen not of their religion?
- Do the Jews born in France, and treated by the law as French citizens, consider France as their country? Are they bound to defend it? Are they bound to obey the laws, and to follow the directions of the civil code?
- What kind of police-jurisdiction have the Rabbis among the Jews?
- What judicial power do they exercise among them?
- Are the forms of the elections of the Rabbis and their police-jurisdiction regulated by the law, or are they only sanctioned by custom?
- Are there professions from which the Jews are excluded by their law?
- Does the law forbid the Jews from taking usury from their brethren?
- Does it forbid or does it allow usury toward strangers?

Paul R. Mendes Flohr and Jehuda Reinharz, eds., The Jew in the Modern World: A Documentary History, New York, 1995

The Answers to Napoleon

Resolved, by the French deputies professing the religion of Moses, that the following Declaration shall precede the answers returned to the questions proposed by the Commissioners of His Imperial and Royal Majesty.

The assembly, impressed with a deep sense of gratitude, love, respect, and admiration, for the sacred person of His Imperial and Royal Majesty, declares, in the name of all Frenchmen professing the religion of Moses, that they are fully determined to prove worthy of the favors His Majesty intends for them, by scrupulously conforming to his paternal intentions; that their religion makes it their duty to consider the law of the prince as the supreme law in civil and political matters; that consequently, should their religious code, or its various interpretations, contain civil or political commands, at variance with those of the French code, those commands would, of course, cease to influence and govern them, since they must, above all, acknowledge and obey the laws of the prince.

That, in consequence of this principle, the Jews have, at all times, considered it their duty to obey the laws of the state, and that, since the revolution, they, like all Frenchmen, have acknowledged no others.

First Question: *Is it lawful for Jews to marry more than one wife?*

Answer: It is not lawful for Jews to marry more than one wife: in all European countries they conform to the general practice [of] marrying only one.

Moses does not command expressly to take several, but he does not forbid it. He seems even to adopt that custom as generally prevailing, since he settles the rights of inheritance between children of different wives. Although this practice still prevails in the East, yet their ancient doctors have enjoined them to restrain from taking more than one wife, except when the man is enabled by his fortune to maintain several.

The case has been different in the West; the wish of adopting the customs of the inhabitants of this part of the world has induced the Jews to renounce polygamy. But as several individuals still indulged in that practice, a synod was convened at Worms in the eleventh century, composed of one hundred Rabbis, with Gershom at their head. This assembly pronounced an anathema against every Israelite who should, in future, take more than one wife.

Although this prohibition was not to last for ever, the influence of European manners has universally prevailed.

Second Question: *Is divorce allowed by the Jewish Religion? Is divorce valid when not pronounced by courts of justice by virtue of laws in contradiction with those of the French Code?*

Answer: Repudiation is allowed by the Law of Moses; but it is not valid if not previously pronounced by the French code.

In the eyes of every Israelite, without exception, submission to the prince is the first of duties. It is a principle generally acknowledged among them, that, in every thing relating to civil or political interests, the law of the state is the supreme law. Before they were admitted in France to share the rights of all citizens, and when they lived under a particular legislation which set them at liberty to follow their religious customs, they had the ability to divorce their wives; but it was extremely rare to see it put into practice. Since the revolution, they have acknowledged no other laws on this head but those of the empire. At the epoch when they were admitted to the rank of citizens, the Rabbis and the principal Jews appeared before the municipalities of their respective places of abode, and took an oath to conform, in every thing to the laws, and to acknowledge no other rules in all civil matters. . . .

Third Question: *Can a Jewess marry a Christian, and a Jew a Christian woman? Or does the law allow the Jews to marry only among themselves?*

Answer: The law does not say that a Jewess cannot marry a Christian, nor a Jew a Christian woman; nor does it state that the Jews can only marry among themselves. The only marriages expressly forbidden by the law, are those with the seven Canaanite nations, with Amon and Moab, and with the Egyptians. The prohibition is absolute concerning the seven Canaanite nations: with regard to Amon and Moab, it is limited, according to many Talmudists, to the men of those nations, and does not extend to the women; it is even thought that these last would have embraced the Jewish religion. As to Egyptians, the prohibition is limited to the third generation. The prohibition in general applies only to nations in idolatry. The Talmud declares formally that modern nations are not to be considered as such, since they worship, like us, the God of heaven and earth. And, accordingly, there have been, at several periods, intermarriages between Jews and Christians in France, in Spain, and in Germany: these marriages were sometimes tolerated, and sometimes forbidden by the laws of those sovereigns, who had received Jews into their dominions.

Unions of this kind are still found in France; but we cannot deny that the opinion of the Rabbis is against these marriages. According to their doctrine, although the religion of Moses has not forbidden the Jews from intermarrying with nations not of their religion, yet, as marriage, according to the Talmud, requires religious ceremonies called Kiddushin, with the benediction used in such cases, no marriage can be religiously valid unless these ceremonies have been performed. This could not be done towards persons who would not both of them consider these ceremonies as sacred; and in that case the married couple could separate without the religious divorce; they would then be considered as married civilly but not religiously.

Such is the opinion of the Rabbis, members of this assembly. In general they would be no more inclined to bless the union of a Jewess with a Christian, or of a Jew with a Christian woman, than Catholic priests themselves would be disposed to sanction unions of this kind. The Rabbis acknowledge, however, that a Jew, who marries a Christian woman, does not cease on that account, to be considered as a Jew by his brethren, any more than if he had married a Jewess civilly and not religiously.

Fourth Question: *In the eyes of Jews, are Frenchmen considered as their brethren? Or are they considered as strangers?*

Answer: In the eyes of Jews Frenchmen are their brethren, and are not strangers. The true spirit of the Law of Moses is consonant with this mode of considering Frenchmen.

When the Israelites formed a settled and independent nation, their law made it a rule for them to consider strangers as their brethren.

With the most tender care for their welfare, their lawgiver commands to love them, "Love ye therefore the strangers," says he to the Israelites, "for ye were strangers in the land of Egypt." Respect and benevolence towards strangers are enforced by Moses, not as an exhortation to the practice of social morality only, but as an obligation imposed by God himself.

A religion whose fundamental maxims are such—a religion which makes a duty of loving the stranger—which enforces the practice of social virtues, must surely require that its followers should consider their fellow-citizens as brethren.

And how could they consider them otherwise when they inhabit the same land, when they are ruled and protected by the same government, and by the same laws? When they enjoy the same rights, and have the same duties to fulfill? There exists, even between the Jew and Christian, a tie which abundantly compensates for religion—it is the tie of gratitude. This sentiment was at first excited in us by the mere grant of toleration. It has been increased, these eighteen years, by new favors from government, to such a degree of energy, that now our fate is irrevocably linked with the common fate of all Frenchmen. Yes, France is our country; all Frenchmen are our brethren, and this glorious title, by raising us our own esteem, becomes a sure pledge that we shall never cease to be worthy of it.

Fifth Question: *In either case, what line of conduct does their law prescribe towards Frenchmen not of their religion?*

Answer: The line of conduct prescribed towards Frenchmen not of our religion, is the same as that prescribed between Jews themselves; we admit of no difference but that of worshipping the Supreme Being, every one in his own way.

The answer to the preceding question has explained the line of conduct which the Law of Moses and the Talmud prescribe towards Frenchmen not of our religion. At the present time, when the Jews no longer form a separate people, but enjoy the advantage of being incorporated with the Great Nation (which privilege they consider as a kind of political redemption), it is impossible that a Jew should treat a Frenchman, not of his religion, in any other manner than he would treat one of his Israelite brethren.

Sixth Question: *Do Jews born in France, and treated by the laws as French citizens, consider France their country? Are they bound to defend it? Are they bound to obey the laws and to conform to the dispositions of the civil code?*

Answer: Men who have adopted a country, who have resided in it these many generations—who, even under the restraint of particular laws which abridged their civil rights, were so attached to it that they preferred being debarred from the advantages common to all other citizens, rather than leave it—cannot but consider themselves as Frenchmen in France; and they consider as equally sacred and honourable the duty of defending their country.

Jeremiah (chapter 29) exhorts the Jews to consider Babylon as their country, although they were to remain in it only for seventy years. He exhorts them to till the ground, to build houses, to sow, and to plant. His recommendation was so much attended to, that Ezra (chapter 2) says, that when Cyrus allowed them to return to Jerusalem to rebuild the Temple, 42,360 only, left Babylon; and that this number was mostly composed of the poor people, the wealthy having remained in that city.

The love of the country is in the heart of Jews a sentiment so natural, so powerful, and so consonant to their religious opinions, that a French Jew considers himself in England, as among strangers, although he may be among Jews; and the case is the same with English Jews in France.

To such a pitch is this sentiment carried among them, that during the last war, French Jews have been seen fighting desperately against other Jews, the subjects of countries then at war with France.

Many of them are covered with honourable wounds, and others have obtained, in the field of honour, the noble rewards of bravery.

[In response to the remaining questions, the rabbis reiterated their commitment to the laws of the state, their willingness to serve in all honorable professions, and the difference between usury that takes advantage of the impoverished and the taking of interest for commercial transactions.]

Paul R. Mendes Flohr and Jehuda Reinharz, eds., *The Jew in the Modern World: A Documentary History*, New York, 1995

How honest were the rabbis in their response to the third question? Did the rabbis sufficiently hedge their acceptance of intermarriage—a practice that they clearly felt uncomfortable tolerating? Do all these replies accurately convey Jewish attitudes—or were they the "politically correct" answers the rabbis felt forced to give for the sake of survival?

Jews Elsewhere in Europe

A popular saying in the nineteenth century was "When France sneezes, Europe catches a cold." What happened in France was quickly echoed in neighboring lands. In some places, like the Italian peninsula, the French armies physically tore down the gates of the ghettos in which Jews were confined. In other countries, like England and Germany, it was the force of an idea unleashed by the Revolution that proved mightier than centuries of persecution.

Italian Jews Welcoming the French Army: 1798

For, praised be the Almighty, the French have entered the city with great speed, swifter than on the wings of eagles, and more powerful than lions. Immediately they inquired the whereabouts of the Jewish ghetto, and entered the ghetto, and said to the Jews: "Jews, our brothers, fear no longer the wicked Christians who seek to harm you! We have come to save you, for God has shortened our journey so we might rescue you from the hands of these people!" And the Jews, seeing this great deliverance, raised their voices with cries of joy: "God bless you, who come in peace, our brethren, our flesh and blood! May the French nation which saved us from our enemies live forever and ever!" And they kissed and embraced each other with great affection, and many of the Jews, because of their great happiness, went to the synagogue and recited the *Song of the Sea* in strong, loud voices, for the portion of the Bible read in the synagogue that week dealt with the liberation of the Jews from Egypt and their crossing of the Red Sea.

With no interference on the part of the officials of their community, they issued an order at the command of the city authorities—that the candles in every house be lighted outside of the windows, in honor of the French army, and since outside of the ghetto not all the people lit their candles, and inside the ghetto there wasn't a single house where the candles were not burning, the saying, the "Jews had light and joy and happiness and pleasure" [Book of Esther], was materialized. And every member of our congregation, each according to his own understanding and ability, praised and thanked God for the liberation and freedom, for replacing sadness with joy, slavery with freedom.

And now things are different—for all the Christians were very much afraid upon seeing the Frenchmen, and there was no spirit left in them, and their hearts sank and their faces turned dark as soot when they saw the Jews happy and in good spirits. Therefore, we, the sons of Ancona, feel it our duty to thank God, blessed be his name, for all his kindness to us. Blessed is the God of Israel, who alone works such miracles, for surely joy such as ours will not again come to Israel except with the coming of Messiah, which we hope will be in our day, and bring us a complete deliverance.

Abraham Duker, Jewish Survival in the World Today, New York, 1940

As ghetto walls began to crumble and Jews became free to mingle with their non-Jewish neighbors, some Jewish leaders feared that emancipation might prove to be more a curse than a blessing in the long run. What was good for the individual Jew could perhaps spell the end of the Jewish people. As Jean-Paul Sartre put it, "The sole tie that binds the Jewish people together is the hostility and disdain of the societies which surround them. It is the anti-Semite who makes the Jew." That, in fact, was the same conclusion of Albert Einstein: "It may be thanks to anti-Semitism that we are able to preserve our existence as a race; that at any rate is my belief." How much truth is there to this observation? Is an open society antithetical to Jewish survival?

Vienna and Jews in High Society

By the mid-nineteenth century, the right to citizenship had been granted to Jews in most of Western Europe. (Only Switzerland and Spain would hold out until 1874 and 1918.) But perhaps more significant even than gaining rights was achieving respect. In less than a century, Jews went from pariahs to sought-after public figures. An example of the elite status attained by some Jews was Fanny Von Arnstein (1758–1818), a leading figure in Vienna's high society, often referred to as "the most interesting woman in Europe." Here is how C. G. Küttner, a prominent socialite and writer of the time, described her salon:

The Salon of Fanny Von Arnstein

Among these various houses there is one in particular, where, in the course of a winter, one can see more society than perhaps in any other in this city. It is the house I have visited most frequently, and I would name it, if I had not resolved to avoid all names as soon as I enter into a subject in detail. If these letters should fall into the hands of the amiable ladies of this house they will recognize themselves in the description, and receive my thanks for the many pleasant hours I have spent with them the more willingly, because I offer them with discretion. In this house guests are received daily, I might almost say at all hours. It is, from the social point of view, the greatest in Vienna, if one can call that house the greatest that is open at all times, or begins entertaining at any time. One finds there every rank, every station—I had almost added, every religion; but this never makes any difference in Vienna, and in social life is in no way considered. Here I see princes, both Austrian and those from other ruling German houses, archbishops, bishops, prelates, foreign ambassadors, scholars, officers, merchants, artists, bourgeois, people of all nations and all classes.

Hilde Spiel, Fanny Von Arnstein: A Daughter of the Enlightenment, 1758–1818,
Christine Shuttleworth, trans., Berg, 1991

Here is an account by Karl August Varnhagen, another fascinated admirer.

For a long time Frau von Arnstein's house in Vienna was simply the only one of its kind, and if later many others, but surely none like hers, have come into being, then this too is to the credit of this excellent woman, by whom this passage was first opened and made viable for her successors. The free, respected position, removed from the constraint of prejudice, which the adherents of the Mosaic faith have enjoyed and now enjoy in Vienna was quite undeniably first won with and through the influence and activity of Frau von Arnstein.

Spiel, Fanny Von Arnstein

Jewish Emancipation in England

Across the Channel, England began its own journey to Jewish emancipation, helped by the fact that Jews were among the wealthiest and most talented Englishmen. Their achievements and honors, and their struggles for their rights, paved the way to acceptance and civil rights for their people.

The Jewish Knight: Moses Montefiore

Great wealth was joined with formidable intellect in the person of Moses Montefiore, an English Jewish giant of commerce and statesmanship. His contributions to Jewish causes are legendary. His name adorns buildings, streets, and institutions worldwide. In his diary he writes of the day in 1835 that he was knighted by the Queen—an honor thought for the longest time to be far beyond Jewish aspiration.

Thursday, 9th of November

With unspeakable but heartfelt gratitude to the Almighty God, I note the occurrences of the day, a day that can never be forgotten by me; it is a proud one: with the exception of the day I had the happiness of dedicating our Synagogue at Ramsgate, and the day of my wedding, the proudest day of my life. I trust the honour conferred by our most gracious Queen on myself and my dear Judith may prove the harbinger of future good to the Jews generally, and though I am sensible of my unworthiness, yet I pray the Almighty to lead and guide me in the proper path, that I may observe and keep His Holy Law.

At half-past eight I went to the Mansion House, at nine set off in grand procession to London Bridge; there I embarked with the Lord Mayor, &c., for Westminster. The new Lord Mayor was presented to the Judges in several Courts. We then returned the same way to the Mansion House. I went to the Marine. My dear Judith was beautifully dressed, but very unwell. We went to the Mansion House, and soon left there in procession. Our state carriage being in advance, I got out at Temple Bar, and the carriage went on with Judith to the Guildhall. I mounted on horseback, with my brother Sheriffs, some Aldermen, and Members of the Common Council. After many of the Royal carriages had passed, we set forward two and two before the Queen. On her arrival in the hall she reposed herself for some time. The Recorder then read the address, to which she replied. The Lord Mayor was introduced, and made a Baronet; the Aldermen were introduced, and then the Sheriffs were knighted, first George Carrol. On my kneeling to the Queen, she placed a sword on my left shoulder and said, "Rise, Sir Moses." I cannot express all I felt on this occasion. I had, besides, the pleasure of seeing my banner with "Jerusalem" floating proudly in the hall. I hope my dear mother will be pleased. The entertainment was most magnificent, but my poor wife dreadfully ill.

L. Loewe, ed., Diaries of Sir Moses and Lady Montefiore, London, 1890

Baron Lionel de Rothschild Runs for Office

Although most of the restrictions on British Jews had been done away with by the middle of the nineteenth century, one major obstacle remained: they were not admitted to Parliament. Even the wealthiest and most powerful family wasn't immune: the Rothschilds could not be members of the ruling class. In August 1847, Baron Lionel de Rothschild tried to break through this prejudicial barrier. He ran as a Liberal candidate for the City of London. A Jewish American periodical breathlessly recounted his victory in its English News column:

London, August 3, 1847

The sole absorbing topic among all the Jewish circles here is Baron Lionel Rothschild's election as a parliamentary representative of the City of London, which in the words of the Liberal enthusiast is "a glorious triumph of the principles of civil and religious liberty, over those of bigotry and intolerance." For the past two or three weeks the greatest excitement has prevailed throughout the city as well as in other districts where the interest has not been less although naturally less active. The Baron, together with many influential members of his family and friends, have for the last fortnight been prosecuting the most active canvass, the Baron himself addressing the constituents in their several wards, together with the other liberal candidates. Though much was not expected of him by his friends and acquaintances, he managed his address remarkably well, and passed with fair success through the usual ordeal of political catechism to which he was continually submitted by the electors at the various wards. The result of the contest was officially known on Thursday morning, when the Jewish liberal partisans were almost intoxicated with joy at their victory.

The Occident and American Jewish Advocate, Vol. 5, No. 6, September 1847

Frederic Morton, in The Rothschilds: Portrait of a Dynasty, *quotes from the proceedings as Baron Rothschild attempted to take the seat of office to which he was elected without swearing an oath on the New Testament:*

Rothschild's Battle to Take His Seat

Lionel Rothschild: My opponents say that I cannot take my seat. That is rather my affair than theirs. I have taken the best advice. I feel assured that as your representative, as the representative of the most wealthy, the most important, the most intelligent constituency in the world, I shall not be refused admission to Parliament on account of any form of words whatsoever. I desire to be sworn on the Old Testament.

Robert Inglis, leader of the opposing faction: From the time that this has been a Christian nation and that this house has been a Christian legislature, no man—if I may use the word without offence—has ever presumed to take his seat here unless prepared to take it under the solemn sanction of an oath in the name of our common Redeemer. I for one will never give my sanction to his admission.

After much wrangling, the Commons permitted Baron Rothschild to be sworn on the Old Testament. But the battle was far from over. The following day he was required to swear the Oath of Abjuration, ending with the words "upon the true faith of a Christian." Instead of repeating these words, he said, "I omit these words as not binding upon my conscience." With that, he was forced to withdraw.

Altogether Baron Rothschild was elected six times by his constituency. Six times he marched up to the table, demanding to be sworn according to the tenets of his faith. Ten times the Liberals introduced a bill revising the Oath of Abjuration. Ten times Prime Minister Disraeli crossed his own party, the Conservatives, to speak in favor of revising the discriminatory law. Ten times the bill was passed in the Commons, and ten times the Upper Chamber tore it up. Finally, in 1858, the Lords had to relent. On July 26, 1858, Baron Lionel de Rothschild stood before the table and took the oath with his head covered according to Jewish tradition, signed his name to the rolls, and proceeded to his seat. A Jew was at long last recognized as an equal in the lower House. What still seemed insurmountable was for a Jew to become a Lord. The Queen was firmly opposed. "To make a Jew a peer," she said, "is a step Her Majesty could not consent to. It would be ill taken and would do the government great harm." Only through the intervention of her prime minister, William Gladstone, was the final "glass ceiling" for Jews removed.

Gladstone's Letter on Behalf of Rothschild

10 Downing Street
October 28th, 1869
As the head of the great European house of the Rothschilds, even more than by his vast possessions, and his very prominent political position . . . Baron L. de Rothschild enjoys exactly the exceptional position, which disarms jealousy, and which is so difficult to find. . . . It would not be possible, in this view, to find any satisfactory substitute for his name. And if his religion were to operate permanently as a bar, it appears that this would be to revive by [the implication is, royal] prerogative, the disability which formerly existed by statute, and which the Crown and Parliament thought proper to abolish.

Mr. Gladstone has now troubled Your Majesty to the full extent incumbent upon him, and will not think of pressing Your Majesty beyond what Your Majesty's impartial judgment may approve.

Frederic Morton, The Rothschilds: Portrait of a Dynasty, Kodansha, 1998.
(Brackets mine.—B. B.)

Victoria sat tight. It was not until Suez had become British through Jewish money, not until the baptized Disraeli had won her heart, and not until years after Lionel's death in 1879 that she conferred the honor of a peerage on a Jew. On July 9, 1885, Nathaniel Mayer de Rothschild, Lionel's son, walked into the great house in Westminster and did in the Upper Chamber what it had once been forbidden for his father to do in the Lower. The new Lord donned the Jewish ceremonial headgear, the three-cornered hat, and on a Hebrew Bible swore his holy Jewish oath. "It was the first time," an awed witness noted, "that the Peers of the Realm had looked on while one of their number took the oath with head covered, or on another book than that which Christian practice and English tradition prescribed."

Assimilation and Reform

The unfortunate consequence of acceptance is often assimilation. Jews faced with a welcoming, open society often opted to embrace the faith of their neighbors. More than a quarter of a million Jews converted to Christianity in Western Europe in the first half of the nineteenth century. Most of the Jews in France, Italy, and Germany gave up their faith. Others chose to adjust their religious practices in response to their surroundings. In Germany a number of rabbinic leaders tried to "reform" Judaism. In an effort to make Judaism more compatible with modernity, they eliminated those aspects of tradition, such as circumcision and the dietary laws, that emphasized Jewish differences. The Jewish Sabbath was changed to Sunday; synagogues were changed to "temples" to reflect the new idea that Jews no longer needed to look forward to rebuilding the Temple in Jerusalem. Emancipation was viewed as the fulfillment of messianic redemption.

Proceedings of the Reform Rabbinical Conference at Frankfurt
July 20, 1845

The concept of the Messiah is closely linked to the entire ceremonial law. The believer in the Talmud finds his salvation only in the reconstruction of the state, the return of the people, the resumption of sacrifices, etc. Here lies the cause for all our lamentations over the destruction of the Temple, and our yearnings for the ruins of the altar. Ardent belief and unshakable courage were expressed in these hopes, uttered forth from the dark caves of our miserable streets.

But now our concepts have changed. There is no need any more for an extended ceremonial law. The earlier approach restricted divine guidance to the land [of Israel] and the people; the deity, it was believed, enjoyed bloody sacrifices, and priests were needed for penance. With increasing zeal, the prophets spoke up against this restricted view. Everybody knows the passage: "It hath been told thee, O man, what is good, and what the Lord doth require of thee; only to do justly, and to love mercy, and to walk humbly with thy God." The decline of Israel's political independence was at one time deplored, but in reality it was not a misfortune, but a mark of progress; not a degradation, but an elevation of our religion, through which Israel has come closer to fulfilling its vocation. The place of the sacrifices has been taken by sacred devotion. From Israel, the word of God had to be carried to the four corners of the earth, and new religions have helped in carrying out the task. Only the Talmud moves in circles; we, however, favor progress. . . . The wish to return to Palestine in order to create there a political empire for those who are still oppressed because of their religion is superfluous. The wish should rather be for a termination of the oppression, which would improve their lot as it has improved ours. The wish, moreover, is inadmissible. It turns the messianic hope from a religious into a secular one, which is gladly given up as soon as the political situation changes for the better. But messianic hope, truly understood, is religious. It expresses either a hope for redemption and liberation from spiritual deprivation and the realization of a Kingdom of God on earth, or for a political restoration of the Mosaic theocracy where Jews could live according to the Law of Moses. This latter religious hope can be renounced only by those who have a more sublime conception of Judaism, and who believe that the fulfillment of Judaism's mission is not dependent on the establishment of a Jewish state, but rather by a merging of Jewry into the political constellations of the fatherland. Only an enlightened conception of religion can displace a dulled one.

In all contemporary additions to the prayer book our modern conception of the Messiah may clearly be stated, including the confession that our newly gained status as citizens constitutes a partial fulfillment of our messianic hopes. . . .

Resolution adopted by the majority: The messianic idea should receive prominent mention in the prayers, but all petitions for our return to the land of our fathers and for the restoration of a Jewish state should be eliminated from the liturgy.

Paul R. Mendes Flohr and Jehuda Reinharz, eds., The Jew in the Modern World:
A Documentary History, New York, 1995

The twentieth century offers a tragic postscript to the misplaced optimism of German Jewry. It was German Jews who described themselves as "Germans of the Mosaic persuasion" rather than Jews. It was in Germany that they designated their houses of worship as Temples, with the assurance that "*this* place is our Jerusalem and *here* is our Temple." The Holocaust proved how terribly wrong they were. Reform Judaism would subsequently change many of its views regarding Israel and the messianic vision.

20

The Lingering Curse of Anti-Semitism

About five million Jews, approximately 40 percent of the Jewish population worldwide, lived in Eastern Europe during the early part of the nineteenth century. For them the Emancipation was no more than a distant rumor that had no discernible impact on their lives. In Russia, Poland, and the Ukraine, Jewish life only grew more difficult as anti-Semitism became a convenient way for rulers to appease their suffering peasants with a ready-made scapegoat.

Pogroms in the Pale of Settlement

Jews were confined by the czars of Russia to an area known as the Pale of Settlement. Expelled from the major cities and most rural areas, Jews had to subsist in small, self-supporting villages known as shtetls. This was the world of Tevye the dairyman, made famous in Fiddler on the Roof. Its reality, though, was far removed from the romanticized depiction offered in the Broadway musical. Violent outbreaks against Jews that included murder, rape, and pillage of Jewish possessions were not only tolerated by the authorities but very often instigated by them. These orgies of hate, known as pogroms, were so common that in one four-year span, 284 pogroms were recorded. As this account of one of these outbreaks makes clear, Jew hatred was actively fomented by the government while every effort was made to keep the events from being publicized.

Report of a Pogrom

Outrages upon Jews in Russia

The Vienna correspondent of the *Daily Telegraph* telegraphed on Wednesday night: A gentleman who passed through Vienna yesterday on his way home from the Far East, via Baku, Tiflis, and Charkoff, assured me that the agitation against the Jews in South Russia has assumed proportions of which Western Europe is not yet aware. He reached Elizabethgrad during the recent disturbances and gathered the particulars he gave me from residents of that town and the neighbourhood. He accounts for the scarcity of news from that part of Russia by the fact that the telegraph officials will not accept messages in any foreign language, while those written in Russian are revised by the censor prior to transmission. The post is scarcely a safer means of communication, there being at present a regular system of letter opening for foreign postal service. My friend's informants told him that the anti-Jewish movement in Russia is the work of the revolutionists. They understand that it would be of no avail to appeal to an ignorant and bigotedly loyal peasantry on the grounds of political emancipation. Ivan Ivanovitch [a personification of the typical Russian or the Russian people] knows little and is careless about Constitutions and administrative reform. It would be worse than useless to talk to him on such subjects. The revolutionists have consequently, touched another chord, and have excited his religious fanaticism. They have represented the Jew as the source of all the evils with which Russia is afflicted. They are held up to popular reprobation as the assassins of the late Czar and Jessie Helfmann, the Jewess who was implicated, as having been the soul of the whole plot. The Czar's assassination happened on a day that is kept up festively by the Jews in Russia, and after the event they were charged with having made merry in anticipation of what was going to happen. The object of the revolutionists is to create a popular rising, in which the troops would be called upon to defend the Jews against the Christians. They anticipate that either the troops would, under such circumstances, refuse duty, or that the people would be so infuriated that a general rising would ensue. The officers themselves apprehend the former contingency; but in either case the opportunity would be favourable for the revolutionists, and they would know how to turn it to account. The atrocities committed at Elizabethgrad, said my informant, must have been fearful to witness, as an officer who travelled a short distance with him and who was present at the time said he had seen things that sickened him to think of. Neither women nor children were spared, and had not many of the Jews been armed a wholesale massacre would certainly have taken place. At first it was proposed to burn the Jews' houses; but it so happens that at Elizabethgrad they do not live in a distinct quarter of the town. Their houses are not separate from those of the Christians, so the latter would have suffered from a conflagration. It appears that at a small locality named Golta, a massacre of the Jews was actually on the point of commencing when the inhabitants of a neighbouring village called Olviopol, came to the rescue and defended the Jews against their aggressors. According to an evening telegram, there have also been excesses against the Jews in the Government of Kiev.

The Jewish Chronicle, London, May 6, 1881. (Brackets mine.—B. B.)

This Viennese correspondent was shocked by the barbaric behavior of the "uncivilized" Eastern Europeans in 1881. It would take only a little more than half a century for the "civilized" Germans to far outdo the excesses of their Russian Jew-hating counterparts. Did the relative silence of the world during the nineteenth century play a part in permitting the Holocaust to become a reality?

The "Almost" Pogrom and the Future Prime Minister of Israel

A pogrom that almost happened left scars for a lifetime. It is described in the autobiography of Golda Meir. Who knows to what extent the views and political decisions of the future prime minister of Israel were shaped by this event.

My Childhood

In a way, I suppose that the little I recall of my early childhood in Russia, my first eight years, sums up my beginnings, what now are called the formative years. If so, it is sad that I have very few happy or even pleasant memories of this time. The isolated episodes that have stayed with me throughout the past seventy years have to do mostly with the terrible hardships my family suffered, with poverty, cold, hunger and fear, and I suppose my recollection of being frightened is the clearest of all my memories. I must have been very young, maybe only three and a half or four. We lived then on the first floor of a small house in Kiev, and I can still recall distinctly hearing about a pogrom that was to descend on us. I didn't know then, of course, what a pogrom was, but I knew it had something to do with being Jewish and with the rabble that used to surge through town, brandishing knives and huge sticks, screaming "Christ killers" as they looked for the Jews, and who were now going to do terrible things to me and to my family.

I can remember how I stood on the stairs that led to the second floor, where another Jewish family lived, holding hands with their little daughter and watching our fathers trying to barricade the entrance with boards of wood. That pogrom never materialized, but to this day I remember how scared I was and how angry that all my father could do to protect me was to nail a few planks together while we waited for the hooligans to come. And, above all, I remember being aware that this was happening to me because I was Jewish, which made me different from most of the other children in the yard. It was a feeling that I was to know again many times during my life—the fear, the frustration, the consciousness of being different and the profound instinctive belief that if one wanted to survive, one had to take effective action about it personally.

Golda Meir, *My Life*, New York, 1975

The Jews under Nicholas I

In 1827 Czar Nicholas I decided on yet another way to afflict the Jews. He introduced the Cantonist Decrees, which required the forced conscription of Jewish boys into the Russian army. Youngsters between the ages of twelve and eighteen were taken from their homes to fulfill mandatory service for twenty-five years. By that time, the czar assumed, his military conscripts would no longer have any memories of their past and their people. Parents forced to part with their children knew that they would almost certainly never see them again. Alexander Herzen (1812–1870), a Russian journalist, gave an eyewitness account of a group of cantonists taken on a march and the conversation he had with the escorting officer.

The Cantonists under the Czar

"Whom do you carry and to what place?"

"Well, sir, you see, they got together a bunch of these accursed Jewish youngsters between the age of eight and nine. I suppose they are meant for the fleet, but how should I know? At first the command was to drive them to Perm. Now there is a change. We are told to drive them to Kazan. I have had them on my hands for a hundred versts or thereabouts. The officer that turned them over to me told me they were an awful nuisance. A third of them remained on the road (at this the officer pointed with his finger to the ground). Half of them will not get to their destination," he added.

"Epidemics, I suppose?" I inquired, stirred to the very core.

"No, not exactly epidemics; but they just fall like flies. Well, you know, these Jewish boys are so puny and delicate. They can't stand mixing dirt for ten hours, with dry biscuits to live on. Again everywhere strange folks. No father, no mother, no caresses. Well then, you just hear a cough and the youngster is dead. Hello, corporal, get out the small fry!"

The little ones were assembled and arrayed in a military line. It was one of the most terrible spectacles I have ever witnessed. Poor, poor children!

The boys of twelve or thirteen managed somehow to stand up, but the little ones of eight and ten. . . . No brush, however black, could convey the terror of this scene on the canvas.

Pale, worn out, with scared looks, this is the way they stood in their uncomfortable, rough soldier uniforms, with their starched, turned-up collars, fixing an inexpressibly helpless and pitiful gaze upon the garrisoned soldiers, who were handling them rudely. White lips, blue lines under the eyes betokened either fever or cold. And these poor children, without care, without a caress, exposed to the wind which blows unhindered from the Arctic Ocean, were marching to their death. I seized the officer's hand, and, with the words: "Take good care of them!", threw myself into my carriage. I felt like sobbing, and I knew I could not master myself.

S. M. Dubnow, *History of the Jews in Russia and Poland:*
From the Earliest Times Until the Present Day, 1916

The Mendel Beilis Trial

Anti-Semitism helped rulers divert attention from their own corruption and thereby to remain in power. The most outrageous libels were spread against the Jews. Among the most frequent accusations was a claim that had been used by the Church in the Middle Ages: the "blood libel" alleging that Jews required the blood of Christian babies for ritual use. It was not until the famous Beilis trial in 1913 that a Russian court finally put this canard to rest. The New York Times *reported:*

"The Czar on Trial"

October 9, 1913

In Kieff, Russia yesterday, there was placed on trial, behind closed doors, one Mendel Beiliss, charged with the murder of a Russian lad, Yuschinsky, in 1911. Beiliss is a Jew, and is accused of "ritual murder," that is to say of having killed a boy to get his blood for alleged use in the rites of the Jewish religion. There are two elements in this case, which make it of great importance and interest to right-thinking persons in all parts of the world.

One is the clear presumption, on all available official Russian testimony, of the entire innocence of the accused. Immediately after the murder of the boy, M. Minschuk, Chief of the Detective Service in Kieff, with several assistants, investigated the case and reported, first, that there was no evidence against Beiliss, the accused, and second, that the boy was murdered by a gang of criminals whom he was suspected of betraying. For this report M. Minschuk was accused of manufacturing evidence to hinder the prosecution and to protect Jews, and though acquitted on one trial, was retried and condemned to prison for a year, with his assistants. That fact clearly discredits the whole case of the prosecution.

The second significant fact in the case is the nature of the accusation, the allegation of murder for Jewish ritual purposes. The crime does not and cannot exist. It has been shown over and over again, and long ago, that there is nothing in the religious belief or practice of the Jews that remotely requires or sanctions or suggests the thing charged. Strict and searching inquiry by eminent men of science, theologians, historians, physicians, not Jews, in Great Britain, in Germany, in France, has resulted in the distinct and unqualified verdict that the belief in this crime has not the slightest foundation in fact, and that it is a foolish, blind superstition bred of prejudice upon ignorance.

It has so been held and denounced by the Pope, by the head of the Orthodox Church, by living Bishops of that Church, and by a Czar of Russia, Alexander I, in 1817, confirmed by Nicholas I in 1835. What renders this base and baseless accusation more revolting at this late day, and by the officials of a Government professedly Christian, is the fact that in the twentieth century there could be the revival of a device used by the pagans in the first century to justify the oppression and slaughter of Christians. The Government of Russia, and especially the Czar of Russia, the authoritative head of a great branch of the Christian Church, in the mad, stupid war on the Jews, is 2000 years behind the times.

For the Russian peasants who are the helpless victims of this superstition, and who accept it as a like superstition was accepted by the savage crowds of the Roman Arena, we can have pity, and even with the brutal action inspired by it we can have patience. But for educated men, particularly for Russian officials who deliberately appeal to the superstitious and incite to brutal action, we can have only indignant detestation. And that feeling is in no wise affected by the fact that this outrage is directed to those of one or another race, one or another religion. The outrage is upon humanity.

Every humane, every decently human instinct condemns it. It is true that the offense is one that cannot be dealt with in the ordinary way of international communication, though it is by no means wholly beyond them, as was very properly shown in the case of Rumania as conducted by the late Secretary Hay. But in the court of public opinion such an offense can and must be dealt with. Fortunately there is a large number of educated and fair-minded Russians who not only will recognize the jurisdiction of that court and respect its verdict, but will contribute to it. And this element in Russia is bound to gain in strength and influence. If the second trial at Kieff results in the conviction of the hapless Beiliss, and that is followed by the disorders it is calculated to produce, this element will be not weakened, but reinforced. In view of this fact and of the general protest that has been aroused it may be said the Czar and the autocracy are now on trial.

The *New York Times*, October 9, 1913

The Dreyfus Affair

While Jews in Eastern Europe continued to suffer, the emancipated Jews of the "enlightened" Western lands came to believe they had outlived the prejudices of the past. Sadly, they were in for a rude awakening. Most painful of all, it was France— the very place where religious tolerance first flowered at the beginning of the nineteenth century—that would, at the close of that same century, be the scene of a dramatic episode that illustrated how powerful a force anti-Semitism remained.

The story that made headlines around the world became known simply as L'Affaire. A Jewish captain in the French army, Alfred Dreyfus, was accused of spying and was convicted of treason in a closed courtroom before a military tribunal. As would later be proven, the real spy was a Colonel Esterhazy, who had forged documents against the "Jewish traitor." Although the government knew the truth, it didn't back away from convicting Dreyfus. France had become virulently anti-Semitic—the most widely read book in 1886 was La France Juive, *a vicious diatribe against the Jews—and after the humiliating defeat in the Franco-Prussian War, the authorities were secretly pleased to give the people a way to vent their rage against the "secret Jewish influence." On January 3, 1895, Dreyfus was paraded in shame through the streets of Paris. The mob howled not "Death to Dreyfus" but "Death to the Jews." Dreyfus later recalled the ordeal that followed.*

From the Memoirs of Alfred Dreyfus

The degradation took place on Saturday, the 5th of January. I underwent the horrible torture without breaking down.

Previously to the terrible ordeal I waited for an hour in the garrison adjutant's room at the Ecole Militaire. During those trying moments I summoned all my strength; the remembrance of the fearful months which I had just passed came back to me. In broken accents I recalled the last visit which Commandant du Paty de Clam had made to me at the prison. I protested against the vile accusation which had been brought against me. I reminded those around me that I had again written to the Minister to assure him of my innocence. By distorting the words I then uttered, Captain Le-Brun Renault, with a strange lack of conscientious scruples, afterward gave currency to the story of a so-called confession, of which I first learned even the existence only in January, 1899. If I had been informed of it before my departure from France, which took place in February, 1895, that is to say more than seven weeks after my public degradation had taken place, I should have endeavored to stifle this fable at the outset.

After the interval of waiting, I was conducted by an officer and four men to the center of the square.

Nine o'clock struck. General Barras, who commanded the squad of execution, gave the order to shoulder arms.

I was suffering martyrdom, but I straightened myself and made a supreme effort to rally my strength, trying to sustain myself by the remembrance of my wife and children. Immediately after the formal reading of the sentence I exclaimed to the troops:

"Soldiers, an innocent man is degraded. Soldiers, an innocent man is dishonored! *Vive la France! Vive l'armée!*"

An adjutant of the Republican Guard came up to me and rapidly tore the buttons from my coat, the stripes from my trousers, and the marks of my rank from my cap and coat sleeves, and then broke my sword across his knee. . . . I saw all these emblems of honor fall at my feet. Then, in the midst of my agony, but with head erect, I shouted again and again to the soldiers and the assembled people, "I am innocent!"

The parade continued. I was compelled to march round the entire square. I heard the howls of a deluded mob; I could feel the shudder with which it looked upon me in the belief that the condemned man in their presence was a traitor to his country, and I made a superhuman effort to create in their hearts the commiseration due to an innocent man unjustly condemned.

The march round the square was at last completed, the torture was over as I thought, but in truth the agony of that memorable day had only just begun.

I was handcuffed, and was taken in the prison van to the common lockup on the other side of the Alma bridge. . . .

On reaching the end of the bridge I saw through the grated ventilator of the van the windows of the house where many pleasant years of my life had been passed, and where all my happiness was centered. My anguish at this pathetic sight was unspeakable. On arriving at the lockup, in my torn and ragged uniform, I was dragged from room to room, searched, photographed, and measured. At length, toward noon, I was taken to the Sante prison and locked in a convict's cell.

Alfred Dreyfus, Five Years of My Life, 1894–1899, New York, 1901

The Aftermath: "J'Accuse"

Emile Zola, widely regarded as one of France's greatest writers, stunned the country with a damning indictment of the miscarriage of justice in the Dreyfus trial. Entitled "J'Accuse" (I accuse), it remains one of history's most inspiring examples of a lone individual speaking out against evil. Zola, not a Jew himself, challenged the military and the government out of his dedication to truth and to principle and paid for it with a conviction for slander and temporary exile to England. Yet in the end, even after a wave of riots against the Jews and untold numbers of anti-Semitic writings, the truth came out. Dreyfus was finally pardoned and restored to his former military rank (although not fully exonerated until 1906!).

"J'Accuse" was published on January 13, 1898, as the full front page of a Paris newspaper and was phrased as an open letter to Félix Faure, the president of the republic.

"J'Accuse . . . !"

Letter to: the President of the Republic

These, then, Monsieur Le President, are the facts which explain how a judicial error could be committed; and the moral proofs, the wealthy position of Dreyfus, the absence of motives; his continual cry of innocence, finish in showing him to have been a victim of the extraordinary imagination of Commandant du Paty de Clam, of his clerical surroundings, of the hunt after "dirty Jews," which dishonours our era.

As I have demonstrated, the Dreyfus case was the affair of the War Office, an officer of the staff, denounced by his comrades on the Staff, condemned through the pressure of the Chiefs of the Staff. How many people do I not know who, in presence of a possible war tremble with anguish, knowing in what hands the national defence is placed! And what a nest of low intrigues, title-tattle, and dilapidations this sacred asylum has become, where the fate of the fatherland is decided! We are scared before the terrible light which the Dreyfus affair has just thrown upon it, this human sacrifice of an unfortunate being, of a "dirty Jew"! All this madness and trickery, the silly imaginations, the practices of a base police, the methods of inquisition and tyranny, the good pleasure of some epauletted individuals, placing their heels on the nation, stifling its cry for truth and justice under the false and sacrilegious pretext of reasons of State!

And it is still another crime to be supported by a vile press, to allow oneself to be defended by all the riffraff of Paris, with the result that this riffraff triumphs insolently in the defeat of justice and simple honesty. It is a crime to accuse of disturbing France, those who wish her to be generous, and at the head of free and just nations, whilst hatching oneself an impudent plot to impose error upon the whole world. It is a crime to mislead public opinion, to utilize for a deadly task this opinion which has been perverted until it becomes delirious. It is a crime to poison the minds of the little and the humble, to exasperate the passions of reaction and intolerance, while seeking refuge behind that odious anti-Semitism of which great liberal France, France of the rights of man, will die, unless she is cured of her disease. It is a crime to exploit patriotism for works of hatred, and, finally, it is a crime to make of the sword a modern God when all human science is labouring for the coming work of truth and justice.

Such is the plain truth, Monsieur Le President; it is terrible, and will remain a blot on your Presidency. I doubt whether you have any power in this matter, whether you are not the prisoner of the Constitution and of your surroundings. But you have nevertheless the duties of a man, of which you will think, and which you will fulfill. Not that I despair in the least of ultimate triumph. I repeat with the most vehement certainty, truth is advancing, and nothing will stop it. . . .

But this letter is long, Monsieur Le President, and it is time to conclude. . . .

I accuse Lieutenant-Colonel du Paty de Clam of having been the diabolical author of the judicial error, unconsciously I am willing to believe, and of having then defended his pernicious work for three years by the most absurd and culpable machinations.

I accuse General Mercier of having rendered himself the accomplice, at least through want of firmness, of one of the greatest iniquities of the century.

I accuse General Billot of having had in his hands certain proofs of the innocence of Dreyfus, and of having suppressed them, of having rendered himself guilty of the crime of treason to humanity and treason to justice with a political object, and in order to screen the compromised Staff. . . .

I accuse the War Office of having carried on in the press, particularly in the *Eclair* and the *Echo de Paris,* an abominable campaign in order to mislead public opinion and screen their error.

Lastly, I accuse the first Court-Martial of having violated the law by condemning an accused person on one document kept secret, and I accuse the second Court-Martial of having, in obedience to orders, covered this illegality by committing in its turn the judicial crime of knowingly acquitting a guilty person. . . .

I have but one passion—that of light. This I ask for in the name of humanity, which has suffered so much, and which has a claim to happiness. My passionate protest is but the cry of my soul.

Emile Zola, in Paul R. Mendes Flohr and Jehuda Reinharz, eds.,
The Jew in the Modern World: A Documentary History, New York, 1995

21

Zionism: "To Dream the Impossible Dream"

The Dream of a Jewish State

Theodore Herzl was probably the most unlikely person to found a movement that would alter the course of Jewish history. A lawyer turned journalist and correspondent, he wrote plays, sketches, reviews, stories, and literary essays for the Neue Freie Presse in Vienna, which he edited. A sophisticated and thoroughly modern German, he hardly concerned himself with his Jewish heritage or the fate of his people. Call it a quirk of fate or divine destiny, but all that dramatically changed when Herzl found himself covering the Dreyfus trial. As he wrote in his diary, "I suffered when Captain Dreyfus was accused of high treason." Herzl witnessed the furious anti-Semitic campaign that attended the trials and came to a forceful conclusion: the only solution to the age-old problem of Jewish persecution was a national homeland. His plan, he realized, was no less than insane. Yet, with a passion that bordered on the fanatic and a personal philosophy—as he put it—that "If you will it, it is not a dream," he fulfilled what he hoped would serve as his final epitaph:

> *One day, when the Jewish state will be in existence, everything will appear petty and self-evident. Perhaps a fair-minded historian will find that it was something, after all, that an impecunious Jewish journalist, in the midst of the deepest degradation of the Jewish people and at a time of the most disgusting anti-Semitism, made a flag out of a rag and a people out of a decadent rabble, and was able to rally this people around such a flag.*

In his diary, Herzl described how the vision he outlined in The Jewish State *consumed him so that he wrote "lying down, in the street, at dinner, at night, when it hounded away sleep." Of his ideas, he wrote, "Who wants to be right in thirty years must be thought crazy the first two weeks."*

From *The Jewish State*

I believe that I understand Anti-Semitism, which is really a highly complex movement. I consider it from a Jewish standpoint, yet without fear or hatred. I believe that I can see what elements there are in it of vulgar sport, of common trade jealousy, of inherited prejudice, of religious intolerance, and also of pretended self-defense. I think the Jewish question is no more a social than a religious one, notwithstanding that it sometimes takes these and other forms. It is a national question, which can only be solved by making it a political world-question to be discussed and settled by the civilized nations of the world in council.

We are a people—one people.

We have honestly endeavored everywhere to merge ourselves in the social life of surrounding communities and to preserve the faith of our fathers. We are not permitted to do so. In vain are we loyal patriots, our loyalty in some places running to extremes; in vain do we make the same sacrifices of life and property as our fellow-citizens; in vain do we strive to increase the fame of our native land in science and art, or her wealth by trade and commerce. In countries where we have lived for centuries we are still cried down as strangers. And often by those whose ancestors were not yet domiciled in the land where Jews had already had experience of suffering. The majority may decide which are the strangers; for this, as indeed every point which arises in the relations between nations, is a question of might. I do not here surrender any portion of our prescriptive right, when I make this statement merely in my own name as an individual. In the world as it now is and for an indefinite period will probably remain, might precedes right. It is useless, therefore, for us to be loyal patriots, as were the Huguenots who were forced to emigrate. If we could only be left in peace. . . .

But I think we shall not be left in peace.

Oppression and persecution cannot exterminate us. No nation on earth has survived such struggles and sufferings as we have gone through. Jew-baiting has merely stripped off our weaklings; the strong among us were invariably true to their race when persecution broke out against them. This attitude was most clearly apparent in the period immediately following the emancipation of the Jews. . . .

For old prejudices against us still lie deep in the hearts of the people. He who would have proofs of this need only listen to the people where they speak with frankness and simplicity: proverb and fairy-tale are both Anti-Semitic. A nation is everywhere a great child, which can certainly be educated; but its education would, even in most favorable circumstances, occupy such a vast amount of time that we could, as already mentioned, remove our own difficulties by other means long before the process was accomplished. . . .

No human being is wealthy or powerful enough to transplant a nation from one habitation to another. An idea alone can achieve that and this idea of a State may have the requisite power to do so. The Jews have dreamt this kingly dream all through the long nights of their history. "Next year in Jerusalem" is our old phrase. It is now a question of showing that the dream can be converted into a living reality.

For this, many old, outgrown, confused and limited notions must first be entirely erased from the minds of men. Dull brains might, for instance, imagine that this exodus would be from civilized regions into the desert. That is not the case. It will be carried out in the midst of civilization. We shall not revert to a lower stage, we shall rise to a higher one. We shall not dwell in mud huts; we shall build new more beautiful and more modern houses, and possess them in safety. We shall not lose our acquired possessions; we shall realize them. We shall surrender our well-earned rights only for better ones. We shall not sacrifice our beloved customs; we shall find them again. We shall not leave our old home before the new one is prepared for us. Those only will depart who are sure thereby to improve their position; those who are now desperate will go first, after them the poor; next the prosperous, and, last of all the wealthy. Those who go in advance will raise themselves to a higher grade, equal to those whose representatives will shortly follow. Thus the exodus will be at the same time an ascent of the class.

The departure of the Jews will involve no economic disturbances, no crises, no persecutions; in fact, the countries they abandon will revive to a new period of prosperity. There will be an inner migration of Christian citizens into the positions evacuated by Jews. The outgoing current will be gradual, without any disturbance, and its initial movement will put an end to Anti-Semitism. The Jews will leave as honored friends, and if some of them return, they will receive the same favorable welcome and treatment at the hands of civilized nations as is accorded to all foreign visitors. Their exodus will have no resemblance to a flight, for it will be a well-regulated movement under control of public opinion. The movement will not only be inaugurated with absolute conformity to law, but it cannot even be carried out without the friendly cooperation of interested Governments, who would derive considerable benefits from it.

Although I speak of reason, I am fully aware that reason alone will not suffice. Old prisoners do not willingly leave their cells. We shall see whether the youth whom we need are at our command—the youth, who irresistibly draw on the old, carry them forward on strong arms, and transform rational motives into enthusiasm.

Theodore Herzl, The Jewish State, 1896, the Theodore Herzl Foundation

> Herzl believed that a Jewish state would bring about the end of anti-Semitism. Clearly that has not happened in modern times. Why was Herzl wrong? What other causes of anti-Semitism did he not take into consideration?

Herzl was that rare combination of thinker and doer. He didn't merely propose a plan; he acted on it with a daring and genius beyond anyone's imagination. In 1897 he called for the First Zionist Congress to meet in Basel, Switzerland, in order "to establish for the Jewish people a publicly and legally assured home in Palestine." For the first time in more than eighteen hundred years, Jews representing communities from around the world got together to discuss a solution to the problem of Jewish survival. "In Basel," Herzl had the audacity to declare, "I founded the Jewish state."

Herzl met with the great Jewish financiers and the heads of nations, the sultan and the kaiser, the foreign ministers of Russia and Austria, and even the pope. From the latter he got the promise that the Church would do nothing to oppose a Jewish return to Israel, but "We will have priests and churches ready to baptize all of you"! The most sympathetic response came from the British colonial secretary, Joseph Chamberlain, who suggested that instead of settling in Palestine, Jews might consider "the attractive lands in Uganda in British East Africa where you can raise sugar and cotton." The Sixth Zionist Congress in 1903 seriously considered this option as a temporary solution, permitting a haven for victims of pogroms and persecution. After bitter infighting and much soul-searching, the view of those who were opposed prevailed: "East Africa is not Zion, and can never become it." But the exertions and demands of leadership took their toll. Herzl died suddenly in 1904 at the age of forty-four. Tragically, he would never know the remarkable fulfillment, almost to the year, of his 1897 declaration.

Israel was declared a Jewish State on May 5, 1948, fifty years and nine months later.

Palestine in the Late Nineteenth Century

It was clearly not the beauty of the landscape that motivated the Zionist leaders to resist any alternative to Palestine as national homeland. Mark Twain gives us an eyewitness account of what Palestine looked like when he made a pilgrimage to the Holy Land in 1867:

We stayed all night with the good monks at the convent of Ramleh, and in the morning got up and galloped the horses a good part of the distance from there to Jaffa, or Joppa, for the plain was as level as a floor and free from stones, and besides this was our last march in holy Land. These two or three hours finished, we and the tired horses could have rest and sleep as long as we wanted it. This was the plain of which Joshua spoke when he said, "Sun, stand thou still on Gibeon, and thou moon in the valley of Ajalon." As we drew near to Jaffa, the boys spurred up the horses and indulged in the excitement of an actual race—an experience we had hardly had since we raced on donkeys in the Azores islands.

We came finally to the noble grove of orange-trees in which the Oriental city of Jaffa lies buried; we passed through the walls, and rode again down narrow streets and among swarms of animated rags, and saw other sights and had other experiences we had long been familiar with. We dismounted, for the last time, and out in the offing, riding at anchor, we saw the ship! I put an exclamation point there because we felt one when we saw the vessel. The long pilgrimage was ended, and somehow we seemed to feel glad of it.

Of all the lands there are for dismal scenery, I think Palestine must be the prince. The hills are barren, they are dull of color, they are unpicturesque in shape. The valleys are unsightly deserts fringed with feeble vegetation that has an expression about it of being sorrowful and despondent. The Dead Sea and the Sea of Galilee sleep in the midst of a vast stretch of hill and plain wherein the eye rests upon no pleasant tint, no striking object, no soft picture dreaming in a purple haze or mottled with the shadows of the clouds. Every outline is harsh, every feature is distinct, there is no perspective—distance works no enchantment here. It is a hopeless, dreary, heart-broken land.

Small shreds and patches of it must be very beautiful in the full flush of spring, however, and all the more beautiful by contrast with the far-reaching desolation that surrounds them on every side. I would like much to see the fringes of the Jordan in springtime, and Shechem, Esdraelon, Ajalon and the borders of Galilee—but even then these spots would seem mere toy gardens set at wide intervals in the waste of a limitless desolation.

Palestine sits in sackcloth and ashes. Over it broods the spell of a curse that has withered its fields and fettered its energies. Where Sodom and Gomorrah reared their domes and towers, that solemn sea now floods the plain, in whose bitter waters no living thing exists—over whose waveless surface the blistering air hangs motionless and dead—about whose borders nothing grows but weeds, and scattering tufts of cane, and that treacherous fruit that promises refreshment to parching lips, but turns to ashes at the touch. Nazareth is forlorn; about that ford of Jordan where the hosts of Israel entered the Promised Land with songs of rejoicing, one finds only a squalid camp of fantastic Bedouins of the desert; Jericho the accursed, lies a moldering ruin, to-day, even as Joshua's miracle left it more than three thousand years ago; Bethlehem and Bethany, in their poverty and their humiliation, have nothing about them now to remind one that they once knew the high honor of the leader's presence; the hallowed spot where the shepherds watched their flocks by night, and where the angels sang Peace on earth, good will to men, is untenanted by any living creature, and unblessed by any feature that is pleasant to the eye. Renowned Jerusalem itself, the stateliest name in history, has lost all its ancient grandeur, and is become a pauper village; the riches of Solomon are no longer there to compel the admiration of visiting Oriental queens; the wonderful temple which was the pride and the glory of Israel, is gone, and the Ottoman crescent is lifted above the spot where, on that most memorable day in the annals of the world, they reared the holy cross. The noted Sea of Galilee, where Roman fleets once rode at anchor and the disciples of the leader sailed in their ships, was long ago deserted by the devotees of war and commerce, and its borders are a silent wilderness; Capernaum is a shapeless ruin; Magdala is the home of beggared Arabs; Bethsaida and Chorazin have vanished from the earth, and the "desert places" round about them where thousands of men once listened to the leader's voice and ate the miraculous bread, sleep in the hush of a solitude that is inhabited only by birds of prey and skulking foxes.

Palestine is desolate and unlovely. And why should it be otherwise? Can the curse of the Deity beautify a land?

Palestine is no more of this workday world. It is sacred to poetry and tradition—it is dream-land.

Mark Twain, The Innocents Abroad, or, the New Pilgrim's Progress, 1869

For some, Zionism meant diplomacy, discussion, debates, and literary endeavors. For others, Zionism required no less than a personal commitment to emigrate to Palestine, to physically work the land and bring it back to productivity. The earliest pioneers, called chalutzim *in Hebrew, bought parcels of land and braved Arab attacks as well as bitter conditions to found communes—many under the rules of a daring socialistic concept known as the* kibbutz—*that would become major cities and settlements in years to come. Highly idealistic, moved by both spiritual and nationalistic prompting, they literally turned deserts into farms and orchards. Among them were "plough women" like Techiah Liberson, whose story illustrates the determination of these earliest settlers.*

Those First Years

When I came to Petach Tikvah in 1905 some Jewish workers were already there. There were only four girls among them: two seamstresses, one stocking knitter, and one who received remittances from her parents. In the season both seamstresses would turn orange packers. But my heart was set on plain labor on the soil. Three days after my arrival I went out to work with the spade for one bishlik (twelve and a half cents) a day. I worked in Gissin's vineyard, and my job was to fill up the holes around the trees.

I used to come home evenings to the colony without any tools, and for a whole month I would leave the regular path and make my way through backyards, so that no one should know that I was working with the men. The workers themselves were against my choice—they were genuinely afraid that I would break down under the labor. They urged me to work with the other girls at the orange packing—but I would not listen. I wanted to work with the spade.

It was comrade S. who first gave me courage to continue. He was the teacher in the colony: and he shifted the school hours so as to be able to come out and take turns with me at the work. In this way, while our comrades took only one hour's rest during the middle of the day, I took three. S. also talked about me to the owner of the vineyard, who assured him that in time I would become a good worker.

Two weeks later the owner raised my pay by half a piastre—making a full three piastres a day. I was astonished, and asked him whether he had done this because I was a Jewish girl or because I was really worth it. He answered frankly that I was really worth a great deal more.

And yet for a long time I was tormented by the question whether I had chosen the right path. The doubts of my fellow workers crept into me too, and I needed someone who would give me more faith in myself and in my own strength.

There worked among us at that time a comrade who was much older than any of us—the man who later became famous in Palestine as A. D. Gordon. His good humor and unflagging cheerfulness were a source of strength to all of us. He composed a great many Jewish songs, which we learned to sing together with him. From the beginning I conceived a deep affection for this old man—but I had not the courage to seek his advice. Often, seeing me sit apart, completely exhausted, he would call out to me: "Cheer up! Look at me. An old man, working as hard as the rest, and always happy." But before I could answer him, and pour out my troubles, he would be gone.

My work with the spade lasted a month, and after that I passed over to orange picking. During the first two days I worked for nothing. When my first basket was filled, I submitted it to the overseer, who went through it, orange by orange. He found three which had been touched by the scissors. My heart was in my mouth—I was certain he would send me home. But in the second basket there was only one damaged orange—and from then on I was a perfect orange picker. When my work on this orchard was finished the overseer sent me to a second. I became known as a skilled orange picker, and work was easy to find.

When the season was over I went to the employment bureau of the colony to look for work. I was told that there were only three colonists who were prepared to take women workers, and none of them had a place for me. For the second time I was seized with despair. I came home, and sat down in loneliness, and brooded over the life I had chosen for myself. I remembered then the letters that I had received from a well-known Zionist leader before I set out for Palestine. He had warned me against coming to Palestine. "You will find no work there," he wrote. "You will suffer hunger and want, and no one will be any the better for it."

For three days I sought work in vain and at the end of the third day, when I sat again in my room, beaten, the old man came to me. He invited me over to his little shack, and there we talked for many, many hours. He gave me courage to hold out; and in the next few days I found employment together with him. He became my teacher in the work.

Before long I was dissatisfied with the simple work; I wanted the more responsible task of grafting trees. A comrade undertook to teach me. He told me to lay off work with the spade for a couple of days, and to bring him his meals in the orchard. At that hour the owner was away, and he would then be able to show me how to graft. I fell in with this plan. Two days later the worker told his boss that I was a skilful grafter and that I had already been employed for that purpose in other orchards. The owner took me on trial, was satisfied with me, and let me remain.

When I had been working for a year and a half I was told that another woman and worker had appeared in Rechoboth—Miriam Zavin. And in 1907 several other women workers came from Russia and went up to Galilee, to work on the farm of Sedjera.

I worked in Petach Tikvah for a total of three years, till 1908. Some time before the end of that year a group of our men workers had gone up to the farm of Kinereth. They applied to the director to let me join them—but not in the kitchen, as was the almost invariable rule with women. Up in Kinereth I worked side by side with the men. First I helped to clear the soil of stones, later I took a hand in the mowing and threshing. There were no houses for the workers in those days. In the summer we slept out in the open. In the winter the woman who worked in the kitchen and I slept in the barn. Raids and attacks by our neighbors were fairly frequent in those days.

With the beginning of the new year the two of us joined the little *kvutzah* or commune which began to work on its own initiative and responsibility in Um-Djuni. And there at last I began to feel that I had become a full-fledged worker. The year's work in Um-Djuni ended with a profit, and yet for a variety of reasons the group fell to pieces. A second group came up to the same ground. I was away then, being down for several months with yellow fever. When I recovered, I joined the new group and out of this group grew the present settlement of Deganiah.

Techiah Liberson, in Rachel Katznelson-Shazar, ed., *The Plough Woman: Memoirs of the Pioneer Women of Palestine*, Maurice Samuel, trans., 1975

> The women who came as early pioneers to Palestine shared a dream of an egalitarian society with the full emancipation of women. In the late nineteenth and early twentieth centuries, this tiny spot in the Middle East became a precursor of the feminist movement. Why would it take so much longer for this "novel idea" to penetrate the culture of the modern Western world?

At the beginning of the twentieth century, Jews could look back at tremendously positive changes. For the most part, they had gained a great measure of equality and acceptance. Facing persecution, they now had the option to emigrate to America and other more hospitable havens. Zionism offered hope for the future. No one could have foretold that the century ahead would present the Jewish people with the worst of times and the best of times. What lay ahead, we now know, were both the greatest tragedy and the greatest miracle of Jewish history. Our final section will encompass the unbearable sorrow of the Holocaust as well as the unbounded joy of Jewish national redemption.

Book VI

Modern Times: The Twentieth Century to the Present

Date (c.e.)	Event
1981	Refusenik Iosef Mendelevitch freed from Soviet prison and emigrates to Israel
1987	Palestinian Intifada begins
1989	Berlin Wall is demolished
1991	Gulf War
1991	Communist-controlled USSR collapses, breaking up into independent states
1993	Rabin and Arafat shake hands in Washington
1994	Israeli-Jordanian Peace Treaty
2000	Arafat rejects Clinton-proposed peace plan at Camp David; New Intifada; suicide bombings

22

"Give Me Your Tired, Your Poor": The American Melting Pot

W henever God closes one door, goes the famous Jewish saying, he opens another. The oppression in Eastern Europe forced Jews to find another home, and America offered its welcome. The words inscribed on the Statue of Liberty couldn't be clearer:

> Give me your tired, your poor,
> Your huddled masses yearning to breathe free,
> The wretched refuse of your teeming shore,
> Send these, the homeless, tempest-tossed to me,
> I lift my lamp beside the golden door.

How fitting that this sentiment was written by Emma Lazarus, a Jew. It would be another Jew, Irving Berlin, who would compose God Bless America, the song that became America's unofficial national anthem. Jews, more than any other people, could truly appreciate the one place on earth where their religion would offer no obstacle to acceptance and to success. In 1880 there were approximately 250,000 Jews in the United States. As a result of the pogroms and persecution in Poland, Russia, Lithuania, Hungary, Romania, and adjacent territories, another half million Jews came by 1900; by 1925, there were about four million Jews in what Jews called the goldene medina—the land of gold.

Coming to the Land "Flowing with Milk and Money"

In a 1912 autobiography that became a classic of the immigrant experience, Mary Antin recalled her family's move to America when she was a child.

From The Promised Land

The Exodus

On the day when our steamer ticket arrived, my mother did not go out with her basket, my brother stayed out of heder [Hebrew school], and my sister salted the soup three times. I do not know what I did to celebrate the occasion. Very likely I played tricks on Deborah, and wrote a long letter to my father.

Before sunset the news was all over Polotzk that Hannah Hayye had received a steamer ticket for America. Then they began to come. Friends and foes, distant relatives and new acquaintants, young and old, wise and foolish, debtors and creditors, and mere neighbors—from every quarter of the city, from both sides of the Dvina, from over the Polata, from nowhere—a steady stream of them poured into our street, both day and night, till the hour of our departure. And my mother gave audience. Her faded kerchief halfway off her head, her black ringlets straying, her apron often at her eyes, she received her guests in a rainbow of smiles and tears. She was the heroine of Polotzk, and she conducted herself appropriately. She gave her heart's thanks for the congratulations and blessings that poured in on her; ready tears for condolences; patient answers to monotonous questions; and handshakes and kisses and hugs she gave gratis.

What did they not ask, the eager, foolish, friendly people? They wanted to handle the ticket, and Mother must read them what is written on it. How much did it cost? Was it all paid for? Were we going to have a foreign passport or did we intend to steal across the border? Were we not all going to have new dresses to travel in? Was it sure that we could get kosher food on the ship? And with the questions poured in suggestions, and solid chunks of advice were rammed in by nimble prophecies. Mother ought to make a pilgrimage to a "Good Jew"—say, the Rebbe of Lubavitch—to get his blessing on our journey. She must be sure and pack her prayer books and Bible, and twenty pounds of zwieback at the least. If they did serve trefah [non-kosher] on the ship, she and the four children would have to starve, unless she carried provisions from home.—Oh, she must take all the featherbeds! Featherbeds are scarce in America. In America they sleep on hard mattresses, even in winter. Haveh Mirel, Yachne the dressmaker's daughter, who emigrated to New York two years ago, wrote her mother that she got up from childbed with sore sides, because she had no featherbed.—Mother mustn't carry her money in a pocketbook. She must sew it into the lining of her jacket. The policemen in Castle Garden take all their money from the passengers as they land, unless the travelers deny having any.

And so on, and so on, till my poor mother was completely bewildered. And as the day set for our departure approached, the people came oftener and stayed longer, and rehearsed my mother in long messages for their friends in America, praying that she deliver them promptly on her arrival, and without fail, and might God bless her for her kindness, and she must be sure and write them how she found their friends.

Hayye Dvoshe, the wig-maker, for the eleventh time repeating herself, to my mother, still patiently attentive, thus:

"Promise me, I beg you. I don't sleep nights for thinking of him. Emigrated to America eighteen months ago, fresh and well and strong, with twenty-five rubles in his pocket, besides his steamer ticket, with new phylacteries, and a silk skullcap, and a suit as good as new—made it only three years before—everything respectable, there could be nothing better; sent one letter, how he arrived in Castle Garden, how well he was received by his uncle's son-in-law, how he was conducted to the baths, how they bought him an American suit, everything good, fine, pleasant—wrote how his relative promised him a position in his business—a clothing merchant is he—makes gold—and since then not a postal card, not a word, just as if he had vanished, as if the earth had swallowed him. *Oi, vey!* What haven't I imagined, what haven't I dreamed, what haven't I lamented! Already three letters have I sent—the last one, you know, you yourself wrote for me, Hannah Hayye, dear—and no answer. Lost, as if in the sea!"

And after the application of a corner of her shawl to eyes and nose, Hayye Dvoshe, continuing: "So you will go into the newspaper, and ask them what has become of my Moshele, and if he isn't in Castle Garden, maybe he went up to Balti-moreh—it's in the neighborhood, you know— and you can tell them, for a mark, that he has a silk handkerchief with his monogram in Russian, that his betrothed embroidered for him before the engagement was broken. And may God grant you an easy journey, and may you arrive in a propitious hour, and may you find your husband well, and strong, and rich, and may you both live to lead your children to the wedding canopy, and may America shower gold on you. Amen." . . .

The weeks skipped, the days took wing, an hour was a flash of thought; so brimful of events was the interval before our departure. And no one was more alive than I to the multiple significance of the daily drama. My mother, full of grief at the parting from home and family and all things dear, anxious about the journey, uncertain about the future, but ready, as ever, to take up what new burdens awaited her; my sister, one with our mother in every hope and apprehension; my brother, rejoicing in his sudden release from heder and the little sister, vaguely excited by mysteries afoot; the uncles and aunts and devoted neighbors, sad and solemn over their coming loss; and my father away over in Boston, eager and anxious about us in Polotzk—an American citizen impatient to start his children on American careers—I knew the minds of everyone of these, and I lived their days and nights with them after an apish fashion of my own. . . .

Our turn came at last. We were conducted through the gate of departure, and after some hours of bewildering maneuvers, described in great detail in the report to my uncle, we found ourselves—we five frightened pilgrims from Polotzk—on the deck of a great big steamship afloat on the strange big waters of the ocean.

For sixteen days the ship was our world. My letter dwells solemnly on the details of the life at sea, as if afraid to cheat my uncle of the smallest circumstance. It does not shrink from describing the torments of seasickness; it notes every change in the weather. A rough night is described, when the ship pitched and rolled so that people were thrown from their berths; days and nights when we crawled through dense fogs, our foghorn drawing answering warnings from invisible ships. The perils of the sea were not minimized in the imaginations of us inexperienced voyagers. The captain and his officers ate their dinners, smoked their pipes, and slept soundly in their turns, while we frightened emigrants turned our faces to the wall and awaited our watery graves.

All this while the seasickness lasted. Then came happy hours on deck, with fugitive sunshine, birds atop the crested waves, band music and dancing and fun. I explored the ship, made friends with officers and crew, or pursued my thoughts in quiet nooks. It was my first experience of the ocean, and I was profoundly moved. . . .

And so suffering, fearing, brooding, rejoicing, we crept nearer and nearer to the coveted shore, until, on a glorious May morning, six weeks after our departure from Polotzk, our eyes beheld the Promised Land, and my father received us in his arms.

Mary Antin, The Promised Land, Boston, 1912. (Brackets mine.—B. B.)

> Why did some Jews leave and others remain behind? Was it lack of funds that prevented more people from emigrating, or fear of the unknown? What would determine whether those who left would cut ties with their past— even forsaking fiancées and brides—or faithfully save money until they could afford to bring their loved ones to them? What characteristics would the new immigrants usually share in terms of their personalities (were they risk takers?), their economic position (those who had the least to lose by leaving?), and their level of piety (was the threat of assimilation a deterrent to the deeply religious?)? Was American Jewry destined to be different because of the unique circumstances that brought it into being?

Culture Shock

The immigrants entered a world that was totally different—strange and, in many ways, threatening. In 1903 the New York Tribune *featured an interview with Dr. David Blaustein, head of the Educational Alliance in New York City, a settlement house devoted to helping those recently arrived to adjust to their new world, in which he described the culture shock faced by these new Americans.*

From the *New York Tribune*, August 16, 1903

"It is impossible to understand the Lower East Side," said Dr. David Blaustein, head of the Educational Alliance, speaking apropos of his recent statistical investigations of conditions in that section, "or the attitude of the people there toward American institutions without knowing the conditions from which these people came in Eastern Europe. . . .

Religious Life

"You can imagine the confusion in the immigrant's mind when he reaches America. He finds his church of no account whatever. No one cares what church he belongs to or whether he belongs to any church or not. The state delegates no rights or powers to the church. All that is asked is whether he is an American or not and whether he is loyal to his adopted Country. No one cares anything about his loyalty to his church or regards his religious belief as a matter of any importance to anyone but himself. In place of finding the congregation all-powerful and all embracing, he finds when he joins a congregation that he has simply joined a liberal society.

Social Life

"The change in social life is as peculiar and puzzling to the immigrant as that in the religious life. In Eastern Europe the social life centers in the Church and the home, and is pervaded by a devotional atmosphere. It is spontaneous. It flows from natural occasions. The social life to which we are accustomed—balls, receptions, banquets, class reunions—is not spontaneous; it is organized. All these affairs are arranged.

"For instance, it is the custom in the Jewish church to celebrate the eighth day after the birth of a son. This festival in Europe is always an occasion of much rejoicing. Suppose the day falls on a weekday, when there is work in the shop. The man goes to the shop, and the celebration is postponed until the following Sunday. Then the host knows and his guests know that it is not the right day. Their consciences smile then, and the occasion is one of secret sadness rather than rejoicing. They fall to mourning over the economic conditions which will not permit them to observe the old customs, rather than enjoying themselves.

"Always, before, the immigrant had room in which to entertain his friends. In the crowded condition of the quarter where he now lives, he cannot do this. The wedding is the pinnacle of Jewish social life. But on the Lower East Side the wedding must take place in a hall. The guest must pay at the door for his hat and coat check, and this at the very start takes away all the old feeling of openhanded hospitality. The hall wedding is a cold and comfortless function.

"So economic conditions prevent him from enjoying himself in his home with his family and his religion in the old way. If he seeks social enjoyment, he finds he must accommodate his time to that of others. A ball is to be held at a certain time. There is no special reason for it at that time, but the date has been fixed by a committee of arrangements, and he is asked to purchase a ticket. Remembering his good times in the old country, he goes, hoping to enjoy himself once more. He finds himself in a sea of strangers, with nothing as he has been used to it. He goes away weary and disheartened. It is the same in summer when he buys a ticket for one of the mammoth picnics. When he compares such a picnic with the harvest festival at home, a thing as happy and spontaneous as the play of children, his heart is sick. Often he says that America is no good and he would rather be back in the old country.

Position of the Woman

"As the woman in Eastern Europe has no religious life, so she has no social life. If you call at a house, you are received by the man of the house, not the woman. There are certain social feasts and celebrations of the church, but the men participate in them, not the women. If invitations are sent out to a wedding they are sent to the males of a family, not to the women. At the wedding, the highest social function of Judaism, there are five men present to one woman.

"The woman is also a minor. She belongs to her father before her marriage, to her husband after. She cannot own property in her own name. Her testimony is not received in the ecclesiastical courts, although in the civil courts it has recently been admitted.

"Can you imagine what all this means to the immigrant? He goes to church here and finds women in the majority. He goes to the schools and finds women teaching most of them. He finds them behind every counter, beside him in every shop. What is the result? The result is that he loses all his respect for women."

Dr. Blaustein paused to let this declaration sink in and then went on to explain: "You may think," he said, "that from what I have said of the position of women among the Jews of Eastern Europe that she is despised. On the contrary, she is an idolized being. She is adored. She is the queen of the home. The theory upon which she is excluded from all the things I have mentioned is not that she is not entitled to them, but that being busy with her household duties she is excused from them. She is excused from religious duties because something at home may require her attention. She is excused from education because more important duties await her. She is excused from looking after her own property. The men of her family will do that for her and protect all her rights. She is even excused from social duties," concluded Dr. Blaustein gravely.

"The immigrant sees woman in America excused from nothing. She bears the heat and burden of the day at his side. She has become his equal, and he supposes she is to be treated as an equal. He loses all respect for women and acts accordingly. Then he goes out into the American world and finds to his astonishment that women have privileges in America. He finds that there is a rule, 'ladies first.' It surprises him very much. He can't understand the apparent contradiction of things. It requires another mental readjustment.

Athletics

"There is nothing that disturbs the Jew so much as to see his boy, and still more his girl, taking part in the athletics of the schools. The rage is something incomprehensible to him. He has cultivated his mind so long at the expense of his body that the American maxim 'a sound mind in a sound body' is something he cannot understand.

"All these things may explain to a slight degree the puzzled condition of the immigrant's mind, the difficulty he has in assimilating and adjusting himself to new conditions, his heavyheartedness, oftentimes, and his frequent estrangement from his own children."

Reprinted in Eliezer Ehrmann, *Readings in Modern Jewish History,* New York, 1977

> Did any of these early immigrant attitudes remain with the following generations? Did the melting pot of American life destroy older cultural mores? Is that a desirable goal—that all Americans become as much alike as possible? Do any of these stereotypes—for example, that Jews hate athletics—have any validity? Did the immigrants who came in great numbers after the Holocaust share any of these older perspectives?

Hardship and Opportunity

Those who had come expecting the apocryphal streets filled with gold faced harsh disillusionment. America didn't offer every newcomer a life of ease and affluence. What it promised was opportunity. Far too often, though, the reality for most immigrants was stifling sweatshops and merciless employers. The hardships they endured led to the Jewish role in founding labor unions that would help secure basic rights for employees throughout the country.

Morris Hillquit, the founder of the Arbeiterzeitung *(Workers Newspaper), one of the first Yiddish-language newspapers in the United States, recalled the early struggles of the union movement.*

From the Autobiography of Morris Hillquit

Sweatshops

In 1890 there were about one thousand knee pants makers employed in New York, all "green" and most of them illiterate. It was a sweat-shop industry par excellence. The work was done entirely on the contracting system. A contractor employed about ten workers on the average and usually operated his shop in his living-rooms. His sole function consisted of procuring bundles of cut garments from the manufacturer and having them made up by the workers. He did not even furnish the sewing machines. The operator provided his own machine as well as the needles and thread. The workday was endless, and the average earnings of experienced operators ran from six to seven dollars per week. Often the contractor would abscond with a week's pay; often the worker would be discharged because he was not fast enough to suit the contractor, and often he would be compelled to quit his job because of maltreatment or intolerable working conditions. Every time a knee pants maker changed contractors, he was compelled to put his sewing machine on his back and carry it through the streets to his new place of employment. It was at this point that their patience finally gave out. In the early part of 1890, they struck. The movement was spontaneous, without program, leadership, or organization. It was a blind outbreak of revolt and was destined to collapse if left to itself, sharing the fate of many similar outbursts in the past.

Strikes and Victory

In this case the United Hebrew Trades stepped in during the very first hours of the strike. Through a committee of five, of whom I was one, it took complete charge of the situation.

Our first step was to hire a meeting hall large enough to accommodate all the strikers. There were about nine hundred, and we gathered them in from all shops and street corners. In the hall we held them in practically continuous session, day and night, allowing them only the necessary time to go home to sleep. We feared to let them go, lest they be tempted to return to work, and we entertained them all the time with speeches and such other forms of instruction and amusement as we could devise.

While the continuous performance was going on in the main hall, we tried to bring order and system into the strike and to organize the strikers into a solid and permanent union.

In consultation with the most intelligent men and women from the ranks of the strikers, we worked out a list of demands centering upon the employer's obligation to furnish sewing machines and other work tools at his own expense. Then we chose pickets, relief committees, and settlement committees, all operating under our direct supervision and guidance.

The men did not know how to conduct meetings or transact business of any kind. They had never acted in concert. Our discourses on the principles of trade unionism and the philosophy of Socialism were interspersed with elementary lessons in parliamentary procedure and practical methods of organization. We tried to pick out the most promising among them and train them for leadership of their fellows. The strike was a course of intensive training and education, but it was of short duration. After one week without a break in the ranks of the workers, the contractors weakened; one Saturday night they became panicky and stormed the meeting hall of the strikers in a body, demanding an immediate and collective settlement on the workers' terms.

The United Hebrew Trades had scored a great victory and was encouraged to new efforts in other fields.

Morris Hillquit, Loose Leaves from a Busy Life, New York, 1934

Was the major role played by Jews in the labor movement rooted in biblical ideals of justice and righteousness? Was the success of the struggle a fulfillment of the prophetic mission preached by Isaiah to be "a light unto the nations"? In the capitalistic struggle between labor and management, has the balance of power shifted too sharply to labor in the years since unions have assumed a considerable degree of control? Did the early unions seek dominance or merely equitable treatment? Why did other minority groups eventually replace Jewish leadership of the unions?

The transition from immigrant to American was, incredibly enough, usually accomplished in one generation. The secret of this success story was beautifully captured by Hutchins Hapgood, a perceptive non-Jewish observer, in a 1902 work, reissued in 1965 with additional comments (in italics) by Harry Golden:

From *The Spirit of the Ghetto*

The Public Schools
No one knew in 1902 that the free public school would become the most important factor in the development of the Jewish community of America. But so it became probably because the free public school became as important a development to modern America itself. Not a day went by that we didn't see new immigrants walking down the middle of the street, each with a tag around the neck bearing a surname and with a piece of paper in hand, which was the address of a relative. And on the next Monday, the children of these immigrants enrolled in the public school. And it was the public school that proceeded to

make citizens out of immigrants and do it within a single generation, surely the most successful endeavor in the history of personal relationships.

We learned history and English. When a new greenhorn came to the class, frightened and confused, unable to manage any English, all knew that within six months he would be able to stand before us and, heavy accent and all, recite:

> *I love the name of Washington,*
> *I love my country, too.*
> *I love the flag, the dear old flag,*
> *The red, the white, the blue.*

This public-school system also provided many of us with an understanding of the Christian world, which heretofore had been a strange and forbidding world. The first Christians the younger Jews knew were the public-school teachers, far different from those Christians our parents muttered about who had populated Europe. These public-school teachers were sexless saints to most of us, and we fully believed they were unencumbered by the usual physical apparatus that slowed everyone else down. We considered these teachers the most wonderful people in the world, and it is surprising to remember the awe in which the Jewish community held them. . . .

Libraries

The vast majority of the immigrants wanted their children to reflect the life and culture of America, and as quickly as possible. There were mothers unable to speak a word of English who went to the branch library on Rivington Street and simply held up to the librarian a finger for each child. And the librarian issued cards, one for each finger. The mother went home and distributed the cards to her offspring and instructed them: "Go. Go and learn. Go now."

I have insisted that the public school was the greatest influence on the immigrant Jews. Next in importance was the library, followed by the settlement house and the clubs they fostered.

Night Schools, Colleges, and Clubs

The night schools of the East Side are used by practically no other race. City College, New York University, and Columbia University are graduating Russian Jews in numbers rapidly increasing. Many lawyers, indeed, children of patriarchal Jews, have very large practices already, and some of them belong to solid firms on Wall Street, although as to business and financial matters they have not yet attained to the most spectacular height. Then there are innumerable boys' debating clubs, ethical clubs, and literary clubs in the East Side. Altogether there is an excitement in ideas and an enthusiastic energy for acquiring knowledge which has interesting analogy to the hopefulness and acquisitive desire of the early Renaissance. It is a mistake to think that the young Hebrew turns naturally to trade. He turns his energy to whatever offers the best opportunities for broader life and success. Other things besides business are open to him in this country, and he is improving his chance for the higher education as devotedly as he has improved his opportunities for success in business.

Hutchins Hapgood, *The Spirit of the Ghetto: Studies of the Jewish Quarter in New York,*
New York, 1965. With preface and notes by Harry Golden.

Immigrants were troubled as they realized that the Americanization of their children was often accompanied by a rejection of their past and their traditions. Would that spell the end of Judaism, they wondered. The sociologist Marcus Lee Hansen, however, noted a remarkable phenomenon that is now known as Hansen's Principle: "What the son wishes to forget, the grandson wishes to remember." Can this account for the tremendous resurgence of interest in Judaism in our times?

Advice to the Immigrants

Before Ann Landers and Dear Abby, the Jewish Daily Forward, *in 1906, conceived the idea of a daily advice column to "greeners"—the newly arrived and confused immigrants struggling to understand American life. This daily feature, known as* A Bintel Brief *(A Bundle of Letters), became extremely popular, and its reflection of the problems, the mind-sets, and the mores of the writers gives us perhaps the best insight into Jewish life of those days.*

Selections from *A Bintel Brief*

Yiddish or English? (1933)
Worthy Editor,

I am sure that the problem I'm writing about affects many Jewish homes. It deals with immigrant parents and their American-born children.

My parents, who have been readers of your paper for years, came from Europe. They have been here in this country over thirty years and were married twenty-eight years ago. They have five sons, and I am one of them. The oldest of us is twenty-seven and the youngest twenty-one.

We are all making a decent living. One of us works for the State Department. A second is a manager in a large store, two are in business and the youngest is studying law. Our parents do not need our help because my father has a good job.

We, the five brothers, always speak English to each other. Our parents know English too, but they speak only Yiddish, not just among themselves but to us too, and even to our American friends who come to visit us. We beg them not to speak Yiddish in the presence of our friends, since they can speak English, but they don't want to. It's a sort of stubbornness on their part, and a great deal of quarreling goes on between our parents and ourselves because of it.

Their answer is: "Children, we ask you not to try to teach us how to talk to people. We are older than you."

Imagine, even when we go with our father to buy something in a store on Fifth Avenue, New York, he insists on speaking Yiddish. We are not ashamed of our parents, God forbid, but they ought to know where it's proper and where it's not. If they talk Yiddish among themselves at home, or to us, it's bad enough, but among strangers and Christians? Is that nice? It looks as if they're doing it to spite us. Petty spats grow out of it. They want to keep only to their old ways and don't want to take up our new ways.

We beg you, friend Editor, to express your opinion on this question, and if possible send us your answer in English, because we can't read Yiddish.

Accept our thanks for your answer, which we expect soon,

Respectfully,

I and the Four Brothers

Answer:

We see absolutely no crime in the parents' speaking Yiddish to their sons. The Yiddish language is dear to them and they want to speak in that language to their children and all who understand it. It may also be that they are ashamed to speak their imperfect English among strangers so they prefer to use their mother tongue.

From the letter, we get the impression that the parents are not fanatics, and with their speaking Yiddish they are not out to spite the children. But it would certainly not be wrong if the parents were to speak English too, to the children. People should and must learn the language of their country.

Eating Non-Kosher Meat (1952)

Dear Editor,

The question came up in our family as to how religious parents who keep strictly kosher should act when they come to visit their children who do not keep kosher homes. Should religious people eat non-kosher meat when they are at their children's homes in order not to insult them?

My opinion is that non-religious children respect their religious parents more when they live up to their beliefs and don't eat non-kosher foods. Others in the family do not agree with me.

I say that in America, where, thank God, there is enough food, everyone can indulge himself with whatever food he desires. And when children know that their parents keep a kosher home, they should not even think of serving them non-kosher meat.

The parents do not visit that often, and the children should not find it difficult to make a dinner that they know is kosher and can eat. They should do this out of respect for their parents. But not everybody in the family agrees with me. Therefore I decided to write to you for your opinion. The fact is that parents are concerned because they think their children will be insulted if they don't eat the food they prepare.

With respect and thanks, M.A.

Answer:

We cannot imagine that children would demand of their religious parents that they eat their non-kosher food. In such a case, the parents do not have to adapt to the children's way, but just the opposite. Not the children but the parents should feel insulted when they come to visit and are served a non-kosher meal.

The "Good Old Days" (1956)

Dear Friend Editor,

I was sitting with a group of old friends who were speaking nostalgically about the "good old days," and I interrupted with the question, Were the old days really that good? In connection with the discussion we had, we would like to hear your opinion.

I think that when older people long for the old days and say it was better then, it's only because they were young and still had their whole lives before them. But the truth is that those times were not so good.

I still remember my hometown in Russia, our simple little house lighted at night by a small kerosene lamp, the door thatched with straw nailed down with sackcloth to keep it warm in winter. I still remember the mud in the streets of the town, so deep it was difficult to get around; our fear of the Gentiles; and who can forget the poverty—the times when there wasn't even a crust of bread?

When we came to New York, I thought we were entering heaven. But here in the new land, in those old days, we lived on the East Side in tenements and had to climb to the fourth and fifth floors to tiny rooms that were dark and airless. There were no bathrooms in the flats. A large bathtub stood in the kitchen near the old iron stove that was heated with coal in which mothers also did the laundry.

In those "good days" we worked in the shops fourteen and sixteen hours a day, six days a week, and the bosses treated the workers like slaves. Summertime, in the great heat, we couldn't breathe in the house at night and we slept on the roofs or on the sidewalks.

When I think of the modern conveniences we live with now, of the wonderful inventions, achievements in various fields that we enjoy, and about the opportunities for everyone in this blessed country, I see there's nothing to be nostalgic about. I say we now have the good times and we do not have to long for the past.

Not all my friends agree with me, and it will be interesting for us to hear what you have to say about it.

With great respect, K.S.

Answer:

Your conclusion is correct. The little town with its mud, the poor hut with the kerosene lamp, the bitter life in czarist Russia and the old-time sweatshops here, contrast dramatically with today's comfortable life in our country. It's like the difference between day and night.

But it is natural for the older immigrant to see that past in beautiful colors. His longing is actually not for that time but for his childhood, his youth, when he was happy with very little.

Isaac Metzker, *A Bintel Brief,* New York, 1971

American Success Story: Louis D. Brandeis

The ladder of success has many rungs. Of course anti-Semitism had its share of disciples even in America—no less prominent a figure than Henry Ford was behind a spate of scurrilous, brutal attacks against Jews in papers such as the Dearborn Independent—*but that didn't prevent the talented from rising to the very top. Perhaps the United States hasn't been ready for a Jewish president, but it is mind-boggling to realize that a Jew, Louis D. Brandeis, was appointed to serve on the Supreme Court in 1916, a position he held with great distinction until his retirement in 1939. In an interview given in 1910, Brandeis made clear what he thought of the role of the Jew in America and what limitations he might have to face because of his religion:*

From *The Advocate* (December 2, 1910)

Question: "Do you believe in a Jewish mission; that is, do you agree with those who say that the Jews are a chosen people whose mission it is to preserve and spread their religion?" asked the interviewer.

Brandeis replied affirmatively and added:

> I believe further that the Jews can be just as much of a priest people today as they ever were in the prophetic days. Their mission is one that will endure forever. The Jewish prophet may struggle for truth and righteousness today just as the ancient prophets did. Nobody takes greater pride than I do in the success of the individual Jews. I mean success in the higher sense, not success that spells dollars. And the opportunity for Jewish success was never greater here than it is today. The Jews in America will be what they themselves decide. America has done its share for the Jew, just as it has done its part for others. It is now for the Jew to say where he will stand in American life. America needs his help.

> Allon Gal, *Brandeis of Boston*, Cambridge, Mass., 1980

With the passage of time, other Jews filled the prestigious position of Supreme Court Justice. What is more remarkable, as Supreme Court Justice Ruth Bader Ginsburg pointed out in her address to the University of Louisville's Louis D. Brandeis School of Law in 2003, the appointment was no longer considered "filling a Jewish seat."

Justice, Guardian of Liberty

The first Jew to accept nomination to the U.S. Supreme Court, of course, was Louis D. Brandeis. Brandeis graduated from Harvard Law School in

1876 at age 20, with the highest scholastic average in that law school's history. He maintained close and continuing relationships with his teachers there and, at age 26, was called back to lecture on the law of evidence.

During his days at the bar, Brandeis was sometimes called "the people's attorney," descriptive of his activity in the great social and economic reform movements of his day. He helped to create the pro bono tradition in the United States. Brandeis made large donations of his wealth from practice to good causes, and he lived frugally at home. A friend recounted that, whenever he went to the Brandeis house for dinner, he ate before and afterward.

Brandeis was appointed to the Court by President Woodrow Wilson in 1916. Like me, he was 60 years old at the time of his appointment. One of his colleagues, James Clark McReynolds, was openly anti-Semitic, as were some detractors at the time of his nomination. When Brandeis spoke in conference, McReynolds would rise and leave the room. No official photograph was taken of the Court in 1924 because McReynolds refused to sit next to Brandeis, where McReynolds, appointed by Wilson two years before Brandeis, belonged on the basis of seniority.

Most people who encountered Brandeis were of a different view. President Franklin Delano Roosevelt, among others, called Brandeis not "Judas," but "Isaiah." Admirers, both Jewish and Gentile, turned to the scriptures to find words adequate to describe his contributions to American constitutional thought.

Brandeis was not a participant in religious ceremonies or services, but he was an ardent Zionist, and he encouraged the next two Jewish Justices—Benjamin Cardozo and Felix Frankfurter—to become members of the Zionist Organization of America.

Jews abroad who needed to flee from anti-Semitism, Brandeis urged, would have a home in the land of Israel, a place to build a new society, a fair and open one, he hoped, free from the prejudices that marked much of Europe; Jews comfortably situated in the United States, in a complementary way, would have a mission, an obligation to help their kinsmen build that new land.

Law as protector of the oppressed, the poor, the minority, the loner, is evident in the life body of work of Brandeis, as it is in the legacies of Cardozo, Frankfurter, Arthur Goldberg and Abe Fortas, the remaining four of the first five Jewish Justices. Frankfurter, once distressed when the Court rejected his view in a case, reminded his brethren, defensively, that he "belong[ed] to the most vilified and persecuted minority in history." I prefer Goldberg's affirmative comment: "My concern for justice, for peace, for enlightenment," he said, "stem[s] from my heritage."

The other Jewish Justices could have reached the same judgment. Justice Stephen Breyer and I are fortunate to be linked to that heritage. But Breyer's situation and mine is distinct from that of the first five Jewish Justices.

Consider President Bill Clinton's appointments in 1993 and 1994 of the 107th and 108th Justices, Breyer and me. Our backgrounds had strong resemblances: We had taught law for several years and served on federal courts of appeals for more years. And we are both Jews. In contrast to Frankfurter, Goldberg and Fortas, however, no one regarded Ginsburg or Breyer as filling a "Jewish seat." Both of us take pride in and draw strength from our heritage, but our religion simply was not relevant to Clinton's appointments.

The security I feel is shown by the command from Deuteronomy displayed in artworks, in Hebrew letters, on three walls and a table in my chambers. "*Zedek, Zedek,*" "Justice, Justice shalt thou pursue," these art works proclaim; they are ever present reminders of what judges must do "that they may thrive." There is also a large silver mezuza mounted on my door post. It is a gift from the super bright teenage students at the Shulamith School for Girls in Brooklyn, N.Y., the school one of my dearest law clerks attended.

Jews in the United States, I mean to convey, face few closed doors and do not fear letting the world know who we are.

American Success Story: Jacob Schiff

"Making it" in America also means achieving financial success. Here too there were many Jews who proved that their religious identity was no barrier to reaching the top. Immigrating to the United States in 1865, Jacob Schiff soon became a multimillionaire, heading the banking firm of Kuhn, Loeb and Company, and playing a crucial role in the nascent railroad industry. Particularly interesting is a decision he made that would prove to have international political ramifications. Remembering the czar's cruelty to his people, Schiff decided to support Japan in its war against Russia in 1904 by arranging for over $196 million in loans. As a result, Japan won the war and a Jew was honored by the emperor with the Order of the Rising Son. In Schiff's diary, he described his feelings at the farewell dinner in his honor in this toast:

We came as strangers, but you received us with open arms and soon we were strangers no longer. I know you desired to show your appreciation of the service it was my good fortune to be able to render your country at a time when it needed friends. But now that this account has been so liberally balanced by you, may I not express the hope, if we should come again, or if it should be our still greater privilege to welcome any of you in our own homes, that no other motive will then be needed for our hearts to open to each other than friend meets friend! By no word in our own language can I so adequately express what I, and with me, no doubt, Mrs. Schiff and our friends, would wish to say in this parting hour than by your own "Sayanora"—"if it must be." And now I lift my glass to your health and to your happiness and to the prosperity of your country—Sayanora.

Jacob Schiff, *The Diary of Jacob Schiff*, New York, 1907

> Sometimes the course of history is guided by a strong feeling of gratitude. In World War II, Japan became Hitler's ally, but it would not join in the German program of genocide. Among the reasons was the Japanese government's memory of a major kindness extended many years before by a Jew that helped save their country!

American Success Story: Hank Greenberg

Jews have enriched the worlds of culture—the media, the arts, and entertainment—far out of proportion to their numbers. Jews became literary lions, social celebrities, trendsetters, and Nobel Prize winners. Some observers of the national scene went so far as to say that in America, Jews went from being hated to being envied. Perhaps most amazing of all, in light of the first immigrants' disdain for athletics, was the fact that Jews became superstars even in sports—and weren't ashamed to maintain their traditions when they came in conflict with the demands of the national pastime. America won't soon forget the World Series game that was played without the bat of Hank Greenberg.

Yom Kippur, the Day of Atonement and the holiest day in the Jewish calendar, fell in the regular season, and in 1934 Greenberg's Detroit Tigers were involved in the pennant race. Greenberg wrote in his autobiography, "The team was fighting for first place, and I was probably the only batter in the lineup who was not in a slump. But in the Jewish religion, it is traditional that one observe the holiday solemnly, with prayer. One should not engage in work or play. And I wasn't sure what to do." Greenberg's rabbi said that Rosh Hashanah was a "festive holiday" and playing on that day would be acceptable. Hank played and hit two home runs, including a ninth-inning game winner. "I caught hell from my fellow parishioners, I caught hell from some rabbis, and I don't know what to do. It's ten days until the next holiday—Yom Kippur." Those words, and his choice not to play on Yom Kippur due to its solemn significance, inspired Edgar Guest to write the following famous piece in the Detroit Free Press:

> Came Yom Kippur—holy fast day world wide over to the Jew,
> And Hank Greenberg to his teaching and the old tradition true
> Spent the day among his people and he didn't come to play.
> Said Murphy to Mulrooney, "We shall lose the game today!
> We shall miss him on the infield and shall miss him at the bat
> But he's true to his religion—and I honor him for that!"

The Tigers lost that game, won the pennant, and lost the World Series. The next year, 1936, they won the series, and Greenberg was voted Most Valuable Player—the first Jewish player to earn MVP status in either league.

> American tradition has it that the "the game must go on." Jewish tradition demands that deeply felt convictions should take priority over other commitments. Where and under what circumstances should we draw the line between the two?

American Success Story: Albert Einstein

There is one man who towers above all others. Forced to flee the country of his birth as a despised Jew, Albert Einstein became not only the most influential person of his lifetime but, as Time *magazine would pronounce him in its issue welcoming the year 2000, "The Man of the Century." An American icon, Einstein redefined "hero" in a way that might well be called Jewish. As* Time *magazine put it, Einstein replaced the cowboy with the intellectual:*

> *He was the first modern intellectual superstar, and he won his stardom in the only way that Americans could accept—by dint of intuitive, not scholarly, intelligence and by having his thought applied to practical things, such as rockets and atom bombs. . . . The recognition of the practical power of his ideas coincided with a time when such power was most needed. Einstein came to America in 1933 as the most celebrated of a distinguished group of European intellectuals, refugees from Hitler and Mussolini, who, as soon as they arrived, changed the composition of university faculties (largely from patrician to Jewish), and who also changed the composition of government. Until F.D.R.'s New Deal, the country had never associated the contemplative life*

with governmental action. Now there was a Brain Trust; being an
"egghead" was useful, admirable, even sexy. One saw that it was pos-
sible to outthink the enemy. Einstein wrote a letter to Roosevelt urging
the making of a uranium bomb, and soon a coterie of can-do intellec-
tuals convened at Los Alamos to become the new cowboys of war
machinery. Presidents have relied on eggheads ever since: Einstein
begat Kissinger begat Rubin, Reich, and Greenspan.

The following letter, signed by Einstein, was delivered to President Roosevelt on
October 11, 1939. It changed the course of history.

The Letter That Saved the World

Sir:

Some recent work by E. Fermi and L. Szilard, which has been communicated to me in manuscript, leads me to expect that the element uranium
may be turned into a new and important source of energy in the immediate future. Certain aspects of the situation which has arisen seem to call
for watchfulness and, if necessary, quick action on the part of the
Administration. I believe therefore that it is my duty to bring to your
attention the following facts and recommendations.

In the course of the last four months it has been made probable—
through the work of Joliot in France as well as Fermi and Szilard in
America—that it may become possible to set up a nuclear chain reaction
in a large mass of uranium, by which vast amounts of power and large
quantities of new radium-like elements would be generated. Now it
appears almost certain that this could be achieved in the immediate future.

This new phenomenon would also lead to the construction of bombs,
and it is conceivable—though much less certain—that extremely powerful
bombs of a new type may thus be constructed. A single bomb of this type,
carried by boat and exploded in a port, might very well destroy the whole
port together with some of the surrounding territory. However, such
bombs might very well prove to be too heavy for transportation by air.

The United States has only very poor ores of uranium in moderate
quantities. There is good ore in Canada and the former Czechoslovakia,
while the most important source of uranium is the Belgian Congo.

In view of this situation you may think it desirable to have some permanent contact maintained between the Administration and the group of
physicists working on chain reactions in America. One possible way of
achieving this might be for you to entrust with this task a person who has

your confidence who could perhaps serve in an unofficial capacity. His task might comprise the following:

a) To approach Government Departments, keep them informed of the further development, and put forward recommendations for Government action, giving particular attention to the problems of securing a supply of uranium ore for the United States.

b) To speed up the experimental work, which is at present being carried on within the limits of the budgets of University laboratories, by providing funds, if such funds be required, through his contacts with private persons who are willing to make contributions for this cause, and perhaps also by obtaining the co-operation of industrial laboratories which have the necessary equipment.

I understand that Germany has actually stopped the sale of uranium from the Czechoslovakian mines which she has taken over. That she should have taken such early action might perhaps be understood on the ground that the son of the German Under-Secretary of State, von Weizaecker, is attached to the Kaiser-Wilhelm-Institut in Berlin where some of the American work on uranium is now being repeated.

A. Einstein

In great part as a result of this letter, America initiated the Manhattan Project in June of 1942. That enabled the United States to complete an atomic weapon before either Germany or Japan, effectively ensuring victory in World War II.

One of the most fascinating games of history is to conjecture "What would have happened if . . . ?" What would have happened if Hitler had not hated the Jews enough to make Einstein flee Europe? What would have happened if there had been no Jews working on the Manhattan Project? And what would have happened to the civilized world if there were no Jews—the very plan that Hitler tried so hard to implement?

23

The Horrors of the Holocaust

Perhaps, as Elie Weisel, the Nobel Prize–winning scribe of the Holocaust put it, the only fitting response to the Holocaust is silence. To do more is to diminish a tragedy that can only be distorted if reduced to mere words. The Holocaust stands in a category all by itself as expression of evil—not only in the history of the Jews but perhaps in the history of mankind. The Holocaust introduced a new word into human vocabulary: genocide, the deliberate and systematic destruction of an entire people. It brought with it the concept of a government-sponsored attempt to eradicate a defined group not for what they believe or for what they do but simply because of who they are. Nazi Germany did not want to convert Jews to any faith or political system; it simply wanted to eliminate them. Had the Third Reich achieved its goal, not a single Jew would have remained alive. It is frightening to realize how close they came. The final tally of Jewish victims is commonly estimated to be about six million. The immensity of the number conceals the deeper truth that every one of these millions was, as Anne Frank made so clear in her now-classic diary, a human being with loved ones, with dreams, and with a longing for life. It is Anne Frank multiplied six million times over who was cruelly and sadistically murdered. It is many untold others, people we ironically label "survivors," who will never survive the horrible nightmares that will continue to hound them until their deaths.

How could the Holocaust have happened? A satisfactory answer will probably never be found. There are those who would lay the blame on one man. Adolf Hitler became chancellor of Germany in 1933 and immediately pursued the vision set forth *in his manifesto,* Mein Kampf. *Two goals consumed him, and he saw them as insep-arable: a new world order with Germany ruling the rest of the world and the total elimination of the Jewish people. Why this obsession with Jews? Hitler himself explained it: "Yes, we are barbarians! We want to be barbarians! It is an honorable title. . . . Providence has ordained that I should be the greatest liberator of human-ity. I am freeing men from . . . the dirty and degrading self-mortifications of a false vision, a Jewish invention called 'conscience' and 'morality.'" Others place the blame on the German people, willing accomplices in the vicious "Final Solution" that included concentration camps and crematoria. Some include an entire world for indictment, a world that stood silently by as atrocities grew progressively greater.*

In 1935 Germany passed the Nuremberg Laws, canceling all the rights Jews had won after the Enlightenment. On November 9, 1938, the infamous Kristallnacht— *"the night of broken glass"—191 synagogues were destroyed, and 91 Jews were killed, many beaten to death. To add further insult, Jews were fined a billion marks (equal to about 400 million dollars) for the damage that was caused by the Germans! The response from the world? Almost none.*

The Germans now understood. They could kill all the Jews, and no one would say a word.

The Plan: Himmler Orders His Soldiers

Address by Heinrich Himmler at Posen, October 4, 1943

I shall speak to you here with all frankness of a very serious subject. We shall now discuss it absolutely openly among ourselves, nevertheless we shall never speak of it in public. I mean the evacuation of the Jews, the extermination of the Jewish race. It is one of those things which is easy to say. "The Jewish race is to be exterminated," says every party member. "That's clear, it's part of our program, elimination of the Jews, extermina-tion, right, we'll do it."

And then they all come along, the eighty million good Germans, and each one has his decent Jew. Of course the others are swine, but this one is a first-class Jew. Of all those who talk like this, not one has watched, not one has stood up to it.

Most of you know what it means to see a hundred corpses lying together, five hundred, or a thousand. To have gone through this and yet— apart from a few exceptions, examples of human weakness—to have remained decent fellows, this is what has made us hard. This is a glorious page in our history that has never been written and shall never be written.

We have taken from them what wealth they had. I have issued a strict order, which SS-Obergruppenführer Pohl has carried out, that this wealth should, as a matter of course, be handed over to the Reich without reserve.

We had the moral right, we had the duty to our people, to destroy this people which wanted to destroy us.

Altogether, however, we can say, that we have fulfilled this most diffi-cult duty for the love of our people. And our spirit, our soul, our charac-ter has not suffered injury from it.

Paul R. Mendes Flohr and Jehuda Reinharz, eds., The Jew in the Modern World:
A Documentary History, New York, 1995

Did the World Know?

Samuel Zygelbojm managed to flee from Poland in 1940. In London in 1942, he tried desperately to draw the attention of the Allied governments to the fate of the Jews. When the news of the revolt in the Warsaw Ghetto came, and with it the final phase of the extermination, Zygelbojm committed suicide as an act of protest against the indifference of the Allied governments to the fate of his people. Before his death he wrote the Polish government the following letter, which was transmitted to the British and American governments:

"A Protest against the Indifference of the World"

With these, my last words, I address myself to you, the Polish Government, the Polish people, the Allied Governments and their peoples, and the con-science of the world.

News recently received from Poland informs us that the Germans are exterminating with unheard-of savagery the remaining Jews in that coun-try. Behind the walls of the ghetto is taking place today the last act of a tragedy which has no parallel in the history of the human race. The respon-sibility for this crime—the assassination of the Jewish population in Poland—rests above all on the murderers themselves, but falls indirectly upon the whole human race, on the Allies and their governments, who so far have taken no firm steps to put a stop to these crimes. By their indiffer-ence to the killing of millions of hapless men, to the massacre of women and children, these countries have become accomplices of the assassins.

Furthermore, I must state that the Polish Government, although it has done a great deal to influence world public opinion, has not taken ade-quate measures to counter this atrocity which is taking place today in Poland. Of the three and a half million Polish Jews (to whom must be added the 700,000 deported from the other countries) in April, 1943, there remained alive not more than 300,000 Jews according to news received from the head of the Bund organization and supplied by government representatives. And the extermination continues.

I cannot remain silent. I cannot live while the rest of the Jewish people in Poland, whom I represent, continue to be liquidated.

My companions of the Warsaw Ghetto fell in a last heroic battle with their weapons in their hands. I did not have the honor to die with them but I belong to them and to their common grave. Let my death be an energetic cry of protest against the indifference of the world which witnesses the extermination of the Jewish people without taking any steps to prevent it. In our day and age human life is of little value; having failed to achieve success in my life, I hope that my death may jolt the indifference of those who, perhaps even in this extreme moment, could save the Jews who are still alive in Poland.

My life belongs to my people in Poland and that is why I am sacrificing it for them. May the handful of people who will survive out of the millions of Polish Jews achieve liberation in a world of liberty and socialist justice together with the Polish people.

I think that there will be a free Poland and that it is possible to achieve a world of justice. I am certain that the President of the Republic and the head of the government will pass on my words to all concerned. I am sure that the Polish Government will hasten to adopt the necessary political measures and will come to the aid of those who are still alive.

I take my leave of all those who have been dear to me and whom I have loved.

Samuel Zygelbojm

Jacob Glatstein, Israel Knox, and Samuel Margoshes, eds.,
An Anthology of Holocaust Literature, New York, 1969

What It Was Like: Testimony from Those Who Were There

The only way to get an inkling of how the German plan of genocide was carried out is to listen to the oral testimony given by survivors. As we hear their voices we have to bear in mind that we are listening only to the "lucky" ones who did not perish; those who did not survive have no one to tell their stories.

Coming to Hell: The Testimony of Lucille Eichengreen

Interviewer: Did you stand the whole way (in the sealed boxcar transporting you to Auschwitz)?

Eichengreen: No, we sort of crouched in corners, there wasn't much room but we sort of crouched together. When the door opened, the first thing we saw was huge spotlights, from the platform onto the train. We saw the SS and the dogs.

I: It was night time?

E: It was four in the morning, three in the morning. A lot of screaming, a lot of commands. They hurried us out of the trains. We were barely out when they said to drop the luggage. The suitcase or whatever we had. My friend dropped hers. I did not. One of the SS came towards me, with I don't know, either a gun or a whip. And she tore it out of my hand and dropped it. I didn't want to give up my passport and my papers and my birth certificate. You know, I can't live without it. Almost immediately they separated the men from the women. It took minutes, seconds. We didn't even say good-bye to Oscar or to Erwin, I mean they were just on the other side. And then they tried to separate the women again. The young ones from the old ones, the children from the . . .

I: There were still children at this point?

E: Oh yes, you know little children, two, three, four, six, you know, any age. Not a great deal, but some. I remember a man in a striped uniform with a hat, with an armband that read Kapo, standing next to us. And my friend asked him in German, where are we? He said, Auschwitz. She said, what's Auschwitz? And he said, you've never heard of Auschwitz? And she said, no. He said, it can't be. When he asked where do you come from, we said from Lodz. He said, do you know Luba? Do you know anybody named Luba, I'm looking for my sister. But I work as sort of a policeman, Kapo, for the Germans. We said, no we don't know anybody and we left. From that, after that separation, you know the young ones from the old ones, we went into a room, into a barracks. They asked to take off all jewelry, all watches, all clothing. And whoever didn't took a terrible beating or worse. And there we stood naked, shivering in the heat, and then they took us to another barracks. Something happened in front of us, we didn't know quite what. The people in front of us sort of moved, moved ahead.

I: Were you all basically in a line?

E: No, it wasn't really a line, it was a line and a line and a line, it was almost like a grouping. When we were in the front line we saw that the Kapos were shaving the hair, all body hair. And if you looked at the women, once the hair was shaven it was just, it was a sight that was so terrible that it really didn't, at that moment, compare to anything we had seen. You saw those bowling balls with protruding ears and those frightened eyes and it was like, something out of a nightmare. They yanked Ellie out of line and they cut her, she had long black hair, they cut her hair and before I knew it I was next. The SS woman who gave the order to the Kapo, who was essentially a prisoner, to shave my hair, was short and blonde and squat. And fat, the uniform didn't fit and she wore glasses. I hated her, I don't think I've ever hated anybody as much. I don't know whether she saw or whether she felt, but she slapped me very hard and I just reeled over to one side. After the hair was gone, they pushed us through sort of a swinging door and the top part of the swinging door was glass. And in one second I saw a reflection that was I. Ears, an oval head, and eyes. It was nobody I knew. It was horrifying, that sight. There was some cold showers, we were sort of rushed through them, if you got a drop of water, yes, if you didn't you didn't. At the other end an SS woman started laughing and she said, the gas chambers are overworked tonight, or today. We'll get you tomorrow. There's plenty of time. We had never heard of gas chambers. We didn't know what it was.

We were thrown a garment at random, just a piece of cloth, whether it was an apron, a dress, just one piece, no underwear, no stockings, nothing. You put that thing on, mine was black and it had sort of a red trim on the top, very strange, very large. It was sort of like cotton. And we were lined up again in groups of five. The fifth in our group, which was my friend Ellie and I, and her mother and her aunt, and the fifth woman was a little woman named Alice, from Vienna. She got some wooden clogs. Nobody else had them, she had wooden shoes, you know these Dutch shoes? And they started marching us, we didn't know that the camp was called Birkenau, start marching us to the barracks. And we passed an orchestra, with the conductor in an impeccable uniform with white gloves, conducting Beethoven, I think it was Beethoven. These people with shaven heads and striped uniforms, playing music. And on the other side we saw three chimneys with black smoke. Somebody whispered in back of us, "The crematorium." We didn't know what it was, why, what for, nothing. But we learned.

We were crammed into the barracks and the center of the barracks had a walkway, and on either side were sort of chessboard squares. Five people were allocated to a square. You could barely seat five people in a square.

But we wondered what we were going to do at night, because you can't sit forever. So Ellie sat down against the back wall, she spread her legs, and the next person would sit against her until all five of us were in that position. And then we would lie down so everybody could lie on somebody's stomach. But you couldn't turn, you couldn't move. Soup came in sometime in the evening, but no plates, no spoons, nothing. Some people scooped it into their hands and it was running through their fingers. Somebody said to Alice, take off your shoes. Alice took off the wooden clogs, and Ellie took one and Alice took one and they stood in line. They filled them up with soup and they ate the soup like animals, out of the shoes. Then they gave them to us and we did the same. And then Alice put the shoes back on. That was the end.

The Kapo in this barracks was a young woman, Jewish, I don't know whether she was from Hungary or from Poland. She yelled a great deal and she ran around with a reed or stick, and anything in her way she would beat. And she took her orders from the Germans.

In the morning they would round us up and we would stand for a spell and they would count us and recount us for hours and hours. It was freezing cold, at five in the morning or whatever, and by noon it was boiling hot, my whole scalp was full of blisters from the sun, the ears. And this went on for a few weeks, maybe two or three weeks I'm not sure of the exact amount of days, and then we were told, she told us, that tomorrow morning Dr. Mengele will inspect. Procedure is, you take off your dress, you carry it over your left arm, and you walk past that committee of three, Mengele and two others, as fast as you can. He'll indicate right or left. So Ellie and I decided that I go first, she follows me. We go very fast, we don't look right we don't look left, just almost run. I almost fell but I made it. And he motioned me to one side and Ellie to the same side.

Holocaust Oral History Project, San Francisco, August 14, 1990

An Ordinary Day: The Testimony of Dov Freiburg

I shall tell the story of one day, an ordinary day, much like any other. That day I worked at cleaning a shed. . . . An umbrella had gotten stuck in a roof beam, and the SS man Paul Groth ordered a boy to get it down. The boy climbed up, fell from the roof and was injured. Groth punished him with 25 lashes. He was pleased with what had happened and called over another German and told him he had found "parachutists" among the Jews. We were ordered to climb up to the roof one after another. . . . The majority did not succeed; they fell down, broke legs, were whipped, bitten by Barry, the German shepherd, and shot.

This game was not enough for Groth. There were many mice around, and each of us was ordered to catch two mice. He selected five prisoners, ordered them to pull down their trousers, and we dropped the mice inside. The people were ordered to remain at attention, but they could not without moving. They were whipped.

But this was not enough for Groth. He called over a Jew, forced him to drink alcohol until he fell dead. . . . We were ordered to lay the man on a board, pick him up and slowly march while singing a funeral march.

This is a description of one ordinary day. And many of them were even worse.

In Yitzchak Arad, *Belzec, Sobibor, Treblinka: The Operation Reinhard Death Camps*, Indianapolis, Ind., 1987

Jewish Resistance

Not all Jews went passively to their deaths like sheep to slaughter. True, since they were unarmed and unprepared, resistance was in most cases simply impossible. Yet there were some remarkable instances of incredible bravery. The Warsaw Ghetto uprising in the spring of 1943 is one of these. For one month, a wildly outnumbered group of ghetto inhabitants held off an army of highly mobilized German soldiers— with 17 rifles against 1,358 pieces of Nazi artillery. The ghetto was finally destroyed, and all those hiding in bunkers were burned alive. But Mordecai Anilewicz, the commander of the uprising, left us this final message.

"The Last Wish of My Life"

It is now clear to me that what took place exceeded all expectations. In our opposition to the Germans we did more than our strength allowed—but now our forces are waning. We are on the brink of extinction. We forced the Germans to retreat twice—but they returned stronger than before.

One of our groups held out for forty minutes; and another fought for about six hours. The mine which was laid in the area of the brush factory exploded as planned. Then we attacked the Germans and they suffered heavy casualties. Our losses were generally low. That is an accomplishment too. Z. fell, next to his machine-gun. I feel that great things are happening and that this action which we have dared to take is of enormous value.

We have no choice but to go over to partisan methods of fighting as of today. Tonight, six fighting-groups are going out. They have two tasks—to reconnoitre the area and to capture weapons. Remember, "short-range weapons" are of no use to us. We employ them very rarely. We need many rifles, hand-grenades, machine-guns and explosives.

I cannot describe the conditions in which the Jews of the ghetto are now "living." Only a few exceptional individuals will be able to survive such suffering. The others will sooner or later die. Their fate is certain, even though thousands are trying to hide in cracks and rat holes. It is impossible to light a candle for lack of air. Greetings to you who are out-side. Perhaps a miracle will occur and we shall see each other again one of these days. It is extremely doubtful.

The last wish of my life has been fulfilled. Jewish self-defense has become a fact. Jewish resistance and revenge have become actualities. I am happy to have been one of the first Jewish fighters in the ghetto.

Where will rescue come from?

Mordecai Anilewicz, in Jacob Glatstein, Israel Knox, and Samuel Margoshes, eds., *An Anthology of Holocaust Literature*, New York, 1969

Spiritual Resistance: Religious Responsa

Unable to physically fight off their oppressors, Jews sought solace in maintaining their faith and their traditions in the face of those who wanted to destroy them. Some of the most moving examples of Jewish spiritual strength are the responsa—accounts of religious questions asked by Jews of their rabbis—during the Holocaust. The selections that follow were recorded by Rabbi Ephraim Oshry, who survived the ghetto of Kovno.

Eventual Danger to Life

Question: Beginning Elul 5701—September 1941, the Jews of Kovno were compelled to work in the airfield next to the city by the Germans who ordered the ghetto Jews to provide 1,000 men daily. Everyone of the slave laborers was allowed one bowl of non-kosher soup as his daily ration plus 100 grams of bread. Many of the laborers understandably refused to defile themselves with this non-kosher soup. But after they grew weak from hunger and from the pressures of hard labor, a number of them came to me in the pre-Yom Kippur days of 5702—late September 1941—and asked if they might be permitted to eat the soup since their lives would ultimately be endangered if they did not eat it.

In brief: Do we look at the present situation, and presently there is no danger to life? Or do we consider that since their lives will eventually be endangered as a result of malnutrition they may already now eat the non-kosher food so as to prevent the eventual danger to their lives?

Response: Medical experts maintained that it was impossible for a person to survive with the nutrition then available to the Jews. The laborers' lives were certainly in danger; famine is an extremely agonizing, drawn-out way to die. I ruled that they might eat the soup now because of the eventual danger to their lives. The rabbi of Kovno, the *gaon* Rav Avrohom DovBer Kahana-Shapira, concurred with me.

Committing Suicide in Order to Be Buried among Jews
Question: On 6 Marcheshvan 5702—October 27, 1941, two days before the horrifying Black Day of the Kovno Ghetto—when some 10,000 men, women, and children were taken away to be butchered—every one of the ghetto dwellers saw his bitter end coming. At that time of confusion, one of the respected members of the community came to me with tears on his cheeks and posed a question of life and death. He felt that he could not bear to see his wife, children, and grandchildren put to death before his very eyes. For the German sadists had a system for extermination. In order for the murderers to enjoy the suffering of their victims, they would kill the children before the eyes of their parents and the women before the eyes of their husbands as a matter of course. Only after satisfying their blood lust in this sadistic fashion, would they put an end to the suffering of the heads of the families. Because he felt certain that it would kill him to witness the horrible suffering of his loved ones, he asked whether he might terminate his own life earlier so as to avoid witnessing the deaths of his loved ones. Besides being spared a horrible death of great suffering at the hands of the accursed murderers, he would also gain burial among Jews in the Jewish cemetery in the ghetto.

Response: Although the man knew he would definitely be subjected to unbearable suffering by the abominable murderers, and so hoped to be buried among Jews, he still was not allowed to commit suicide.

Moreover, permitting suicide in such a case meant surrendering to the abominable enemy. For the Germans often remarked to the Jews, "Why don't you commit suicide as the Jews of Berlin did?" Suicide was viewed as a great desecration of God, for it showed that a person had no trust in God's capability to save him from the accursed hands of his defilers. The murderers' goal was to bring confusion into the lives of the Jews and to cause them the greatest despondency in order to make annihilating them all the easier.

I cite proudly that in the Kovno Ghetto there were only three instances of suicide by people who grew greatly despondent. The rest of the ghetto dwellers trusted and hoped that God would not forsake His People.

Ephraim Oshry, *Responsa from the Holocaust*, trans., Y. Leiman, New York, 1983

> Both responses reflect the overriding emphasis on life in Jewish tradition. To preserve life, one not only *may* eat non-Kosher food, one is *obligated* to do so. That is true with regard to every religious requirement. In the face of death, laws are suspended. The legal rationale for this ruling is that only in life can we continue to serve God. In that light, suicide is a major sin. Even when death is inevitable, it must come about through the hands of others, not our own. How has this passion for life played a role in ensuring Jewish survival?

Fifty million people would perish by the time World War II came to a close in 1945.

For the Jews, the six million victims equaled a third of their world population. In fact, many of those who were liberated thought they were the last living Jews on earth. But the Jews, confronting their greatest challenge of history, had survived.

Hitler's last dispatch before he committed suicide in his bunker demonstrated his obsession with the Jews to the very end: "Above all, I enjoin the leaders of the nation and those under them to uphold the racial laws of their full extent and to oppose mercilessly the universal poisoner of all peoples, International Jewry." Thankfully, he did not succeed.

The Orphan Who Became Chief Rabbi of Israel

Yisrael Meir Lau, the youngest survivor of the Buchenwald concentration camp, was asked, almost fifty years later, to recall his liberation. What makes his story all the more meaningful is that this eight-year-old orphan went on to become chief rabbi of Israel.

"What the State of Israel Means to Me"

What you are about to read happened 48 years ago. It was after our liberation from the Nazis. After spanning the length of Germany from Buchenwald in East Germany, we arrived in a small village not far from France. We were close to 200 children, most of them from Bergen-Belsen. A few, including myself, were from Buchenwald. In Buchenwald, I was the youngest, only eight years old, but from Bergen-Belsen, there were two who were younger than I.

Orphans all, we were placed temporarily in a kind of convalescent home where we were taught how to "eat" again. First, a quarter-slice of bread, then a half slice. We had to learn to be careful that the food did not slip out of our mouths, for we were not used to eating.

In that sanitarium, a lady, Rachel Mintz, of blessed memory, served as our housemother. She came from Poland to France before the war, and later was put in charge of this home. She spoke Polish and was like a mother to us.

One day, after lunch, she requested that we do her a favor. "Today at 4 p.m.," she said, "very important guests will arrive on the lawn in the center of the village. These guests are the heads of all the organizations who fund this institution and they will be accompanied by the army commander of the French region, the police commander, the mayor, the governor, as well as all those who sustain this institution." We were to be at the site no later than 4 p.m. to greet them, behave nicely, and applaud their speeches.

After Mrs. Mintz left the dining hall, two or three of us spontaneously organized a protest meeting and declared that "we are not going!" We didn't want any business with the French or the Poles. The Poles helped the Nazis, while the French just stood idly by. That day they were coming to be photographed with us, the orphans. We were already aware that wherever we came, we were an "attraction." People would request to be photographed with us, and the next day they would arrive in Paris or in America and show off a picture "together with children of the Holocaust."

Our sentiments were: "Leave us alone. We did not come to you. This is only a transit station. We are on our way home to Eretz Yisrael. We're not interested in the French, not in the army, not in the police, and not in the mayor." We then sent a delegation to Mrs. Mintz to tell her that we were not coming. She knew that the fate of this institution, as well as the fate of the next round of refugees who were scheduled to arrive, depended on those guests. So she began to plead with us: "But you must come; they'll bring presents for each of you."

Now, I don't have to tell you what it means, after six years as "guests" of the Nazis, to come to a child and tell him "Here's a present." But we replied, "No, thank you. Where were they when they slaughtered our parents? They did not scream nor did they lift a finger. Now they're coming to take pictures? No! We don't want that!"

Then she made her final plea—the strongest one. "O.K. Then do it for me. I'm asking you." We came up with a compromise. For the sake of Mrs. Mintz, we would all come, but we would not applaud nor would we look them in the face. We would just sit there with our faces lowered into the ground. We would all be there, but in essence we won't be there.

And that was the way it went. About 20 years later, a long article appeared in a French weekly about the "Children of Buchenwald." It was accompanied by a picture showing people in uniform sitting on a dais, a lady holding an old circa-1945 microphone, and behind her, tens of shaven heads. Not one face was visible, only bald heads.

Mrs. Mintz introduced the guests, and then translated their speeches into Polish. There was deafening silence. Then Mrs. Mintz announced, "The last speaker will be Mr. Goldberg. Mr. Goldberg is a Polish Jew from Lodz, who lost his wife and children in Auschwitz. Since he had business in France before the war, he came here after he was rescued and recovered some of his earlier possessions. Since his entire family had been annihilated, he decided to donate his entire possessions to the surviving children. Part of his donation has sustained the sanitarium in this village."

No one pushed or gave us a hint. Spontaneously, 200 pairs of eyes lifted from the ground and stared at him. After all, he is one of us. Against whom then are we protesting? This Goldberg is part of our flesh and bones. We stared at him and waited for him to speak.

Just to come to this place made Mr. Goldberg so emotional. He became even more emotional when he saw our demonstration. And now, seeing all those pairs of eyes staring at him, his emotions apparently overflowed. He held on to the large microphone, his hands trembling, and all he managed to utter were two or three words: "Kinder, tyere kinder!" Children, dear children! Then he burst into tears. Realizing that he was unable to speak, he returned to his seat.

On the lawn there was dead silence, and suddenly it happened. Each of us began to feel our eyesight becoming blurred and our cheeks wet. We were all embarrassed and afraid to be caught crying. After all that we had endured, it was not befitting for us to cry. We were all trying to wipe our cheeks with our sleeves, but to no avail. Tears began to flow like a river. When we couldn't hold out any longer, we started to cry out loud, releasing all the dammed-up emotions and giving way for our pain to burst. All of us, 200 children, cried out loud, continuously, for five minutes. The lawn became the "Valley of Tears."

After we had calmed down, one of us, a 16-year-old boy named Aharon—I found him 30 years later in the Hadassah Hospital in Jerusalem where he served as a doctor—stood up, and spoke in Polish:

"I arose to say thank you to all of you. Thank you! Not for your visit which we did not request, and not even for the presents that we do not want. Thank you for the one present you gave us now, unintentionally— the ability to cry. This is a big present because for the past couple of years, I have been thinking that I am not normal.

"That I did not laugh for the past two or three years is understandable after all that I went through. In the past two or three years when I did not shed a tear, I began to realize that something in me was frozen, numb. I heard there was a concept called 'a heart of stone,' and I thought this had happened to me, that I will no longer be able to laugh or cry. And five minutes ago, we all received this wonderful present from your visit. We are normal! We can cry! For this, thank you."

And Aharon continued: "I want to share with you my feelings now. Six years ago during the summer of 1939, I was 10 years old. I traveled to Warsaw to spend the summer vacation at my grandfather's house. Grandpa would take me out for walks and learn Tanach (Bible) with me. There were paragraphs which I had to memorize by heart. It has been six years now that I haven't held a Tanach, and I forgot almost everything. But there is one chapter that now, after crying, I remember, and part of it I want to recite before you now. It goes as follows:

"The hand of God was upon me and He set me down in the valley. It was full of bones. . . . He said to me. 'Can these bones live again?' Thus said the Lord: 'I will cause breath to enter into you and you shall live again.' And He said to me, 'these bones are the whole House of Israel. They say: Our bones are dried up, our hope is lost, we are doomed.' Thus said God, 'I will open your graves, and lift you from your graves, O my people, and bring you to the land of Israel.'" (Ezekiel 37)

"We," concluded Aharon, "are the dried up bones. God opened our graves. All of Europe is one big grave, and He raised us from our graves, and we are now on our way to the land of Israel."

My dear readers, I know you understand very well what I have just related to you. There is no need for any symposium or debate on the radio or in newspapers. Regardless of political affiliation, education, or religious observance, there is no need to explain what the State of Israel means.

We are like Joshua and Caleb the son of Jephunneh who stood up against the ten spies who belittled the Land of Israel. Contradicting the majority, Joshua and Caleb insisted that *"Tova ha'aretz meod meod,"* The land is very, very good. If something is missing in Israel, we must search for the fault in ourselves. If there are negative manifestations—and indeed there are many—we are at fault. But why complain against the Land?! *Tova Ha'aretz Meod Meod.*

The Jewish Press, May 7, 1993

24

Welcome Home:
Israel Reborn

E ven in retrospect, it is hard to believe. In the span of three years, the
Jewish people went from death to deliverance. In 1945, when World War
II mercifully ended, Jews reeled as they realized the immensity of their losses. Many
wondered aloud, "Where was God during the Holocaust?" Prognosticators of doom
didn't hesitate to announce that at last the story of the Jews had come to its conclud-
ing chapter. And then came 1948 and the creation of the State of Israel. For the religious, it was no less than a modern-day miracle. For the secular, it was the fulfillment
of a dream that had appeared impossible to attain. "Our hope is not yet lost," the key
phrase in what was later adopted as Israel's national anthem, Hatikvah (The Hope),
had been written many years before (1886) by Naftali Herz Imber. But the optimism
of its words was severely challenged by the cataclysmic events of the 1930s and early
1940s. No scriptwriter would have dared write so incredible a turnabout. Yet it truly
happened: Jews went from genocide to Jerusalem.

Chaim Weizmann and the Balfour Declaration

As with all success stories, though, the truth is that it didn't happen overnight. Many
years of intense struggle preceded this moment. There were the political efforts of
Theodore Herzl as well as the Herculean physical labors of the chalutzim, the early
pioneers in Palestine. And there was Chaim Weizmann, the man who saved England
during World War I and was rewarded with the world's first major proclamation of

support for Palestine as the homeland for the Jewish people. Weizmann, a brilliant chemist, invented TNT for the British army, which played a key role in achieving victory for the Allies. In gratitude, the government passed the Balfour Declaration on November 2, 1917, announcing that "His Majesty's Government view with favor the establishment in Palestine of a national home for the Jewish people and will use their best endeavors to facilitate the achievement of this object."

In this passage from his autobiography, Weizmann recalls meeting Lord Balfour:

"My First Meeting with Lord Balfour"

I was brought in to Balfour in a room in the old-fashioned Queen's Hotel, on Piccadilly, which served as his headquarters. The corridors were crowded with people waiting for a word with the candidate. I surmised that Mr. Balfour had consented to see me for a few minutes—"a quarter of an hour," Dreyfus warned me—simply to break the monotony of his routine. He kept me for well over an hour. . . .

I had been less than two years in the country, and my English was still not easy to listen to. I remember how Balfour sat in his usual pose, his legs stretched out in front of him, an imperturbable expression on his face. We plunged at once into the subject of our interview. He asked me why some Jews, Zionists, were so bitterly opposed to the Uganda offer. The British Government was really anxious to do something to relieve the misery of the Jews; and the problem was a practical one, calling for a practical approach. In reply I plunged into what I recall as a long harangue on the meaning of the Zionist movement. I dwelt on the spiritual side of Zionism. I pointed out that nothing but a deep religious conviction expressed in modern political terms could keep the movement alive, and that this conviction had to be based on Palestine and on Palestine alone. . . .

I looked at my listener, and suddenly became afraid that this apparent interest and courtesy might be nothing more than a mask. I remember that I was sweating blood and I tried to find some less ponderous way of expressing myself. I was ready to bow myself out of the room, but Balfour held me back, and put some questions to me regarding the growth of the movement. He had heard of "Dr. Herzl"—a very distinguished leader, who had founded and organized it. I ventured to correct him, pointing out that Herzl had indeed placed the movement on a new footing, and had given the tradition a modern political setting; but Herzl had died young; and he had left us this legacy of Uganda, which we were trying to liquidate.

Then suddenly I said: "Mr. Balfour, supposing I were to offer you Paris instead of London, would you take it?"

He sat up, looked at me, and answered: "But, Dr. Weizmann, we have London."

"That is true," I said. "But we had Jerusalem when London was a marsh."

He leaned back, continued to stare at me, and said two things which I remember vividly. The first was: "Are there many Jews who think like you?"

I answered: "I believe I speak the mind of millions of Jews whom you will never see and who cannot speak for themselves, but with whom I could pave the streets of the country I come from."

To this he said: "If that is so, you will one day be a force."

Shortly before I withdrew, Balfour said: "It is curious. The Jews I meet are quite different."

I answered: "Mr. Balfour, you meet the wrong kind of Jews."

Chaim Weizmann, Trial and Error: The Autobiography of Chaim Weizmann,
New York, 1949

Chaim Weizmann would live to be rewarded in one more way. When the State of Israel was established, he was elected the first president of Israel. The word *Jew* comes from a Hebrew root that means "gratitude." How fitting that the first official Jewish leader in almost two thousand years should be selected in appreciation for his past efforts!

David ben Gurion

The first prime minister of the new state was David ben Gurion, a Polish-born Jew who emigrated to Palestine in 1906. A farmer, fighter, politician, intellectual, and born leader, ben Gurion was chairman of the executive of the Jewish Agency when the high commissioner of the League of Nations called for an investigation of the conflict between Arabs and Jews in the wake of the 1936 Arab riots and insurrection. In January 1937 ben Gurion gave this testimony to the Palestine Royal Commission, which was under the direction of Lord Peel, a former secretary of state for India:

David ben Gurion on the Arab Question

Our right in Palestine is not derived from the Mandate and the Balfour Declaration. It is prior to that. . . . The Bible is our Mandate, the Bible which was written by us, in our own language, in Hebrew, in this very country. That is our Mandate. Our right is as old as the Jewish people. It was only the recognition of this right which was expressed in the Balfour Declaration and the Mandate. It is stated in the Mandate that it recognizes the right of the Jewish people to reconstitute their National Home.

We are here as of right and I believe all those people, first of all the British people and then other European nations and the United States of America, which endorsed the action of Great Britain, for them, too, the Jewish National Home was an end in itself. It was not in order that the Jews should benefit Palestine, but it was to solve the Jewish problem. It was to remove a grievance, a historical grievance of the Jewish people against the whole Christian world for many centuries. There were attempts, very worthy and sincere attempts, by civilized people during the last century to remove the grievance of the Jewish people, their persecutions and their sufferings, by giving them equal rights in England and France and other countries; but it proved to be no solution, because it did not take away the root of our troubles, and the root is that we are in every country a minority at the mercy of the majority. This majority may treat us rightly and fairly, as in England and in France, and it may be otherwise, as in Germany, but we are always at the mercy of others. . . .

We do not intend to create in Palestine the same intolerable position for the Jews as in all other countries. It means a radical change for the Jewish people; otherwise, there is no need for a National Home. It is not to give the Jews equal rights in Palestine. It is to change their position as a people. I want to say one word on why we are here in Palestine. It is not because we once conquered Palestine. Many people have conquered a country and lost it, and they have no claim to that country, but here we are for two reasons unprecedented in history. The first is this—Palestine is the only country in the world that the Jews, not as individuals but as a nation, as a race, can regard as their own country, as their historic homeland, and the second reason is there is no other nation—I do not say population, I do not say sections of a people—there is no other race or nation as a whole which regards this country as their only homeland. All of the inhabitants of Palestine are children of this country and have full rights in this country, not only as citizens but as children of this homeland, but they have it in their capacity as inhabitants of this country. We have it as Jews, as children of the Jewish people, whether we are here already or whether we are not here yet. When the Balfour Declaration was made, there were 60,000 Jews here. It was not only the right of those 60,000. Now we are 400,000, and it is not only the right of these 400,000. It is because we are the children of the Jewish people and it is the only homeland of the Jewish people that we have rights in this country. . . .

I believe that . . . our Arab neighbors in Palestine also will more appreciate the beneficial nature of our constructive work, and they will see that not only is there no conflict of interests between the Jewish people as a whole and the Arab people as a whole but that their interests are complementary.

We need each other. We can benefit each other. I have no doubt that at least our neighbors around us in Syria, Iraq and Egypt will be the first to recognize that fact, and from them this consciousness will also spread in Palestine amongst our Arab neighbors here, because there is no essential conflict. We have never had a quarrel with the Arabs on our side, neither with the Arabs in Palestine nor the Arabs in other countries. On the contrary. We came to this country with the consciousness that, besides saving ourselves and freeing and liberating our own people, we had also a great civilizing task to achieve here and that we could be of great help to our Arab neighbors here and in the surrounding countries, and I believe we have proved it by our work. The stronger we get, the greater our community becomes in Palestine, the greater our colonization work, the more developed our scientific institutions become, the more will be recognized by our neighbors abroad and here the blessing of our work and the mutual interest which exists historically between the Jewish people which is returning to its country, returning with the tradition of European culture, with the blessing of European culture, and the Arab peoples around us, who also want to achieve not only formal political independence but are also interested in achieving an economic, intellectual, spiritual and cultural renaissance, and it is our belief that a great Jewish community, a free Jewish nation in Palestine, with a large scope for its activities, will be of great benefit to our Arab neighbors, and from the recognition of this fact will come a lasting peace and lasting co-operation between the two peoples.

Palestine Royal Commission, Notes of Evidence Taken on Thursday 7 January 1937, in Paul R. Mendes Flohr and Jehuda Reinharz, eds., *The Jew in the Modern World: A Documentary History*, New York, 1995

In light of recent events, how relevant are ben Gurion's insights today? Why were his hopes for cooperation with the Arab world not realized? What additional points might ben Gurion have added to his remarks after the Holocaust? What other justifications for the Jewish claim to Israel did ben Gurion not mention?

Bowing to Arab pressure, England "rethought" its policy as expressed in the Balfour Declaration. The Peel Commission, in 1937, recommended that Palestine, originally promised to the Jews, be partitioned into separate Arab and Jewish states, with a far smaller portion allotted as a Jewish homeland. In what would become an oft-repeated pattern, the Jews, albeit reluctantly, accepted; the Arab leadership rejected any compromise. Further efforts at negotiation proved fruitless.

Exasperated, England issued the White Paper in 1939, effectively nullifying the Balfour Declaration with, as Weizmann put it, "a death sentence." Including as it did additional restrictions against Jewish immigration to Palestine, the White Paper was indeed a death sentence for Jews seeking haven from the decrees that were soon to doom them in Nazi Germany. England applied its restrictive policies not only to Hitler's victims throughout the war, denying fleeing refugees admission to Palestine, but also to the displaced Jewish survivors of the Holocaust as well. Jews who had escaped death in Nazi Europe and attempted to settle in Palestine were placed in specially established detention camps for illegal immigrants in Cyprus. Some met a fate even worse than that.

The *Exodus 1947*

In 1947 the British attacked the refugee ship Exodus 1947 *to prevent it from proceeding to the Promised Land. Seventeen miles from shore, still in international waters, five British destroyers and one cruiser opened fire, threw gas bombs, and rammed the ship. On board were 4,500 refugees; 3 were killed and 217 were wounded. The ship, badly damaged, was towed to Haifa, where the British reloaded the refugees onto prison ships and sent them back to the German concentration camps—now serving as displaced persons' camps—from which they had fled. This episode became the background for the novel* Exodus *by Leon Uris.*

In this passage, an eyewitness describes the scene as the Exodus 1947 *arrived in Haifa.*

The ship looked like a matchbox that had been splintered by a nutcracker. In the torn, square hole, as big as an open blitzed barn, we could see a muddle of bedding, possessions, plumbing, broken pipes, overflowing toilets, half-naked men, women looking for children. Cabins were bashed in; railings were ripped off; the lifesaving rafts were dangling at crazy angles.

Amidst the blare of the loudspeakers ("Come off quietly, women and children first"), the smashing of glass bottles which the refugees took along in which to keep their drinking water, and the explosion of depth bombs by the British to ward off underwater swimmers who might attach floating mines to damage the ships, the slow weary march of unloading began from the *Exodus* on to the prison boats.

The pier began to take on the noise and smell and animal tragedy of a Chicago slaughterhouse. The cattle moved slowly down the tracks.

From a July 17, 1947, Tel Aviv radio broadcast, in Azriel Eisenberg,
Hannah Grad Goodman, and Alvin Kass, eds., *Eyewitnesses to Jewish History:
From 586 B.C.E. to 1967,* New York, 1973

In 1947 England decided that it was in its best interest to give up the Mandate that gave it rule over Palestine. The United Nations was now empowered to settle the problem of Arab and Jewish claims over the land. In a stunning decision, marked by furious debate, the United Nations authorized the establishment of independent Arab and Jewish states in a partitioned Palestine. Some Jews took it as a sign of divine intervention that this was the first time that the Russian and American delegations had voted together.

Although the amount of territory allotted to the Jews was tiny, far smaller than had been promised years before, the Jews ecstatically accepted their recognition, after almost two thousand years, into the family of nations. Their new state, the Jews decided, would be called Israel. A fitting name, they said, for a people mentioned in a famous parchment stele of Mnepthah, one of the earliest of the pharaohs, who had written thirty centuries before, "Israel is no more," using the term Israel for the first time in recorded history.

May 5, 1948: The Birth of Israel

Here, by an Israeli minister, is a memorable description of the scene at the moment when the State of Israel was born.

From *Three Days* by Zeev Sharef

It was a day like any other day. We moved about our duties as usual but as if in a dream. Mingled joy and dread filled us, the present and past were fused. Vision and reality were indistinguishable; the days of the Messiah had arrived, the end of servitude under alien rulers. We hurried . . . toward the Tel Aviv Museum hall, the precious document in hand—our hearts resounding the sing-song chant of the *rebbe,* the teacher, in our boyhood *cheder* [religious class], telling of the great things reserved for the righteous and the just by divine ordainment. . . . What had loomed in the distant future, as nebulous as a dream, now became transposed into the present; and we had been privileged to witness the day. Past chapters had been sealed, new chapters were beginning—the days of the Third Jewish Commonwealth.

The guard around the building was strict, cordon within cordon, and pressing against them a multitude of people hastening from all directions. . . .

Below the steps to the museum entrance stood an honor guard of cadets of the Jewish army's officers' school, their white belts gleaming. The small hall was specially decorated . . . [with] works by Jewish artists, Minkowsky's *Pogroms,* Marc Chagall's *Jew Holding a Scroll of the Law,* S. Hirshenberg's *Exile,* among others. A large portrait of Theodor Herzl hung . . . against a blue-and-white backdrop flanked by the blue-and-white flags. When had he said: "The Jewish state is essential to the world. It will therefore be created"?

The hall was packed. . . . Movie cameramen and newspaper photographers from other countries . . . with their arc-lamp, and flash-bulbs. . . . Newspapermen and reporters. . . . The peoples of Europe and America, to whose culture the Book of Books was integral, were turning their eyes to the tiny corner in which . . . its prophecies [were] being fulfilled. . . .

Exactly at four o'clock Ben-Gurion rose, rapped the gavel of the table, and the gathering rose. Spontaneously they began to sing *Hatikvah* [the national anthem; literally, "The Hope"] not according to plan. It was to have been played by the Philharmonic Orchestra, concealed on the upper floor. . . .

Ben-Gurion said: "I shall now read to you the Scroll of the Establishment of the State. . . .

His face shone. . . .

"The Land of Israel was the birthplace of the Jewish people. Here came Joshua ben-Nun and King David, Nehemiah and the Hasmoneans.

"Here their spiritual, religious, and national identity was formed. Here they achieved independence and created a culture, of national and universal significance.

"Here the prophets and Ezra the Scribe and the men of the Great Assembly wrote and gave the Bible to the world." . . .

"We hereby proclaim the establishment of the Jewish state in Palestine to be called *Medinat Yisrael* [the State of Israel]."

At these words the entire audience rose to its feet and burst into prolonged hand clapping. All were seized by ineffable joy, their faces irradiated.

The chairman read the seven articles arising out of the declaration . . . [concluding]: "With trust in Almighty God, we set our hand to this declaration, at this session of the Provisional State Council, on the soil of the homeland, in the city of Tel Aviv, on this Sabbath eve, the fifth of Iyar, 5708, the fourteenth day of May, 1948."

He added: "Let us stand to adopt the Scroll of the Establishment of the Jewish state." . . .

. . . Rabbi Y. L. Fishman delivered the benediction of "Who hath kept and sustained and brought us unto this day," which the aged rabbi did in a trembling voice choked with emotion. . . .

Suddenly the full impact of what had been done came home.—The significance of the creation of the state. . . .

The "Proclamation" was adopted by acclamation. . . .

As the signing of the document ended, *Hatikvah* was struck up by the orchestra; and it seemed as if the heavens had opened and were pouring out a song of joy on the rebirth of the nation. The audience stood motionless, transfixed. . . .

"The State of Israel is established! This meeting is ended!"

It had taken thirty-two minutes in all to proclaim the independence of a people who, for 1,887 years, had been under the servitude of other nations. . . .

People embraced . . . tears of rejoicing streamed; yet there was grief for sons who had fallen and sons whose fate was in the womb of the future— grief and dread locked in the innermost recesses of the heart.

Outside thousands had gathered. . . . The streets of Tel Aviv were filled with crowds. . . .

Copies of *Day of the State*, jointly issued by all newspapers combined . . . were grabbed from shouting newsboys.

Music played by the *Voice of Israel* lilted from radios in open windows. Overhead, planes dropped leaflets urging subscription to the Independence Loan. . . . City employees posted placards announcing that recruiting for the services would go on throughout the Sabbath and into the night.

Zeev Sharef, *Three Days*, trans., Julian Louis Meltzer, New York, 1962

Through the Eyes of the First President

In his autobiography Chaim Weizmann recalled his first actions as the first president of the new state of Israel.

From *Trial and Error: The Autobiography of Chaim Weizmann*

When I was resting in my hotel [in New York] from the fatigue of the preceding weeks, a message reached me that the provisional council of state had elected me as its president. . . . A few hours later the same message was repeated over the radio and was picked up in the adjoining room where my wife was entertaining friends. Almost at the same moment Aubrey Eban [Abba Eban], then one of our younger aides at the United Nations and at this time of writing the brilliant representative of Israel before that body—and, I might add, one of its most distinguished members—came in with some friends from Madison Square Garden where the Jews of New York were celebrating at a mass rally which I could not attend because of ill-health. They brought definite confirmation of the report. That evening my friends gathered in our hotel apartment and raised glasses of champagne in a toast to the President of Israel.

My first official act as president of the State of Israel . . . was to accept the invitation of the President of the United States to be his guest in Washington and to take up the usual residence at Blair House. I traveled to Washington by special train and arrived to find Pennsylvania Avenue bedecked with the flags of the United States and Israel. I was escorted to the White House by representatives of the United States government and by Mr. Eliahu Epstein, whom the provisional government had appointed its envoy to the United States. . . . I expressed our gratitude to the President. . . .

It had been my intention to go to England. . . . I now felt no longer free to do so. Arab armies were attacking Israel . . . spearheaded . . . by the Arab Legion of Trans-Jordan, equipped by British arms, financed by the British treasury, trained and commanded by British officers. . . . Their main operations were directed against the Holy City. The Hebrew University and Hadassah Medical Center were under bombardment; Jewish shrines . . . which had survived attacks of barbarians in medieval times, were now being laid waste. . . . I had always believed that an anti-Zionist policy was utterly alien to British tradition, but now . . . the ideals of the State of Israel, and the policies of Great Britain, under Mr. Bevin's direction, were brought into bloody conflict. . . . I felt it to be a bitter incongruity that I should not be able to set foot in a country whose people and institutions I held in such high esteem, and with which I had so long sought to link the Jewish people by ties of mutual interest and cooperation. I decided to arrange my affairs in France ... then proceeded to Switzerland for a much needed rest before I went on to Israel to assume my duties.

Chaim Weizmann, *Trial and Error: The Autobiography of Chaim Weizmann,*
New York, 1949

Jews in the Soviet Union

For Jews in the Soviet Union, the twentieth century seemed certain to fulfill the aspirations of their Communist persecutors. The survivors of pogroms and cruel anti-Semitism were denied any contact with Judaism; all religion was suppressed, and the study, teaching, and practice of Judaism were punishable offenses. In St. Petersburg, for example, one solitary synagogue existed in a city with over 100,000 Jews—who were too fearful to attend it. Stalin thought he had succeeded in stamping out any remaining Jewish national consciousness or sense of identification with their people. For Soviet Jewry, the birth of Israel was more than a miracle; it was a moment of resurrection. Its meaning to them was magnificently expressed when Golda Meir, Israel's first minister to the Soviet Union, came to Moscow in the fall of 1948. In this passage from her autobiography, Meir described her reception.

The Soviet Jews Greet Golda Meir

As we had planned, we went to the synagogue on Rosh Hashanah. All of us, the men, women and children of the legation—dressed in our best clothes, as befitted Jews on a Jewish holiday. But the street in front of the synagogue had changed. Now it was filled with people, packed together like sardines, hundreds and hundreds of them, of all ages, including Red Army officers, soldiers, teenagers and babies carried in their parents' arms. Instead of the 2,000-odd Jews who usually came to the synagogue on the holidays, a crowd of close to 50,000 people was waiting for us. For a minute I couldn't grasp what had happened—or even who they were. And then it dawned on me. They had come—those good, brave Jews—in order to be with us, to demonstrate their sense of kinship and to celebrate the establishment of the State of Israel. Within seconds they had surrounded me, almost lifting me bodily, almost crushing me, saying my name over and over again. Eventually, they parted ranks and let me enter the synagogue, but there, too, the demonstration went on. Every now and then, in the women's gallery, someone would come to me, touch my hand, stroke or even kiss my dress. Without speeches or parades, without any words at all really, the Jews of Moscow were proving their profound desire—and their need—to participate in the miracle of the establishment of the Jewish state, and I was the symbol of the state for them.

I couldn't talk, or smile, or wave my hand. I sat in that gallery like a stone, without moving, with those thousands of eyes fixed on me. No such entity as the Jewish people, Ehrenburg had written. The State of Israel meant nothing to the Jews of the USSR! But his warning had fallen on deaf ears. For thirty years we and they had been separated. Now we were together again, and as I watched them, I knew that no threat, however awful, could possibly have stopped the ecstatic people I saw in the synagogue that day from telling us, in their own way, what Israel meant to them. The service ended, and I got up to leave; but I could hardly walk. I felt as though I had been caught up in a torrent of love so strong that it had literally taken my breath away and slowed down my heart. I was on the verge of fainting, I think. But the crowd still surged around me, stretching out its hands and saying *Nasha Golda* (our Golda) and *Shalom, shalom,* and crying.

Out of that ocean of people, I can still see two figures clearly: a little man who kept popping up in front of me and saying, "*Goldele, leben zolst du Shana Tova!*" (Goldele, a long life to you and a Happy New Year), and a woman who just kept repeating, "Goldele! Goldele!" and smiling and blowing kisses at me.

It was impossible for me to walk back to the hotel, so although there is an injunction against riding on the Sabbath or on Jewish holidays, someone pushed me into a cab. But the cab couldn't move either because the crowd of cheering, laughing, weeping Jews had engulfed it. I wanted to say something, anything, to those people, to let them know that I begged their forgiveness for not having wanted to come to Moscow and for not having known the strength of their ties to us. For having wondered, in fact, whether there was still a link between them and us. But I couldn't find the words. All I could say, clumsily, and in a voice that didn't even sound like my own, was one sentence in Yiddish. I stuck my head out of the window of the cab and said, "*A dank eich vos ihr seit geblieben Yidden*" (Thank you for having remained Jews), and I heard that miserable, inadequate sentence being passed on through the enormous crowd as though it were some wonderful prophetic saying.

Golda Meir, *My Life,* New York, 1975

The Ingathering of the Exiles

With his own state, the wandering Jew could at last come home. Throughout the centuries, Jews had prayed three times a day for the "ingathering of the exiles." Now that could become a reality. For Jews oppressed in unfriendly lands, Israel beckoned with a warm welcome. Among the first to take advantage of this new reality were the Jews of Yemen, an ancient community going back to the days before the destruction of the First Temple. Harassed by their Muslim rulers, almost the entire Jewish community decided to settle in Israel. With all land and sea routes denied to them, Israel rescued Yemenite Jewry in an airlift that became known as Operation Magic Carpet. For the Yemenite Jews who had never before seen an airplane, what they witnessed seemed clearly to be replicas of the biblical "wings of eagles" on which God had metaphorically delivered the Jews from Egypt. In this passage an American pilot who took part in Operation Magic Carpet describes one of his trips.

An Eyewitness Account of Operation Magic Carpet

The car drew up alongside our faithful skymaster on the hot desert airfield at Aden. We could see our patient passengers waiting in the shade of the outstretched wings. There were about one hundred fifty in the group, about half of them children, many dressed in colorful Arabian costumes, flowing robes, and stunning headdresses.

I was struck with their stunted, wizened appearance. Many were emaciated from the ordeal of their long trek from Yemen and, although they had already received considerable care at Hashed Camp, it was clear that they . . . would need a good deal of care when they arrived in Israel. It was clear to me now how we could carry so many of them and still not be overloaded.

Most of them were barefoot, but some wore tennis shoes provided by the camp at Hashed. They had very dark hair, rather wiry, and many, including the men, wore it in curls and sidelocks with ringlets down about their ears. Most of the men were bearded and many looked as though they might have stepped right out of the pages of the Old Testament. They sat under the wing, some of them smoking water pipes which stood about three feet high. . . . If they were excited about the trip it certainly was not apparent from their actions. The women and children also sat around in small groups, the children quietly disciplined to remain with their parents and keep out of the way of the ground crews. Their interest in the aircraft appeared casual and they did not wander around, touching and fingering the strange marvel of flight, as might have been expected. It seemed as though they accepted this great metal bird poised on the desert as a part of the Bible and prophecy in which they were so well versed.

They presented a strange picture, squatting in groups on the sand. Some wore the exquisite silver filigree jewelry for which the Yemenites are renowned—bracelets, earrings, and necklaces.

Many were beautiful, deeply tanned, with fine features and aristocratic faces. They were deeply religious, and . . . many were carrying with them their Bible scrolls, some probably hundreds of years old. They had little else. . . .

One swarthy fellow, barefoot in a red and white headdress and brown and white striped robe approached me while I was inspecting the craft. . . . I could see his black curls hanging inside his headdress. He had dark features, bushy eyebrows, piercing black eyes that flashed in the bright sunlight and a hawk nose. He held out to me the most beautiful silver filigree bracelet I had ever seen, probably the only thing he owned besides his clothes. I could not understand what he said, but I'm sure he wanted to sell the bracelet. Unfortunately I did not take advantage of the opportunity. . . .

Before long they climbed the wooden ramp to the main door of the skymaster and were seated on the plywood benches. An attendant who spoke Yemenite Arabic and also knew some English remained with them in the cabin.

One by one the engines were started, and thus began our first flight back to Lydda Airport. The takeoff demanded much of the straining engines in the hot desert air, and almost all of the runway was used up before we were airborne. The load of passengers was noticeable in the performance of our plane, and our rate of climb was low. . . . We finally leveled off at 9,000 feet and after cruise power was set and all was functioning in good order, I took leave of the cockpit for a look at our passengers. Upon opening the door, I saw a scene of crowded tranquility. Most of the passengers had been lulled to sleep by the droning engines. Some were staring through the windows in a relaxed manner, perhaps looking for the Promised Land which they would not see until another seven hours had passed. What a short link of time in the chain spanning thousands of tortured years ere their return! An eternal link forged from the ultimate in a modern technology and fitted to an ancient prophecy which even now was drawing up the anchor of a forgotten age. I thought of the marvel of flight . . . and wondered what they thought of it. I saw one woman thoughtfully touching the circular frame of a window, her delicate fingers vibrating in tune with the quivering pulse of the plane. A mechanical phenomenon, explained in the intricate formulae of vibration mechanics, but, to her, was it perhaps evidence of a living pulse coursing through the great eagle that was winging her homeward?

The return flight was quite beautiful, flying up the middle of the Red Sea toward the Gulf of Aqaba. The sky was a clear, turquoise blue and, below, an occasional ship could be seen plying its way along the sea lanes where three millennia before the ships of King Solomon had sailed. As we droned along in the sky, I thought of the patient people in the cabin behind us . . . and how many centuries they and their ancestors had waited for this moment. No more blocks to their return to Israel now. . . . This time no Red Sea would have to part. . . . We were high above, and some-where down there, west of Suez, there was a crossroads in the sea where only time separated two epochs of history.

Presently we were flying up the Gulf of Aqaba past the rugged terrain of the Sinai Peninsula. Off our left wing in the distance I could see Mt. Sinai, where Moses received the Ten Commandments, which even now were riding with us on ancient Yemenite parchments, and where the Lord had called unto Moses saying, "Ye have seen what I did unto the Egyptians and how I bore you on eagles' wings and brought you unto Myself." Suddenly I understood . . . the attitudes of the other pilots I had met on the airlift and their quiet devotion to their work in this inspired airlift. I became at this moment an integral part of "Operation: Magic Carpet."

Our Yemenite passengers deplaned in orderly fashion, their shining, radiant faces portraying their joy in being at last in the Promised Land. As if in a dream they quietly proceeded to the JDC center at the airport. . . . For these good people the prophecy of Isaiah had been fulfilled: "But they that wait for the Lord shall renew their strength; They shall mount up with wings as eagles; They shall run, and not be weary; They shall walk, and not faint." (Isaiah 40:31)

Edward Trueblood Martin, I Flew Them Home: A Pilot's Story of the Yemenite Airlift,
New York, 1958

Jews came to Israel from most of the surrounding Arab lands, from Egypt, Syria, Iraq, and Ethiopia, leaving behind the possessions they weren't permitted to take with them. Others came from democratic countries in Europe as well as from the United States. They came seeking freedom, a better way of life, and an opportunity to live fully and openly in accord with their beliefs. The largest ethnic group to make aliyah *(literally "ascent"—the word used to describe immigration to Israel) was Russian Jewry. Once the Kremlin opened the gates to a modern-day exodus, over one million Jews left the Soviet Union to become Israeli citizens. The ingathering of the exiles eventually brought the population of Israel to over 6 million—a number impossible to ignore for its symbolic meaning after the Holocaust.*

The chart below gives us a vivid picture of the changes in the distribution of the Jewish population around the world in the past century.

JEWISH POPULATION: AROUND THE WORLD AND IN ISRAEL

Year	World	Israel	% in Israel
1882	7,800,000	24,000	0
1900	10,600,000	50,000	1
1914	13,500,000	85,000	1
1922	14,400,000	84,000	1
1925	14,800,000	126,000	1
1939	16,728,000	449,000	3
1948	11,500,000	650,000	6
1955	11,800,000	1,590,000	13
1970	12,630,000	2,582,000	20
1980	12,840,000	3,283,000	25
1990	12,870,000	3,947,000	30
2000	13,191,500	6,289,000	48

25

War—and Peace?
Hopes for the Future

N o sooner did the British pull out of Israel, on May 15, 1948, than the
    armies of seven surrounding Arab nations attacked the newborn state.
*The outcome was surely a foregone conclusion. The Arabs would easily defeat the
small nation of Jews who, just to make sure of the result, were denied arms by the
British. At the same time, England continued to supply the Arabs with weapons.
England was confident that a newly constituted Arab Palestine would seek British
support and that it could again play the dominant role in the oil-rich Middle East.
Amazingly enough, things didn't go as planned. David once more defeated Goliath.
When asked how they could possibly have triumphed, Israelis were fond of giving the
only answer that made any sense to them:* Eyn b'reyra—We had no choice.

Defending the New State

*A colony comprising mainly Jewish settlers from Poland and Galicia, many of them
survivors of the Warsaw Ghetto, was established in the Negev (south). Dedicated to
the memory of Mordecai Anilewicz, commander of the Warsaw Ghetto uprising, it
was named Yad Mordecai. On May 18, 1948, an Egyptian army attacked it. The
colony's diary records the events as they tried to fight off their enemies—who were in
clear violation of the United Nations decision—and once again notes the world
standing by in silence.*

Friday, May 21

We knew that with such an overwhelming superiority in weapons the enemy should be able to wipe out a small place like ours within a very short time. We steeled ourselves to the last ditch defense and sent out a call for help. But no help arrived. The dead animals lay all about us but it was impossible to bury them. We faced the danger of an epidemic. For the third day we were not able to wash ourselves.

In the afternoon, the enemy placed five big guns on the eastern hills and opened fire. We were unable to understand the purpose of this fire. . . . The buildings were all destroyed and no one could be seen in the yard.

Before evening the riddle was solved. Under cover of cannon fire the enemy transferred a convoy of one hundred twenty vehicles to the north. We faced the danger of being surrounded and cut off from the *Yishuv* [the Jewish community]. Our situation became worse. The injured were unable to receive adequate medical treatment. The doctor, an elderly man, lost his strength running from one position to another. The ammunition was decreasing. . . . The promised outside help had not yet arrived. The enemy now occupied all of the strategic positions around us and we faced . . . attack from all sides.

Saturday, May 22

How had we lost the pill box? It was a position that we were very proud of, believing that it would withstand even a hit from a two-inch mortar. The pill box had been heavily shelled and Yitzchak, the command of the post, injured in the head and close to collapse, ordered his men to withdraw, taking all of the guns and ammunition. One of his men, Zelig, with a paralyzed leg, succeeded in taking a box of ammunition while retreating. . . . All of them reached our lines safely with all of their arms. We ourselves wondered what was the source of this spiritual and physical strength which enabled us to repulse for four days and nights the unceasing enemy attacks.

Sunday, May 23

We are very troubled today. This is the fifth day and no help has reached us. There was not even an attempt to divert the enemy in order to give us a little rest. For the fifth day we drank filthy water, the stench of dead corpses permeated the air, and there was no opportunity to bury the cows, the dogs, the chickens, and the ducks. The condition of the injured became worse. No surgeons around and the Red Cross did not appear. The representatives of Egyptian civilization do not recognize international institutions. . . .

In the afternoon the cannons renewed their concert. . . . We decided to invite the position commanders to a conference to find out what the chances were of breaking through to evacuate the injured and non-combatants. Before evening enemy tanks approached. The *chaverim* were alerted. . . . Our heavy machine gun had been hit and was out of action. The other automatic weapons were covered with sand-as a result of the bombings. However, in spite of this we stormed the tank with grenades and rifles.

It was a hard battle. The tank was followed by Egyptian soldiers firing as they came. Once more our *chaverim* performed exceptionally heroic deeds. Shmulik, with a hand grenade in his hand, ran to the tank and threw his hand grenade at it. He was slain. Nissim, from the *Palmach,* who was in charge of the *Piat* (anti-tank gun), was badly injured and died. Zvi Kestenbaum, the operator of the *Spandau,* who for the past few days could be seen running from position to position constantly under fire, appeared here too . . . but before he was able to shoot he was killed. Clarus, wandering with his mortar from place to place, received a bullet through his heart. Tzvi, from the *Palmach,* the young boy in charge of the Bren gun, who was not afraid of anything and had always appeared wherever needed, lost his life too. But the tank was put out of action and the corpses of many Egyptians lay on the ground beside it. . . .

This attack had been repulsed but our *chaverim* were in bad shape . . . hardly able to fight. Almost all of our ammunition was exhausted. The best of our fighters had fallen. All of the outposts were destroyed. We were unable to relieve *chaverim* that had been fighting in hand-to-hand combat less than a half hour ago. The number of our casualties had grown.

The situation was very clear. . . . We must either surrender . . . or risk an evacuation in order to save the women, the youth, and the remnants of our exhausted fighters. We chose the second alternative despite the extreme danger. Thanks to the *Palmach* and its *Panzers* the task was performed quickly. Only one *chaver,* one *chavera* [feminine member], and one injured person fell into the hands of the enemy.

When we saw our *chaverim* falling during the battle we did not weep. But then, as we said good bye to our *meshek* the tears came to our eyes. Our greatest, most creative force and energy were invested in this place and here it had stood, magnificently, between the hills and the desert. Here too we had stood, as only a man is able to stand. Here we had given everything that is in the realm of man to give. To this place we shall return! The earth of Yad Mordecai, saturated with the blood of our loved ones, will live again under our hands!

Youth and Nation, August 1947; in Azriel Eisenberg, Hannah Grad Goodman, and Alvin Kass, eds., *Eyewitnesses to Jewish History: From 586 B.C.E. to 1967*, New York, 1973

Today Yad Mordechai is a thriving kibbutz. Its members vow not to forget the heroic efforts of its founders. For every inch of land that makes up Israel today, Jews had to fight against enemies who wanted to annihilate them and deny them the small parcel of real estate granted them by the United Nations. Why is Israel, unlike other nations, denied the right to hold on to the fruits of its victories after defeating those who attack it?

The Six-Day War

The miracle of 1948 is eclipsed only by the incredible events of 1967. This time, the Arab nations were so certain they would destroy all of Israel that they jubilantly announced their victory before they even began their offensive. Military strategists still study the amazing success of the Israeli forces as they soundly trounced all the Arab forces aligned against them from every direction in a mere six days. The Six-Day War, as it came to be known, left Israel with a unified and liberated Jerusalem as well as larger and more secure borders. Hoping to give back some of its gains in exchange for lasting peace, Israel offered the return of territory it had conquered with much bloodshed. It was met with the response of the famous "three no's" declared by the Arab world at the Khartoum Summit in 1968: no negotiation, no recognition, and no peace with Israel. Abba Eban provided the most pithy summary of the Arab political strategy in their dealings with Israel: "They have never missed an opportunity to miss an opportunity."

In the meantime, Israel had to deal not only with the external problem of finding peace with its neighbors, but perhaps even more critically with the internal spiritual questions raised by the need to have its children trained for war. In the aftermath of the Six-Day War, some of the soldiers reflected on the moral and ethical dimensions of their involvement in conflict—how it affected them and the price the next generation was paying for the lack of peace.

From *The Seventh Day*, Tape-recorded Conversations of Veterans of the Six-Day War

Going Off to War

I was leaning on a newspaper stall at the time. The newspaper seller was in the very act of stretching out his hand towards the paper I wanted when suddenly the voice caught his attention. His eyes widened, he looked through me rather than at me, and said, as if in surprise, "Oh! They've called me up too." He rolled up his papers and went. The salesgirl came out of the shop opposite, stopped jerkily at the door, adjusted her blouse, a little nervously, snapped her handbag shut, and walked off. The butcher took off his apron, pulled down his shutters, and left. A group of men stood huddled round a transistor in the middle of a patch of lawn. Whenever one of them heard his code word read out by the announcer, he detached himself from the group and left. Without a word, another left. Then a third. Silently the group broke up. Each went his own way. A girl came towards me, clicking along on high heels. She too was struck by the voice, and stopped. She listened, turned around, and left. A unique silence descended on the town.

I have seen cities on mobilization day. I have seen nations go to war— I have seen them marching off to the blare of raucous loudspeakers. I have seen them in the railway stations clasped in the arms of their weeping wives, their despairing mothers. I have watched them pass through the cheering crowds, receiving the embraces of foolish women. I have watched them go off, their bayonets wreathed in gay flowers, their hobnailed boots crashing out the rhythm of the marching songs that swell from their throats. I have seen them smiling, and proud. Always surrounded by crowds waving them on with shouts of 'Hurrah!' 'Vivat!' 'I-Ioch Hoch!' 'Nych Dzhiah!' But never before have I seen a city rise so silently to answer the call of duty. This nation went to war filled with a sense of destiny, gravely and quietly prepared, in a way that cannot be surpassed. (Abba, Kibbutz Ein Hachoresh)

The Will to Fight

We know the meaning of genocide, both those of us who saw the holocaust and those who were born later. Perhaps this is why the world will never understand us, will never understand our courage or comprehend the doubts and the qualms of conscience we knew during and after the war. Those who survived the holocaust, those who see pictures of a father and a mother, who hear the cries that disturb the dreams of those close to them, those who have listened to stories—know that no other people carries with it such haunting visions. And it is these visions which compel us to fight and yet make us ashamed of our fighting. The saying, "Pardon us for winning" is no irony—it is the truth. (Muki, Kibbutz Ein Gev)

Hate of Arab?
Right through the war when boys from your own unit had fallen alongside you—people you'd known for years, whose families and children you knew—even when they'd fallen and been killed and burned, even after all this, there still wasn't any hatred. It simply didn't exist. It was a professional encounter—if you can use a term like that—a question of who could fire first. (Hillel, Kibbutz Giv'at Hashlosha)

When the fighting began, and the mountains around Ein Gev began to spit fire, a group of our reconnaissance troops on one of the hills next to the Syrian border was busy—putting out a fire in a little field belonging to an Arab peasant. "A field is a field," said one of the boys. Could anything be more paradoxical? And yet it seems to me that behavior like this really symbolizes the situation we are caught up in. Our feelings are mixed. We carry in our hearts an oath which binds us never to return to the Europe of the holocaust; but at the same time we do not wish to lose that Jewish sense of identity with the victims. (Muki, Kibbutz Ein Gev)

Respect for Human Life
The big problem is one of education. How—despite the fact that from our point of view this was a just war—are we going to avoid turning into militarists? How are we going to retain respect for human life? This is the contradiction; this is the paradox within the whole business. What we've got to avoid is cheapening life and becoming conquerors. We mustn't become expansionists at the expense of other people. (Nachman, Kibbutz Gevo)

Henry Near, *The Seventh Day: Soldiers' Talk about the Six-Day War*, London, 1970

The Yom Kippur War

The euphoria that resulted from the victory in 1967 was brought to an abrupt end in 1973 on the holiest day of the Jewish year, a day auspiciously called the Day of Judgment. Relying on total surprise, the surrounding Arab nations, led by Egypt, attacked on Yom Kippur—the day by which this war would become known—and for the first time seemed to have the upper hand. Israel was caught off-guard, lulled into a false sense of security and superiority. Israelis understood that the Arabs might lose wars many times and come back to fight again, but one defeat for the Jewish state meant—as the Arab world so clearly announced—total annihilation. Once more, eyn b'reyra, there was no choice. Israel had to win. In a stunning turnabout, General Sharon surrounded and cut off the Egyptian army and forced them to sue for peace. A far humbler Israel had again won the war—but at a terrible cost of killed and wounded.

The mood of the country was movingly captured by an essay written by a veteran of the Yom Kippur War and published in September 1974. Even more fascinating was the flood of responses his comments elicited.

"An Invitation to Weeping"

We lay curled up in a shallow foxhole in the soft sand, Uriel and I. It was an ugly dawn hour, sky and earth were aflame. Uriel, a boy slim and beautiful as a girl, talked about Milan, from whence he had landed the day before yesterday, and I told him about New York which I had left four days before. Uriel was saying he just had to fix me up with this gorgeous girl, Iris, because it wasn't possible that we shouldn't meet—we were simply made for each other.

He was inserting sparkling new bullets into his clip, and I was sucking a mint to freshen my mouth after the night's sleep. Before the order came to leave the foxholes, we made a quick decision to have a big party at his house after the war.

Uriel promised to send me a gilded invitation.

At noon, his body was lying under a blanket in the field hospital.

Funny that we had thought of a party.

I want to send you an invitation to weeping.

The date and the hour don't matter, but the program, I guarantee you, will be a rich one: weeping. We'll cry for hours, and together—because I just can't do it alone. All through the war I wanted to cry but couldn't. This time it will work; it must. Nothing can stop us.

I'll cry for my dead: Avremele, Ilan, Amitai, Dudu, Uzi, Yair, Uriel—and you'll cry for yours.

And we'll cry together for the dreams out of which we've been shaken, for the grand things turned trivial, for the gods that failed, for the meaninglessness, the lack of will, the impotence, the present devoid of even a single ray of light. . . .

We'll cry for the fast friendships that have been cut off, the pricked illusions . . . the plans that will never be carried out, the dark cloud that will now hang forever over every celebration.

And we'll feel sorry for ourselves, because we deserve pity—a lost generation of a tormented people in "a land that consumes its inhabitants."

The big deciders, the oh-so-sober ones, won't be allowed in. This isn't for them.

Oh, will we cry. Bitterly we'll cry. Heartrendingly. Hugely. We'll cry cupfuls. Kettlefuls. Rivers.

Anyone feeling that he's had it, that he's all dried up, that he hasn't a tear left in him—will sneak out. On tiptoe, so as not to spoil the evening. Most likely, I'll be the last one left.

But, anytime at all—next month, in two months, next year—you can come again. The door's open. It's a standing invitation: from now on, my place is always open for crying.

> Arnon Lapid, "An Invitation to Weeping," *Hadassah Magazine,* September 1974;
> in Eliezer Ehrmann, *Readings in Modern Jewish History,* New York, 1977

The "Invitation" drew a flood of responses, opening up a public exchange of feelings on this painful issue.

Israelis Respond to the "Invitation to Weeping"

From Lotte Aharon, member of the same kibbutz as Arnon Lapid and mother of two boys who fell in the Yom Kippur War—Yehuda (the Dudu mentioned in the "invitation") and Hanokh:

No, Arnon, I don't agree with you. I'm the mother of Dudu and Hanokh, and they wouldn't have agreed with you either. They wouldn't want to see us cry. . . .

Not cry. Let's all sit down together—you and those who loved them: Amitai and Avremele and Yair and Hanokh and all the rest of them—and think! Think hard, and not about "failures" or "wars of the generals" or political parties. Think about how to go on, how to build a society that really knows what's special about itself. They didn't come here to get killed or to kill. They came because this is where their roots are. Here is where they were shaped. Let's sit together and think about how to build a society, a nation, a homeland.

And let's help the widows, the orphans, the brothers and sisters, the friends . . . till we hear them laugh again. Let's feel the confidence they felt. No, Arnon—when Yisrael fell, Dudu shouted at me: "Mama, you mustn't cry! Paratroopers don't cry." (I know he cried—but out of sight, alone; and we also cry—but alone, each one of us separately, and then smoothen ourselves out for each other.)

In his last postcard, Dudu wrote me to "keep up the company's good name." No, Dudu, we'll be worthy of you. We'll sit and plan. Be strong, Arnon. That's the way they would have wanted us.

From Yehoshua, a soldier then stationed on the western shore of the Suez Canal:
Such sensitivity and courage. What bravado and cheek it takes to write so
sincerely and intimately on weeping and pain without paying lip service to
"strength" and "valor" and "manliness," to "happy end" and "glimmering
hope," the way everybody is doing with nauseating banality. How wise of
you to forego politics and "constructive suggestions." I hate, I hate (maybe
because I fail to understand) those who don't allow themselves to bow
their heads, to weep absolutely, cathartically, pessimistically.

I know, Arnon: tomorrow or the next day, in a month or two, you'll get
over it, and then you'll be the same optimistic, hedonistic, cynical Arnon
I've known for years. But promise you'll never be ashamed of having written what you did. . . .

From Alex Barzel, of Kibbutz Kfar Hahoresh:
My door has also been open, for years, for people to come and weep with
me. But I'll come, Arnon, I'll come to you. Now I must stand weeping
alongside you so that you may be able to help me carry my burden. . . .

I have wept for the shadowy column of women being led off to slave
labor and worse, for the children and old people—of my own family as
well—being tormented, and all the rest of that suffering throng, of all
nations and languages, around me. I was shaken, and I wept in Rome's
gloomy railway station when I faced that 30-foot wall on which hung pictures of my dear ones with all the details written underneath. . . .

Afterwards, I wept for a blue-eyed boy with whom I had plowed in
Galilee, a boy who was the personification of love, of life, of tomorrow and
who now lies buried at Huleikat. I wept for the husky boy in the next
bunker after a shell tore a hole in his chest.

And I wept for the driver of the armored vehicle with whom I traveled
to the Negev one pitch-black, menacing night, and who two days later was
one of the shattered monuments in Shaar Hagai.

And I wept for the father of five who was still alive as we carried him
under a rain of mortar shells at Sharm el-Sheikh. Then, in the years that
followed, as Welfare Sergeant of the brigade that never forgot, I wept with
his widow and orphans.

In the Six-Day War, my heart went out to the fallen sons of my friends,
to my fallen pupils.

Today, too.

You see, Arnon, I'm carrying a frightful burden. I came into the world two decades before you, and in so short a time this world has become filled with so much hate, so much bereavement—but also, always, so much hope. . . .

I'll come to weep with you. But not over ourselves. I've never wept over myself as though I were a "lost generation." There have been, and there are today, people who are far more lost than I.

No Arnon, there is no time now to cry over myself, because in an hour, tomorrow, I have to get on with building a world which may somehow be better. . . . We will bring to that world a burden of never-ceasing weeping, but also renewed vitality. I will not "sneak out on tiptoe." I will stay so that, between cries, we will be able, together, to look the future in the face.

From Nira, of Kibbutz Hulda:
This winter, Arnon, we will join you for the big weeping party. But after the winter comes the spring, and then we'll have to put an end to the weeping. . . .

It will be necessary to harvest the winter crops. And others will be sitting on the tractors in place of those who are gone. They will be young and beautiful, and we shall not wish to weep with them—we will want to live with them.

You've invited us to come and weep with you always. But we are a people that cannot weep endlessly. We've had enough weeping since the days of the "Waters of Babylon," through the pogroms and expulsions, to the European Holocaust. . . . This coming summer many babies will be born, children of those who are gone and those still with us, a new generation recalling those left on the battlefield. These babies will grow up and laugh, and we will smile along with them, knowing that this is the way, the *only* way.

So forgive me, Arnon, if, come spring, I don't show up at the weeping party. I hereby invite you to the living party, the living that thrusts forward toward hope.

Hadassah Magazine, September 1974; in Eliezer Ehrmann,
Readings in Modern Jewish History, New York, 1977

Even today, peace has not come to Israel. All efforts at compromise have come to a dead end. In 2000, as a new millennium dawned, it almost seemed as if the Camp David summit engineered by President Clinton might bring the bitter conflict to a close. But Palestinian leadership chose the way of intifada rather than peaceful resolution. Again, the Arabs didn't miss the opportunity to miss an opportunity.

Negotiations once more gave way to terrorism, to ongoing violence, and, most horrendous of all, to suicide bombings against civilians going about their daily lives in buses, malls, and shopping centers.

How will the story end?

Only a prophet can answer.

But thankfully, a prophet has answered, telling us what to expect in the end of days. These words from Isaiah, Chapter 2, have given Jews throughout history the courage and will to go on:

2: And it shall come to pass in the last days, that the mountain of the Lord's house shall be established in the top of the mountains, and shall be exalted above the hills; and all nations shall flow unto it.

3: And many people shall go and say, Come ye, and let us go up to the mountain of the Lord, to the house of the God of Jacob; and he will teach us of his ways, and we will walk in his paths: for out of Zion shall go forth the law, and the word of the Lord from Jerusalem.

4: And he shall judge among the nations, and shall rebuke many people: and they shall beat their swords into plowshares, and their spears into pruning hooks: nation shall not lift up sword against nation; neither shall they learn war any more.

Jewish tradition holds that Jews have survived all of the travails of the centuries, all of their suffering since the slavery of Egypt, in order to fulfill a divinely ordained mission. Jews are meant to serve as "a light unto the nations" in order to hasten the arrival of the time that will usher in universal love, peace, and brotherhood.

We can only hope.

Further Reading

Alpher, Joseph, ed. *Encyclopedia of Jewish History: Events and Eras of the Jewish People.* New York: Facts on File, 1986.

Bamberger, Bernard. *The Story of Judaism.* New York: Schocken Books, 1970.

Barnavi, Eli. *A Historical Atlas of the Jewish People: From the Time of the Patriarchs to the Present.* New York: Schocken Books, 1995.

Baron, Salo W. *A Social and Religious History of the Jews.* 19 vols to date. New York: Columbia University Press, 1952.

Ben-Sasson, H. H., ed. *A History of the Jewish People* (by scholars at the Hebrew University, Jerusalem). Cambridge, Mass.: Harvard University Press, 1976.

Ben-Sasson, H. H., and S. Ettinger, eds. *Jewish Society Through the Ages.* New York: Schocken Books, 1971.

Blech, Benjamin. *The Complete Idiot's Guide to Jewish History and Culture.* New York: Alpha Books, 1999.

Brook, Kevin Alan. *The Jews of Khazaria.* Northvale, N.J.: Jason Aronson, 1999.

Cahill, Thomas. *The Gifts of the Jews: How a Tribe of Desert Nomads Changed the Way Everyone Thinks and Feels.* New York: Doubleday, 1998.

Cohen, Mark R. *Under Crescent and Cross: The Jews in the Middle Ages.* Reissue edition. Princeton, N.J.: Princeton University Press, 1995.

Cohn-Sherbok, Dan. *Atlas of Jewish History.* New York: Routledge, 1996.

Dimont, Max I. *Jews, God, and History.* New York: Simon and Schuster, 1962.

Finkelstein, Louis. *The Pharisees: The Sociological Background of Their Faith.* Philadelphia: Jewish Publication Society, 1938.

Finkelstein, Louis, ed. *The Jews: Their Role in Civilization.* 4th ed. New York: Schocken Books, 1971.

Glick, Leonard B. *Abraham's Heirs: Jews and Christians in Medieval Europe.* Syracuse, N.Y.: Syracuse University Press, 1999.

Gribetz, Judah, Edward L. Greenstein, and Regina Stein. *The Timetables of Jewish History: A Chronology of the Most Important People and Events in Jewish History.* New York: Simon and Schuster, 1993.

Isaacs, Ronald H., and Kerry M. Olitzky, eds. *Critical Documents of Jewish History: A Sourcebook.* Northvale, N.J.: Jason Aronson, 1995.

Johnson, Paul. *A History of the Jews.* New York: HarperCollins, 1988.

Kaiser, Walter C. *A History of Israel: From the Bronze Age Through the Jewish Wars.* Nashville, Tenn.: Broadman & Holman, 1998.

Mendes-Flohr, Paul R.; and Jehuda Reinharz, eds. *The Jew in the Modern World: A Documentary History.* New York: Oxford University Press, 1995.

Potok, Chaim. *Wanderings: Chaim Potok's History of the Jews.* New York: Fawcett Books, 1990.

Sachar, Howard Morley. *The Course of Modern Jewish History.* New York: Vintage Books, 1990.

———. *A History of Israel: From the Rise of Zionism to Our Time.* 2nd ed. New York: Knopf, 1996.

Wein, Berel. *Triumph of Survival: The Story of the Jews in the Modern Era, 1650-1990.* Suffern, N.Y.: Shaar Press, 1990.

Permissions
Acknowledgments

Permission to quote from the following works is gratefully acknowledged.

The Jew in the Medieval World: A Source Book, 315–1791 by Jacob Marcus (New York: Hebrew Union College Press, 2000). Reprinted with the permission of the publisher.

Reprinted from *The Jews of Arab Lands,* ©1991 by Norman Stillman, published by the Jewish Publication Society, with the permission of the publisher, The Jewish Publication Society.

The Karaite Anthology, Leon Nemoy, ed. (New Haven, Conn.: Yale University Press, 1987), © 1987 Leon Nemoy. Reprinted with the permission of the publisher.

Jewish Prince in Moslem Spain: Selected Poems of Samuel Ibn Nagrela by Leon J. Weinberger (Tuscaloosa, Ala.: University of Alabama Press, 2001). Reprinted with the permission of the publisher.

Reprinted from *Hebrew Ethical Wills,* ©1976 by Israel Abrahams, published by the Jewish Publication Society, with the permission of the publisher, The Jewish Publication Society.

"A Jewish Peddler's Diary" by Abraham Kohn, Abram Vossen Goodman, trans., American Jewish Archives, vol. 3, 1951. Reprinted with permission of the Jacob Rader Marcus Center of the American Jewish Archives.

My Life by Golda Meir, copyright © 1975 by Golda Meir. Used by permission of G.P. Putnam's Sons, a division of Penguin Group (USA) Inc.

The Jewish State by Theodore Herzl, 1896, the Theodore Herzl Foundation; originally published by Hertzl Press. Reprinted with the permission of the publisher.

The Plough Woman: Memoirs of the Pioneer Women of Palestine, Rachel Katznelson-Shazar, ed. (New York: Herzl Press, 1975). Reprinted with the permission of the publisher.

Belzec, Sobibor, Treblinka: The Operation Reinhard Death Camps by Yitzchok Arad (Indianapolis, Ind.: Indiana University Press, 1987). Reprinted with the permission of Yad Vashem, the Holocaust Martyrs' and Heroes' Remembrance Authority.

Responsa from the Holocaust by Ephraim Oshry (New York: Judaica Press, 1983). Reprinted with the permission of the Oshry family.

"What the State of Israel Means to Me" by Rabbi Yisrael Meir Lau, in the *Jewish Press,* May 7, 1993. Reprinted with the permission of Rabbi Lau.

Trial and Error: The Autobiography of Chaim Weizmann by Chaim Weizmann. Copyright 1949 by the Weizmann Foundation, renewed © 1977 by Abraham Levin. Reprinted by permission of HarperCollins Publishers, Inc.

Three Days by Zeev Sharef, translated by Julian Louis Meltzer, copyright © 1962 by Zeev Sharef. Used by permission of Doubleday, a division of Random House, Inc.

I Flew Them Home: A Pilot's Story of the Yemenite Airlift by Edward Trueblood Martin, in *Eyewitnesses to Jewish History: From 586 B.C.E. to 1967,* edited by Azriel Eisenberg, Hannah Grad Goodman, and Alvin Kass (New York: Union of American Hebrew Congregations, 1973). Originally published by Herzl Press. Reprinted with the permission of Herzl Press.

Youth and Nation, August 1948. In *Eyewitnesses to Jewish History: From 586 B.C.E. to 1967,* edited by Azriel Eisenberg, Hannah Grad Goodman, and Alvin Kass (New York: Union of American Hebrew Congregations, 1973). Reprinted with the permission of Hashomer Hatzair.

Index